D1254995

THE JOHANNINE SYNOPSIS
OF THE GOSPELS

REMOVED FROM THE
ALVERNO COLLEGE LIBRARY

111396

THE JOHANNINE SYNOPSIS
OF THE GOSPELS

H. F. D. SPARKS, D.D., F.B.A.

Oriel Professor of the Interpretation of Holy Scripture
in the University of Oxford

226.5
S73L

HARPER & ROW, PUBLISHERS
NEW YORK, EVANSTON, SAN FRANCISCO, LONDON

Alverno College Library
Milwaukee, Wisconsin

THE JOHANNINE SYNOPSIS OF THE GOSPELS. Copyright © 1974 by Hedley Frederick
Davis Sparks. All rights reserved. Printed in Great Britain. No part of this book may
be used or reproduced in any manner whatsoever without written permission except
in the case of brief quotations embodied in critical articles and reviews. For informa-
tion address Harper & Row, Publishers, Inc., 10 East 53rd Street, New York, N.Y.
10022.

FIRST UNITED STATES EDITION

ISBN: 0-06-067474-1

LIBRARY OF CONGRESS CATALOG CARD NUMBER: 74-5379

INTRODUCTION

The primary purpose of *The Johannine Synopsis* and its companion volume, *A Synopsis of the Gospels*, is to enable the Greekless student of the gospels to read through any one of them continuously in English, with the parallel passages in the other three printed in parallel columns alongside.

For the editor of such a synopsis there is no serious problem so long as he confines his attention to the first three gospels. They are generally known as 'The Synoptic Gospels' precisely because they share so much common subject-matter, which appears in much the same order in each. Consequently, the editor of a synopsis of these gospels can with no great difficulty start by setting out opposite one another the parallel passages that occur in all three, and then sandwich in between them in the appropriate places the material which is in fact found between them in each separate gospel.

Theoretically there is no reason why this procedure should not be equally applicable in the construction of a synopsis which sets out all four gospels in parallel. The amount of material shared in common by the fourth gospel with the other three is relatively small: very little of even this small amount is in the same order: the 'fixed points' are therefore few; and the result is that in the arrangement of the 'sandwich' material (especially in the arrangement of the 'sandwich' material found in the fourth gospel only) the widest possible discretion is left to the editor. One editor will arrange the material in one way and another in another—with no more, and no less, justification; and the danger is that the unwary student will be misled into thinking that, say, a particular incident (or series of incidents) in the fourth gospel belongs by right between two consecutive incidents in the first three gospels, merely because his editor has seen fit to place it there. For this reason it has seemed necessary to publish the text of St. John with the Synoptic Parallels as a separate volume.

In *A Synopsis of the Gospels* the Synoptic gospels were arranged in the traditional order, starting with Matthew in the extreme left-hand column, and followed by Mark and Luke, with the Johannine parallels on the extreme right and separated by a thick black line to mark the distinction. In *The Johannine Synopsis* the positions have been reversed: the text of John occupies the first column on the left-hand side of the page, with the Synoptic parallels arranged in order on the right-hand side of the thick black line. And just as in *A Synopsis of the Gospels* the text of each of the Synoptic gospels, which was to be read through continuously, was printed in normal size type, and the text of the parallels in smaller size, so now in *The Johannine Synopsis* the continuous text of John is printed in normal size and that of the parallels (both of the parallels in the Synoptics and of the parallels in John in different contexts) in smaller.

As previously, great care has been taken in setting out the parallels to ensure that identical or alternative words and phrases are printed *exactly* parallel. The student thus has his attention drawn immediately to what is significant on the parallel without having to search through up to (perhaps) twenty or so lines of text in the neighbourhood in order to discover for himself what may, or may not, be significant.

Similarly, with the references. Very occasionally a reference consists of just chapter and verse numbers—e.g., in § 2, '11 10' appears in the Matthew column and '7 27' in the Luke column opposite Mark 1 2: in these cases attention is drawn to what is in fact a parallel, though for one reason or another it has not been printed in full. But usually the chapter and verse numbers are preceded by '*cp.*' (= 'compare'): these are in no sense parallels, but references proper; and they are of several kinds. Sometimes they draw attention to similar or comparable incidents or situations, as when Jesus is said to have 'come again unto Cana' at John 4 46 or an attempt is made by his Jewish opponents to stone him at John 8 59. Sometimes the point of comparison is theological rather than factual, as when Jesus is referred to as a 'prophet' at John 4 19, or what is popularly known as a 'universalistic' note is struck, as at John 10 16. At other times a reference may apply to a word or phrase characteristic of the evangelist: examples here are the fourth evangelist's regular description of the miracles or 'mighty works' of Jesus as 'signs' (2 11, 23; etc.) and his repeated use of 'the hour cometh' (4 21, 23; etc.). If the reader is so inclined, he will find the following up of this last class of reference of very great value indeed in appreciating the evangelists' stylistic peculiarities and theological preferences, and particularly those of St. John.

Again, as in *A Synopsis of the Gospels*, the Revised Version of 1881 has been used for the English text. Despite the subsequent appearance of a number of more modern versions, and despite their unquestionable merits in many directions, there can be no doubt that the Revised Version still provides the most satisfactory basis for an English synopsis of the gospels, whatever may be said against it on other grounds. The prime requisite in a version, which is to serve as a basis for an English synopsis, is that it shall as clearly and unambiguously as possible reflect in English the agreements and disagreements between the gospels as they exist in Greek; and judged by this criterion, none of the other more modern versions is comparable. The Revised Version was deliberately designed as a 'faithful' rendering of the Greek; and when it first appeared it was widely castigated for being far too mechanically exact and over-literal—indeed, one reviewer even described it as resembling 'an interlinear translation' prepared 'for incompetent schoolboys'. Admittedly, for most purposes, this is not an attractive feature. But if we are looking for a version to serve as the basis for a synopsis, where accuracy in detail is of such supreme importance, the Revised Version's mechanical exactness and word-for-word literalness, so far from being a drawback, is a decisive recommendation.

Finally, the sections into which the text is divided are the Reviser's paragraphs, numbered, and with headings. The headings of many of the sections have been suggested by popular usage (as, e.g., the heading for § 24—'The Feeding of the Five Thousand'). It is hoped that the headings supplied for the remaining sections will not be found too much out of keeping with their neighbours.

TABLE OF CONTENTS

§		John	Matt.	Mark	Luke	Page

THE GOSPEL ACCORDING TO ST JOHN
WITH THE SYNOPTIC PARALLELS

A. The Preparation for the Ministry (§§ 1-5)

(i) The Prologue (§ 1)

§ 1. The Incarnation of the Word and the Mission of John the Baptist

John 1 1-18

1 In the beginning was the Word, and the Word was with God [*cp.* 17 5, 24: *also verse* 18 *and* 17 11], and the Word was God. **2** The same was in the beginning with God. **3** All things were made [1]by him [*cp. verse* 10]; and without him [2]was not anything made that hath been made. **4** In him was life [*cp.* 5 26; 6 57; 11 25; 14 6: *also* 3 15; *etc.*]; and the life was the light [*cp.* 8 12; 9 5; 12 35, 46: *also* 3 19] of men. **5** And the light shineth in the darkness [*cp.* 8 12; 12 35, 46]; and the darkness [3]apprehended it not [*cp.* 12 35: *also* 3 19-20]. **6** There came a man, sent from God [*cp.* 1 33; 3 28], whose name was John. **7** The same came for witness [*cp. verse* 15: *also* 1 19-36; 3 26-36; 5 33-36; 10 41], that he might bear witness of the light, that all might believe through him. **8** He was not the light [*cp.* 5 35], but *came* that he might bear witness of the light. **9** [4]There was the true [*cp.* 6 32; 15 1: *also* 6 55: *and* 17 3] light, *even the light* which lighteth [5]every man, coming into the world [*cp.* 3 19; 12 46: *also* 6 14; 9 39; 10 36; 11 27; 16 28; 17 18; 18 37: *and* 12 35]. **10** He was in the world, and the world was made [1]by him [*cp. verse* 3], and the world knew him not [*cp.* 1 26, 31, 33; 8 19; 14 9; 16 3: *also* 20 14; 21 4: *and* 8 55; 14 17; 17 25]. **11** He came unto [6]his own [*cp.* 8 44; 15 19; 16 32; 19 27], and they that were his own [*cp.* 13 1] received him not [*cp.* 5 43: *also* 3 11, 32: *and* 4 44]. **12** But as many as received him, to them gave he the right to become children of God [*cp.* 11 52: *also* 12 36], *even* to them that believe on his name [*cp.* 2 23; 3 18]: **13** which were [7]born [*cp.* 3 3, 5-7], not of [8]blood, nor of the will of the flesh, nor of the will of man, but of God. **14** And the Word became flesh [*cp.* 6 51], and [9]dwelt among us (and we beheld his glory [*cp.* 2 11; 12 41; 17 5, 22, 24], glory as of [10]the only begotten [*cp. verse* 18 *and* 3 16, 18] from the Father [*cp.* 5 44; 6 46; 7 29; 9 16, 33; 16 27, 28; 17 8]), full of grace [*cp. verse* 17] and truth [*cp. verse* 17: *also* 5 33; 8 32; 14 6; 18 37]. **15** John beareth witness [*cp. verse* 7: *also* 1 19-36; *etc.*] of him, and crieth, saying, [11]This was he of whom I said, He that cometh [*cp.* 1 27; 3 31; 6 14; 11 27; 12 13] after me is become before me: for he was [12]before me [*cp.* 1 26-27, 30; 3 26-30]. **16** For of his fulness we all received, and grace for grace. **17** For the law was given [1]by Moses [*cp.* 7 19: *also* 1 45; 7 23; 8 5]; grace [*cp. verse* 14] and truth [*cp. verse* 14: *also* 5 33; 8 32; 14 6; 18 37] came [1] by Jesus Christ. **18** No man hath seen God at any time [*cp.* 5 37; 6 46: *also* 14 7-9]; [13]the only begotten [*cp. verse* 14: *also* 3 16, 18] Son, which is in the bosom of the Father [*cp. verse* 1 *and* 17 5, 24: *also* 17 11: *and* 6 46; 7 29; 8 19; 10 15], he hath declared *him* [*cp.* 3 11, 32; 8 26, 40; 15 15; 17 6, 25-26].	*cp.* 3 1. *cp.*13 53-58; 21 37-39. *cp.* 5 9: *also* 8 12; 13 38: *and* 5 45 *cp.* 19 28; 25 31. *cp.* 3 17; 12 18; 17 5. *cp.*3 11; 11 3; 21 9; 23 39. *cp.* 3 11. *cp.* 3 17; 12 18; 17 5. *cp.* 11 27.	*cp.* 1 4. *cp.* 6 1-6; 12 6-8. *cp.* 10 37. *cp.* 1 11; 9 7; 12 6. *cp.* 11 9. *cp.* 1 7-8. *cp.* 1 11; 9 7; 12 6.	*cp.* 3 2-3. *cp.* 18 28. *cp.* 4 16-30; 20 13-15. *cp.* 20 36: *also* 6 35; 16 8. *cp.*9 26, 32; 24 26. *cp.* 3 22; 9 35; 20 13. *cp.*7 19, 20; 13 35; 19 38. *cp.* 3 16. *cp.* 3 22; 9 35; 20 13. *cp.* 10 22.

[1] Or, *through*
[2] Or, *was not anything made. That which hath been made was life in him; and the life &c.*
[3] Or, *overcame.* See ch. 12 35 (Gr.).
[4] Or, *The true light, which lighteth every man, was coming*
[5] Or, *every man as he cometh*   [6] Gr. *his own things.*   [7] Or, *begotten*
[8] Gr. *bloods.*   [9] Gr. *tabernacled.*   [10] Or, *an only begotten from a father*
[11] Some ancient authorities read (*this was he that said*).
[12] Gr. *first in regard of me.*   [13] Many very ancient authorities read *God only begotten.*

(ii) The Witness of John the Baptist (§§ 2-3)

§ 2. John's Witness concerning himself and his Relationship to the Christ

[*Cp.* Matt. 3 14; Luke 1 41-44; John 1 15, 29-34, 35-36; 3 26-36: *also* Matt. 11 2-19;
17 10-13; 21 24-32; Mark 9 11-13; 11 29-33; Luke 7 18-35; 16 16; 20 3-8; John 1 1-8;
5 33-36; 10 41; Acts 1 5; 11 16; 18 25; 19 1-7.]

John 1 19-28	Matt. 3 3, 11	Mark 1 2-3, 7-8	Luke 3 15, 4, 16	Acts 13 25
19 And this is the witness of John, when the Jews sent unto him from Jerusalem [*cp.* 5 33] priests and Levites to ask him, Who art thou [*cp.* 8 25; 21 12]? **20** And he confessed, and denied not; and he confessed, I am not the Christ [*cp.* 3 28: *also* 1 8]. **21** And they asked him, What then? Art thou Elijah? And he saith, I am not. Art thou the prophet [*cp.* 6 14; 7 40]? And he answered, No. **22** They said therefore unto him, Who art thou? that we may give an answer to them that sent us. What sayest thou of thyself? **23** He said, I am			**15** And as the people were in expectation, and all men reasoned in their hearts concerning John, whether haply he were the Christ;	**25** And as John was fulfilling his course, he said, What suppose ye that I am? I am not *he.*
	cp. 3 4; 11 10, 14; 17 10-13.	*cp.* 1 2, 6; 9 11-13.	*cp.* 1 17, 76; 7 27.	
	3 For this is he that was spoken of [1]by Isaiah the prophet, saying, 11 10	**2** Even as it is written [1]in Isaiah the prophet, Behold, I send my messenger before thy face, Who shall prepare thy way;	**4** as it is written in the book of the words of Isaiah the prophet, 7 27	

the voice of one crying in the wilderness,
    Make straight the way of the Lord,
	The voice of one crying in the wilderness,
	    Make ye ready the way of the Lord,
	    Make his paths straight.
		3 The voice of one crying in the wilderness,
		    Make ye ready the way of the Lord,
		    Make his paths straight.
			The voice of one crying in the wilderness,
			    Make ye ready the way of the Lord,
			    Make his paths straight.	

as said Isaiah the prophet. **24** [1]And they had been sent from the Pharisees [*cp.* 5 33]. **25** And they asked him, and said unto him, Why then baptizest thou, if thou art not the Christ, neither Elijah, neither the prophet? **26** John answered them, saying,				
	cp. 3 6, 7.	*cp.* 1 4.	*cp.* 3 7.	
		7 And he preached, saying,	**16** John answered, saying unto them all, I indeed baptize you with water;	
I baptize [2]with water [*cp.* 1 31, 33]:	**11** I indeed baptize you [2]with water unto repentance:			

John	Matt. 3 11	Mark 1 7	Luke 3 16	Acts 13 25
in the midst of you standeth one whom ye know not [cp. 1 10, 31, 33; 8 19; 14 9; 16 3: also 20 14; 21 4: and 8 55; 14 17; 17 25], 27 even he that cometh [cp. 1 15, 30; 3 31; 6 14; 11 27; 12 13] after me,	but he that cometh [cp. 11 3; 21 9; 23 39] after me is mightier than I, whose shoes	There cometh [cp.11 9] after me he that is mightier than I, the latchet of whose shoes	but there cometh [cp. 7 19, 20; 13 35; 19 38] he that is mightier than I, the latchet of whose shoes	But behold, there cometh one after me,
the latchet of whose shoe I am not worthy to unloose.	I am not ³worthy to bear:	I am not ²worthy to stoop down and unloose. 8 I baptized you ³with water; but	I am not ¹worthy to unloose:	the shoes of whose feet I am not worthy to unloose.
cp. 1 33. 28 These things were done in ³Bethany beyond Jordan, where John was baptizing [cp. 3 26; 10 40: also 3 23].	he shall baptize you ²with the Holy Ghost and with fire.	he shall baptize you ³with the ⁴Holy Ghost.	he shall baptize you ²with the Holy Ghost and with fire.	cp. 11 16: also 1 5; 19 6.
	cp. 3 1, 6.	cp. 1 4-5.	cp. 3 3.	

¹ Or, And certain had been sent from among the Pharisees.
² Or, in
³ Many ancient authorities read Bethabarah, some, Betharabah.

¹ Or, through
² Or, in
³ Gr. sufficient.

¹ Some ancient authorities read in the prophets.
² Gr. sufficient.
³ Or, in
⁴ Or, Holy Spirit: and so throughout this book.

¹ Gr. sufficient.
² Or, in

John 1 21: cp. Mal. 4 5 and Deut. 18 15.   Mark 1 2 = Exod. 23 30; Mal. 3 1.
John 1 23 || Matt. 3 3 || Mark 1 3 || Luke 3 4 = Is. 40 3.

§ 3. John bears Witness to Jesus

John 1 29-34

29 On the morrow [cp. 1 35, 43; 2 1: also 6 22; 12 12] he seeth Jesus coming unto him, and saith, Behold, the Lamb of God [cp. 1 36], which ¹taketh away the sin of the world [3 16-17; 4 42; 12 47]! 30 This is he of whom I said, After me cometh a man which is become before me: for he was ²before me [cp. 1 15, 26-27; 3 26-30]. 31 And I knew him not [cp. 1 10, 26, 33; 8 19; 14 9; 16 3: also 20 14; 21 4: and 8 55; 14 17; 17 25]; but that he should be made manifest [cp. 2 11; 3 21; 7 4; 9 3; 17 6; 21 1, 14: also 14 21, 22] to Israel, for this cause came I baptizing ³with water [cp. 1 26, 33]. 32 And John bare witness, saying,

cp. 27 62.   cp. 11 12.

cp. 16 12, 14.

Matt. 3 13-17	Mark 1 9-11	Luke 3 21-22
13 Then cometh Jesus from Galilee to the Jordan unto John, to be baptized of him. 14 But John would have hindered him, saying, I have need to be baptized of thee, and comest thou to me? 15 But Jesus answering said unto him, Suffer ¹it now: for thus it becometh us to fulfil all righteousness [cp. 5 6, 10, 20; 6 1, 33; 21 32]. Then he suffereth him.	9 And it came to pass in those days, that Jesus came from Nazareth of Galilee, and was baptized of John	21 Now it came to pass, when all the people were baptized,

John (col. 1)

cp. 11 41-42; 12 27-28; 17 1-26.

I have beheld the Spirit descending as a dove out of heaven; and it abode upon him.

cp. 12 28.
verse 34
cp. 1 14, 18; 3 16, 18: *also* 1 34, 49; *etc.*

33 And I knew him not [cp. *verse* 31]: but he that sent me [cp. 1 6; 3 28] to baptize [3]with water [cp. 1 26, 31], he said unto me, Upon whomsoever thou shalt see the Spirit descending, and abiding upon him, the same is he that baptizeth [3]with the Holy Spirit. **34** And I have seen, and have borne witness that this is the Son of God [cp. 1 49; 3 18; 5 25; 9 35; 10 36; 11 4, 27; 19 7; 20 31: *also* 1 18; 3 16-17, 35-36; *etc.*].

[1] Or, *beareth the sin*
[2] Gr. *first in regard of me.*
[3] Or, *in*

Matthew (col. 2)

16 And Jesus, when he was baptized,
cp. 14 23; 19 13; 26 36, 39, 42, 44: *also* 11 25-26.
went up straightway from the water: and lo, the heavens were opened [2]unto him, and he saw the Spirit of God descending as a dove, and coming upon him; **17** and lo, a voice out of the heavens [cp. 17 5], saying, [3]This is my beloved Son [cp. 12 18; 17 5: *also* 4 3; *etc.*], in whom I am well pleased [cp. 17 5: *also* 11 26; 12 18].

cp. 3 11.

verse 17

cp. 4 3, 6; 8 29; 14 33; 16 16; 26 63; 27 40, 43, 54: *also* 3 17; 17 5.

[1] Or, *me*
[2] Some ancient authorities omit *unto him.*
[3] Or, *This is my Son; my beloved in whom I am well pleased.* See ch. 12 18.

Mark (col. 3)

[1]in the Jordan. **10** And
cp. 1 35; 6 46; 14 32, 35, 39.
straightway coming up out of the water, he saw the heavens rent asunder, and the Spirit as a dove descending upon him: **11** and a voice came out of the heavens [cp. 9 7], Thou art my beloved Son [cp. 9 7; 12 6: *also* 1 1; *etc.*], in thee I am well pleased.

cp. 1 8.

verse 11

cp. 1 1; 3 11; 5 7; 15 39: *also* 1 11; 9 7.

[1] Gr. *into.*

Luke (col. 4)

that, Jesus also having been baptized, and praying [cp. 5 16; 6 12; 9 18, 28, 29; 11 1; 22 41, 44: *also* 10 21],

the heaven was opened, **22** and the Holy Ghost descended in a bodily form, as a dove, upon him, and a voice came out of heaven [cp. 9 35], Thou art my beloved Son [cp. 9 35; 20 13: *also* 1 35; *etc.*]; in thee I am well pleased [cp. 2 14; 10 21; 12 32].

cp. 3 16.

verse 22

cp. 1 35; 4 3, 9, 41; 8 28; 22 70: *also* 3 22; 9 35.

John 1 29: *cp.* Is. 53 4, 7, 11-12.   John 1 32, 33 ‖ Matt. 3 16 ‖ Mark 1 10 ‖ Luke 3 22: *cp.* Is. 11 2. Matt. 3 17 ‖ Mark 1 11 ‖ Luke 3 22: *cp.* Ps. 2 7; Is. 42 1.

(iii) The First Disciples (§§ 4-5)

§ 4. Andrew, Simon, and One Other

John 1 35-42

35 Again on the morrow [cp. 1 29, 43; 2 1: *also* 6 22; 12 12]

John was standing, cp. 6 1; 21 1: *also* 6 16, *etc.*
and two of his disciples [cp. 3 25; 4 1];
verse 42

Matt. 4 18-20; 16 16-18

cp. 27 62.

4 **18** And walking by the sea of Galilee [cp. 15 29: *also* 8 24; *etc.*], he saw two cp. 9 14; 11 2; 14 12. brethren, Simon who is called Peter [cp. 10 2; 16 16-18], and Andrew his brother,

Mark 1 16-18; 8 29

cp. 11 12.

1 **16** And passing along by the sea of Galilee [cp. 7 31: *also* 2 13; *etc.*], he saw [cp. 2 14] cp. 2 18; 6 29. Simon cp. 3 16. and Andrew the brother of Simon

Luke 5 1-2, 10-11; 9 20

5 **1** Now it came to pass, while the multitude pressed upon him and heard the word of God, that he was standing by the lake of Gennesaret [cp. 5 2; 8 22, 23, 33], **2** and he saw two cp. 5 33; 7 18-19; 11 1.

cp. 6 14.

boats standing by the lake: but

John

cp. 1 43; 12 26; 21 19, 22.

36 and he looked upon Jesus as he walked, and saith, Behold, the Lamb of God [cp. 1 29]! 37 And the two disciples heard him speak, and

they   followed Jesus.
38 And Jesus turned, and beheld them following, and saith unto them, What seek ye [cp. 18 4, 7; 20 15: also 4 27]? And they said unto him, Rabbi [cp. 1 49; 3 2; 4 31; 6 25; 9 2; 11 8: also 20 16: and 3 26] (which is to say, being interpreted, ¹Master [cp. 20 16: also 8 4]), where abidest thou? 39 He saith unto them, Come, and ye shall see [cp. 1 46; 4 29; 11 34]. They came therefore and saw where he abode; and they abode with him that day: it was about the tenth hour [cp. 4 6, 52; 19 14]. 40 One of the two that heard John *speak*, and followed him, was Andrew [cp. 1 44; 6 8; 12 22], Simon Peter's [cp. 6 8, 68; etc.] brother. 41 He findeth first his own brother Simon,
and saith unto him, We have found the Messiah [cp. 4 25] (which is, being interpreted, ²Christ [cp. 4 25, 29; 7 26, 41; 9 22; 10 24; 11 27: also 4 26, 42]).
cp. 1 34, 49; 3 18; 5 25; 9 35; 10 36; 11 4, 27; 19 7; 20 31: also 1 18; etc.

42 He brought him unto Jesus.   Jesus looked upon him, and said,
Thou art Simon [cp. 21 15, 16, 17] the son of ³John [cp. 21 15, 16, 17]:

thou   shalt be called Cephas (which is by interpretation, ⁴Peter).
cp. 21 15-17.

¹ Or, Teacher   ² That is, Anointed.
³ Gr. Joanes: called in Matt. 16 17, Jonah.
⁴ That is, Rock or Stone.

Matthew

casting a net into the sea; for they were fishers. 19 And he saith unto them, Come ye after me [cp. 8 22; 9 9; 16 24; 19 21], and I will make you fishers of men.

20 And they straightway left the nets, and followed him [cp. 4 22; 9 9; 19 27].
cp. 9 22; 16 23.

cp. 26 25, 49: also 23 7, 8: and 8 19; etc.

cp. 4 18; 10 2.
cp. 16 16.

16 16 And Simon Peter answered and said,
Thou art the Christ [cp. 26 63: also 26 68; 27 17, 22], the Son [cp. 4 3, 6; 8 29; 14 33; 26 63; 27 40, 43, 54: also 3 17; 17 5] of the living [cp. 26 63] God.

17 And Jesus answered and said unto him, Blessed art thou, Simon [cp. 17 25] Bar Jonah: for flesh and blood hath not revealed it unto thee [cp. 11 25], but my Father which is in heaven [cp. 5 16, 45; 6 1, 9; 7 11, 21; 10 32, 33; 12 50; 18 10, 14, 19: also 5 48; 6 14, 26, 32; 15 13; 18 35; 23 9]. 18 And I also say unto thee, that thou art [cp. 4 18; 10 2]

¹Peter, and upon this ²rock [cp. 7 24] I will build my church [cp. 18 17].

¹ Gr. Petros.   ² Gr. petra.

Mark

casting a net in the sea: for they were fishers. 17 And Jesus said unto them, Come ye after me [cp. 2 14; 8 34; 10 21], and I will make you to become fishers of men.

18 And straightway they left the nets, and followed him [cp. 1 20; 2 14; 10 28].
cp. 5 30; 8 33.

cp. 9 5; 11 21; 14 45: also 10 51: and 4 38; etc.

cp. 1 16, 29; 3 18; 13 3.

8 29 Peter answereth and saith unto him,
Thou art the Christ [cp. 14 61: also 15 32].
cp. 1 1; 3 11; 5 7; 15 39; also 1 11; 9 7.

cp. 14 37.

cp. 11 25, 26.

cp. 3 16.

Luke

the fishermen had gone out of them, and were washing their nets . . . .

10 And Jesus said unto Simon, Fear not;
cp. 5 27; 9 23, 59; 18 22.
from henceforth thou shalt ¹catch men.

11 And when they had brought their boats to land, they   left all,   and followed him [cp. 5 28; 18 28].
cp. 7 9, 44; 9 55; 10 23; 14 25; 22 61; 23 28.

cp. 7 40; etc.

cp. 6 14.
cp. 5 8.

9 20 And   Peter answering   said,
The Christ [cp. 22 67: also 23 2, 35, 39]
cp. 1 35; 4 3, 9, 41; 8 28; 22 70: also 3 22; 9 35. of God [cp. 23 35].

cp. 22 31.

cp. 10 21.

cp. 11 13.

cp. 6 14.

cp. 6 48.
cp. 22 32.

¹ Gr. take alive.

§ 5. Philip and Nathanael

John 1 43-51

43 On the morrow [cp. 1 29, 35; 2 1; 6 22; 12 12] he was minded to go forth into Galilee [cp. 4 3, 43; 6 1], and he findeth Philip [cp. 6 5-7; 12 21-22; 14 8-9]: and Jesus saith unto him, Follow me [cp. 12 26; 21 19, 22]. **44** Now Philip was from Bethsaida [cp. 12 21], of the city of Andrew [cp. 1 40; 6 8; 12 22] and Peter. **45** Philip findeth Nathanael [cp. 21 2], and saith unto him, We have found him, of whom Moses in the law, and the prophets [cp. 5 46; 12 41], did write, Jesus of Nazareth [cp. 18 5, 7; 19 19], the son of Joseph [cp. 6 42]. **46** And Nathanael said unto him, Can any good thing come out of Nazareth [cp. 7 41, 52]? Philip saith unto him, Come and see [cp. 1 39; 4 29; 11 34]. **47** Jesus saw Nathanael coming to him, and saith of him, Behold, an Israelite indeed, in whom is no guile! **48** Nathanael saith unto him, Whence knowest thou me? Jesus answered and said unto him, Before Philip called thee, when thou wast under the fig tree, I saw thee [cp. 2 24, 25; 4 19, 29; 5 6, 42; 6 61, 64; 11 14; 13 11, 18; 16 19, 30; 18 4; 21 17]. **49** Nathanael answered him, Rabbi [cp. 1 38; 3 2; 4 31; 6 25; 9 2; 11 8: also 20 16: and 3 26],

Matthew cross-references: cp. 27 62. — cp. 10 3. — cp. 4 19; 8 22; 9 9; 16 24; 19 21. — cp. 11 21. — cp. 4 18; 10 2. — cp. 2 23; 26 71: also 21 11. cp. 13 55. — cp. 26 25, 49: also 23 7, 8.

Mark cross-references: cp. 11 12. — cp. 3 18. — cp. 1 17; 2 14; 8 34; 10 21. — cp. 6 45; 8 22. — cp. 1 16, 29; 3 18; 13 3. — cp. 1 24; 10 47; 14 67; 16 6. — cp. 9 4; 12 25; 16 8. — cp. 9 5; 11 21; 14 45: also 10 51.

Luke cross-references: cp. 6 14. — cp. 5 27; 9 23, 59; 18 22. — cp. 10 13. — cp. 6 14. — cp. 16 29, 31; 24 27, 44. — cp. 4 34; 18 37; 24 19. cp. 3 23; 4 22. — cp. 2 8; 8 17. — cp. 5 22; 6 8; 9 47; 11 17.

Matt. 26 63 And the high priest said unto him, I adjure thee by the living God, that thou tell us whether thou be the Christ,

Mark 14 61 Again the high priest asked him, and saith unto him, Art thou the Christ,

Luke 22 67 If thou art the Christ, tell us. But he said unto them, If I tell you, ye will not believe: **68** and if I ask *you*, ye will not answer. **69** But from henceforth shall the Son of man be seated at the right hand of the power of God. **70** And they all said, Art thou then the Son of God [cp. 4 41; 8 28: also 1 35; 4 3, 9: and 3 22; 9 35]?

John: thou art   cp. 10 24-25.

verse 64   *verse 62*

John: the Son of God [cp. 11 27: also 6 69; 20 28: and 1 34; 3 18; 5 25; 9 35; 11 4; etc.]; thou art King of Israel [cp. 12 13: also 18 33, 39; 19 3, 19, 21: and 6 15; 12 15; 18 37]. **50** Jesus answered and said unto him, Because I said unto thee, I saw thee underneath the fig tree, believest thou? thou shalt see greater things than these [cp. 5 20; 14 12]. **51** And he saith unto him, Verily, verily, I say unto you, Ye shall see the heaven

Matt: the Son of God [cp. 8 29; 14 33; 16 16; 27 54: also 4 3, 6; 27 40, 43: and 3 17; 17 5]. cp. 27 42: also 2 2; 27 11, 29, 37: and 21 5.

Mark: the Son of cp. 3 11; 5 7; 15 39: also 1 1: and 1 11; 9 7. the Blessed? cp. 15 32: also 15 2, 9, 12, 18, 26.

Luke: cp. 23 3, 37, 38: also 19 38; 23 2: and 1 33.

Matt: **64** Jesus saith unto him, Thou hast said: nevertheless I say unto you, Henceforth ye shall see

Mark: **62** And Jesus said, I am: and ye shall see

Luke: And he said unto them, [1]Ye say that I am.

opened, and the angels [cp. 12 29] of God ascending and descending upon the Son of man [cp. 6 62].	cp. 3 16. cp. 4 11; 26 53.	cp. 1 10. cp. 1 13.	cp. 3 21. cp. 22 43.
	the Son of man sitting at the right hand of power, and coming on the clouds of heaven.	the Son of man sitting at the right hand of power, and coming with the clouds of heaven.	verse 69
			¹ Or, *Ye say* it, *because I am.*

John 1 47: cp. Ps. 32 2; Zeph. 3 13.   John 1 51: cp. Gen. 28 12.

B. The Ministry in Galilee, Samaria, and Judæa (§§ 6-48)

(i) In Galilee I (§§ 6-7)

§ 6. The Marriage Feast at Cana

John 2 1-11

1 And the third day [cp. 1 29, 35, 43] there was a marriage in Cana [cp. 4 46; 21 2] of Galilee; and the mother of Jesus was there: **2** and Jesus also was bidden, and his disciples, to the marriage. **3** And when the wine failed, the mother of Jesus saith unto him, They have no wine. **4** And Jesus saith unto her, Woman [cp. 19 26: *also* 4 21; 20 13, 15], what have I to do with thee? mine hour is not yet come [cp. 7 6, 8, 30; 8 20: *also* 12 23; 13 1; 17 1: *and* 12 27]. **5** His mother saith unto the servants, Whatsoever he saith unto you, do it. **6** Now there were six waterpots of stone set there after the Jews' manner of purifying [cp. 3 25], containing two or three firkins apiece. **7** Jesus saith unto them, Fill the waterpots with water. And they filled them up to the brim. **8** And he saith unto them, Draw out now, and bear unto the ¹ruler of the feast. And they bare it. **9** And when the ruler of the feast tasted the water ²now become wine [cp. 4 46], and knew not whence it was (but the servants which had drawn the water knew), the ruler of the feast calleth the bridegroom, **10** and saith unto him, Every man setteth on first the good wine; and when *men* have drunk freely, *then* that which is worse: thou hast kept the good wine until now. **11** This beginning of his signs [cp. 2 23; 3 2; 4 54; 6 2, 14, 26; 7 31; 9 16; 11 47; 12 18, 37; 20 30] did Jesus in Cana of Galilee, and manifested [cp. 1 31; 3 21; 7 4; 9 3; 17 6; 21 1, 14: *also* 14 21, 22] his glory [cp. 1 14; 12 41; 17 5, 22, 24]; and his disciples believed on him [cp. 2 23; 4 39, 41; 7 31; 8 30; 10 42; 11 45; 12 11, 42: *also* 3 16; 6 35; etc.].

¹ Or, *steward*   ² Or, *that it had become*

	cp. 15 28. cp. 8 29. cp. 26 18, 45.	cp. 1 24; 5 7. cp. 14 35, 41.	cp. 13 12. cp. 4 34; 8 28. cp. 22 14, 53.
		cp. 7 3-4.	
			cp. 5 39.
			cp. 23 8.
		cp. 16 12, 14.	
	cp. 19 28; 25 31.	cp. 10 37.	cp. 9 26; 32; 24 26.
	cp. 18 6.	cp. 9 42.	

§ 7. Jesus at Capernaum

John 2 12

12 After this he went down to Capernaum, he, and his mother, and *his* brethren [cp. 7 3, 5, 10], and his disciples: and there they abode not many days.

	cp. 4 13. cp. 12 46-50. 13 55.	cp. 1 21. cp. 3 31-35; 6 3.	cp. 4 23, 31. cp. 8 19-21.

(ii) In Judæa I (§§ 8-13)

§ 8. The Cleansing of the Temple

[*Cp.* Mal. 3 1; Zech. 14 21]

John 2 13-22	Matt. 21 12-13; 26 60-61	Mark 11 15-17; 14 57-58	Luke 19 45-46
13 And the passover of the Jews was at hand [*cp.* 6 4; 11 55: *also* 5 1 *and* 7 2], and Jesus went up to Jerusalem [*cp.* 5 1; 7 10: *also* 7 14]. **14** And he found in the temple those that sold oxen and sheep and doves, and the changers of money sitting: **15** and he made a scourge of cords, and cast all out		11 **15** And they come to Jerusalem:	
	21 12 And Jesus entered into the temple [1]of God,	and he entered into the temple,	*cp.* 2 41. **19 45** And he entered into the temple,
of the temple, both the sheep and the oxen; and he poured out the changers' money, and overthrew their tables; **16** and to them that sold the doves	and cast out all them that sold and bought in the temple,	and began to cast out them that sold and them that bought in the temple,	and began to cast out them that sold,
	and overthrew the tables of the money-changers, and the seats of them that sold the doves;	and overthrew the tables of the money-changers, and the seats of them that sold the doves; **16** and he would not suffer that any man should carry a vessel through the temple.	
he said, Take these things hence; make not my Father's house [*cp.* 14 2]	**13** and he saith unto them, It is written, My house shall be called a house of prayer: but ye make it a den of robbers.	**17** And he taught, and said unto them, Is it not written, My house shall be called a house of prayer for all the nations? but ye have made it a den of robbers.	**46** saying unto them, It is written, And my house shall be a house of prayer: but ye have made it a den of robbers.
a house of merchandise. **17** His disciples remembered that it was written, The zeal of thine house shall eat me up. **18** The Jews therefore answered and said unto him, What sign shewest thou unto us [*cp.* 6 30: *also* 4 48], seeing that thou doest these things [*cp.* 5 27; 17 2]?	*cp.* 12 38; 16 1.	*cp.* 8 11.	*cp.* 11 16.
	cp. 21 23: *also* 7 29; 9 6; 28 18. 26 **60** . . . But afterward came two,	*cp.* 11 28: *also* 1 22, 27; 2 10. 14 **57** And there stood up certain, and bare false witness against him, saying, **58** We heard him say,	*cp.* 20 2: *also* 4 32, 36; 5 24.
19 Jesus answered and said unto them, Destroy this [1]temple,	**61** and said, This man said, I am able to destroy the [2]temple of God,	I will destroy this [1]temple that is made with hands, and	
and in three days	and to build it in three days [*cp.* 27 40: *also* 12 40; 16 21; 17 23; 20 19; 27 63, 64].	in three days [*cp.* 15 29: *also* 8 31; 9 31; 10 34].	*cp.* 9 22; 13 32; 18 33; 24 7, 21, 46.
I will raise it up. **20** The Jews therefore said, Forty and six years was this [1]temple in building, and wilt thou raise it up in three days [*cp.* 8 57]?		I will build another made without hands.	

21 But he spake of the ¹temple of his body [*cp.* 10 18]. **22** When therefore he was raised from the dead, his disciples remembered [*cp.* 12 16: *also* 14 26; 16 4] that he spake this; and they believed the scripture [*cp.* 20 9], and the word which Jesus had said [*cp.* 3 14; 12 32–33].	*cp.* 26 75. *cp.* 16 21-23; 17 9, 12, 22-23; 20 17-19, 28; 26 2, 32: *also* 26 12, 24.	*cp.* 14 72. *cp.* 8 31-33; 9 9, 12, 30-32; 10 32-34, 45; 14 28: *also* 14 8, 21.	*cp.* 24 6, 8: *also* 22 61. *cp.* 24 45-46. *cp.* 9 22, 43-45; 13 32-33; 17 25; 18 31-34; 24 7: *also* 22 22.
¹ Or, *sanctuary*	¹ Many ancient authorities omit *of God.* ² Or, *sanctuary*	¹ Or, *sanctuary*	

John 2 16 *and* Mark 11 16: *cp.* Zech. 14 21.   Matt. 21 13 ‖ Mark 11 17 ‖ Luke 19 46 = Is. 56 7: *cp.* Jer. 7 11. John 2 17 = Ps. 69 9.

§ 9. Jesus in Jerusalem

John 2 23-25

23 Now when he was in Jerusalem at the passover, during the feast, many [*cp.* 4 45] believed [*cp.* 2 11; 4 39, 41; 7 31; 8 30; 10 42; 11 45; 12 11, 42: *also* 3 16; 6 35; *etc.*] on his name [*cp.* 1 12; 3 18], beholding [*cp.* 6 2; 7 3; 11 45] his signs [*cp.* 2 11; 3 2; 4 54; 6 2, 14, 26; 7 31; 9 16; 11 47; 12 18, 37; 20 30] which he did. **24** But Jesus did not trust himself unto them, for that he knew all men [*cp.* 1 48; 2 25; 14 19, 29; 5 6, 42; 6 61, 64; 11 14; 13 11, 18; 16 19, 30; 18 4; 21 17], **25** and because he needed not that any one should bear witness concerning ¹man; for he himself knew what was in man [*see verse* 24 *above*].	*cp.* 18 6. *cp.* 9 4; 12 25; 16 8.	*cp.* 9 42. *cp.* 2 8; 8 17.	*cp.* 23 8. *cp.* 5 22; 6 8; 9 47; 11 17.
¹ Or, *a man; for* . . . *the man*			

§ 10. Jesus and Nicodemus (i)

John 3 1-15

1 Now there was a man of the Pharisees, named Nicodemus [*cp.* 7 50; 19 39], a ruler [*cp.* 7 26, 48; 12 42] of the Jews: **2** the same came unto him by night [*cp.* 9 22; 12 42], and said to him, Rabbi [*cp.* 1 38, 49; 4 31; 6 25; 9 2; 11 8: *also* 20 16: *and* 3 26], we know [*cp.* 4 42; 9 24, 29, 31; 16 30; 21 24] that thou art a teacher come from God: for no man can do these signs [*cp.* 2 11, 23; 4 54; *etc.*] that thou doest, except God be with him [*cp.* 9 16, 33; 10 21: *also* 5 36; 10 25]. **3** Jesus answered and said unto him, Verily, verily, I say unto thee, Except a man [*cp.* 3 5; 6 53; 8 24: *also* 13 8]	*cp.* 9 18. *cp.* 26 25, 49: *also* 23 7, 8. *cp.* 22 16. Matt. 18 **3** Verily I say unto you, Except ye turn, and become	*cp.* 5 22. *cp.* 9 5; 11 21; 14 45: *also* 10 51. *cp.* 12 14. Mark 10 **15** Verily I say unto you, Whosoever shall not receive	*cp.* 14 1; 18 18; 23 13, 35; 24 20: *also* 8 41; 13 14. *cp.* 20 21. Luke 18 **17** Verily I say unto you, Whosoever shall not receive

John	Matt.	Mark	Luke
be born [cp. 1 12-13; 3 5-7] ¹anew, he cannot see [cp. 3 36] the kingdom of God. **4** Nicodemus saith unto him, How can a man be born when he is old [cp. 3 9; 6 42, 52; 8 33; 12 34: also 4 9; 6 60; 7 15]? can he enter a second time into his mother's womb, and be born? **5** Jesus answered, Verily, verily, I say unto thee, Except a man [cp. verse 3] be born [cp. 1 12-13; 3 3] of water and the Spirit, he cannot enter [cp. 10 1, 2, 9] into the kingdom of God.	as little children, ye shall in no wise enter [cp. 5 20; 7 21; 19 23, 24; 21 31; 23 13: also 7 13; 18 8, 9; 19 17; 25 21, 23] into the kingdom of heaven.	the kingdom of God as a little child, cp. 9 1. he shall in no wise enter [cp. 9 47; 10 23, 24, 25: also 9 43, 45] therein.	the kingdom of God as a little child, cp. 9 27. he shall in no wise enter [cp. 18 24, 25: also 11 52; 13 24; 24 26] therein.

6 That which is born of the flesh [cp. 1 13] is flesh; and that which is born of the Spirit is spirit [cp. 6 63]. **7** Marvel not [cp. 5 28] that I said unto thee, Ye must be born ¹anew. **8** ²The wind bloweth where it listeth, and thou hearest the voice thereof, but knowest not whence it cometh, and whither it goeth [cp. 8 14; etc.]: so is every one that is born of the Spirit. **9** Nicodemus answered and said unto him, How can these things be [cp. 3 4; 6 42, 52; 8 33; 12 34: also 4 9; 6 60; 7 15]?

John	Matt.	Mark	Luke
10 Jesus answered and said unto him, Art thou the teacher of Israel, and understandest not these things [cp. 4 33; 8 27, 43; 10 6; 11 13; 12 16; 13 7, 28, 36; 14 5-10, 22; 16 17-18]? **11** Verily, verily, I say unto thee, We speak that we do know [cp. 4 22], and bear witness of that we have seen [cp. 3 32: also 1 18; 8 26, 40; 15 15: and 17 6, 26]; and ye receive not our witness [cp. 3 32: also 1 11; 5 43: and 12 37].	cp. 15 16; 16 8-12.	cp. 4 13; 6 52; 7 18; 8 17-21; 9 10, 32; 16 14.	cp. 2 50; 9 45; 18 34.
12 If I told you earthly things, and ye believe not [cp. 6 64; 14 10; 20 27], how shall ye believe, if I tell you heavenly things? **13** And no man hath ascended into heaven, but he that descended out of heaven [cp. 3 31; 6 32-33, 38, 41-42, 50-51, 58: also 8 23], even the Son of man [cp. 6 62: also 20 17: and 1 51], ³which is in heaven.	cp. 8 26; 14 31; 16 8; 17 20; 21 21; 28 17.	cp. 4 40; 11 22; 16 14.	cp. 8 25; 12 28; 17 5-6; 22 32; 24 25, 38.
14 And as Moses lifted up the serpent in the wilderness, even so must the Son of man be lifted up [cp. 8 28; 12 32-34: also 2 19-22]:	cp. 16 21-23; etc.	cp. 8 31-33; etc.	cp. 9 22; etc.
15 that whosoever ⁴believeth may in him have eternal life [cp. 3 16, 36; 5 24; 6 40, 47: also 11 25-26; 20 31: and 4 14, 36; etc.].	cp. 19 16, 29; 25 46.	cp. 10 17, 30.	cp. 10 25; 18 18, 30.

¹ Or, *from above*   ² Or, *The Spirit breatheth*
³ Many ancient authorities omit *which is in heaven*.   ⁴ Or, *believeth in him may have*

John 3 8: *cp.* Eccl. 11 5.   John 3 13: *cp.* Deut. 30 12; Prov. 30 4.   John 3 14: *cp.* Num. 21 9; Wisd. 16 5-7.

§ 11. Jesus and Nicodemus (ii)

John 3 16-21

John	Matt.	Mark	Luke
16 For God so loved the world, that he gave his only begotten [cp. verse 18 and 1 14, 18] Son, that whosoever believeth on him should not perish [cp. 10 28: also 17 12; 18 9: and 6 39], but have	cp. 3 17; 12 18; 17 5.	cp. 1 11; 9 7; 12 6.	cp. 3 22; 9 35; 20 13.
eternal life [cp. 3 15, 36; 5 24; 6 40, 47: also 11 25-26; 20 31: and 4 14, 36; etc.]. **17** For God sent not the Son into the world [cp. 10 36; 17 18: also 3 34; 5 38; 6 29; 17 3: and 1 9; 3 19; etc.] to judge the world [cp. 8 15; 12 47]; but that the world should be	cp. 19 16, 29; 25 46.	cp. 10 17, 30.	cp. 10 25; 18 18, 30.
saved [cp. 12 47: also 4 42; 5 34; 10 9] through him. **18** He that believeth on him is not judged: he that believeth not hath been judged already [cp. 5 24: also 3 19; 12 31; 16 11: and 5 29; 12 48], because he hath not believed on the name [cp. 1 12: 2 23] of the	cp. 1 21; 18 11: also 20 28.	cp. 10 45.	cp. 9 55; 19 10: also 2 11.

only begotten [cp. verse 16 and 1 14, 18] Son of God. **19** And this is the judgement, that the light is come into the world [cp. 1 9; 12 46: also 1 4, 5; 8 12; 9 5; 12 35-36: and 6 14; 9 39; 10 36; 11 27; 16 28; 17 18; 18 37], and men loved the darkness rather than the light; for their works were evil [cp. 7 7]. **20** For every one that [1]doeth ill hateth the light, and cometh not to the light [cp. 1 5], lest his works should be [2]reproved. **21** But he that doeth the truth cometh to the light, that his works may be made manifest [cp. 1 31; 2 11; 7 4; 9 3; 17 6; 21 1, 14: also 14 21, 22], [3]that they have been wrought in God [cp. 6 28-29; 9 3-4: also 10 25, 32, 37; 14 10: and 4 34; 5 36; 17 4: and 5 17; 7 21].	cp. 3 17; 12 18; 17 5.	cp. 1 11; 9 7; 12 6.	cp. 3 22; 9 35; 20 13.
	cp. 16 12, 14.		

[1] Or, *practiseth*　　[2] Or, *convicted*　　[3] Or, *because*

§ 12. **John again bears Witness to Jesus** (i)

John 3 22-30

22 After these things came Jesus and his disciples into the land of Judæa; and there he tarried with them [cp. 11 54], and baptized [cp. verse 26 and 4 1-2]. **23** And John also was baptizing in Ænon near to Salim [cp. verse 26: and 1 28; 10 40], because there [1]was much water there: and they came, and were baptized. **24** For John was not yet cast into prison. **25** There arose therefore a questioning on the part of John's disciples [cp. 1 35, 37; 4 1] with a Jew about purifying [cp. 2 6]. **26** And they came unto John, and said to him, Rabbi [cp. 1 38; etc.], he that was with thee beyond Jordan [cp. 1 28; 10 40: also verse 23], to whom thou hast borne witness [cp. 1 7, 8, 15, 19-36: also 5 33-36; 10 41], behold, the same baptizeth [cp. verse 22 and 4 1-2], and all men come to him [cp. 12 19]. **27** John answered and said, A man can receive nothing, except it have been given him [cp. 6 65; 19 11] from heaven. **28** Ye yourselves bear me witness, that I said, I am not the Christ [cp. 1 20: also 1 8], but, that I am sent [cp. 1 6, 33] before him [cp. 1 23, 27, 30]. **29** He that hath the bride is the bridegroom: but the friend of the bridegroom, which standeth and heareth him, rejoiceth greatly because of the bridegroom's voice: this my joy therefore is fulfilled [cp. 15 11; 16 24; 17 13]. **30** He must increase, but I must decrease.	cp. 2 6, 20, 21; 4 15; 10 15; 11 24. cp. 3 1, 6. cp. 4 12; 11 2; 14 3. cp. 9 14; 11 2; 14 12. cp. 3 1, 6. cp. 21 25. cp. 3 3, 11; 11 10. cp. 9 15. cp. 3 11.	cp. 1 4-5. cp. 1 14; 6 17. cp. 2 18; 6 29. cp. 1 4-5. cp. 11 30. cp. 1 2-3, 7. cp. 2 19. cp. 1 7.	cp. 3 3. cp. 3 20. cp. 5 33; 7 18, 19; 11 1. cp. 3 3. cp. 20 4. cp. 3 15. cp. 1 17, 76; 3 4; etc. cp. 5 34. cp. 3 16.

[1] Gr. *were many waters.*

§ 13. **John again bears Witness to Jesus** (ii)

John 3 31-36

31 He that cometh [cp. 1 15, 27; 6 14; 11 27; 12 13: also 1 30] from above is above all: he that is of the earth is of the earth, and of the earth he speaketh: [1]he that cometh from heaven [cp. 3 13; 6 32-33, 38, 41-42, 50-51, 58: also 8 23] is above all. **32** What he hath seen and heard, of that he beareth witness [cp. 3 11: also 1 18; 8 26, 40; 15 15: and 17 6, 26]; and no man receiveth his witness [cp. 3 11: also 1 11; 5 43: and 12 37]. **33** He that hath received his witness hath set his seal [cp. 6 27] to *this*, that God is true [cp. 7 28; 8 26: also 17 17]. **34** For he whom God hath sent [cp. 5 38; 6 29; 10 36; 17 3: also 3 17; etc.] speaketh the words of God [cp. 8 26, 47; 12 47-50; 14 10; 17 8, 14: also 6 63, 68]: for he giveth not the Spirit [cp. 7 39: also 1 33; 20 22] by measure. **35** The Father loveth the Son [cp. 5 20; 10 17; 15 9-10; 17 23, 24, 26], and hath given all things into his hand [cp. 5 27; 13 3; 17 2: also Matt. 9 6, 8; 11 27; 28 18: Mark 2 10: Luke 5 24; 10 22]. **36** He that believeth on the Son hath eternal life [cp. 3 15, 16; 5 24; 6 40, 47: also 11 25-26; 20 31: and 4 14, 36; etc.]; but he that [2]obeyeth not the Son shall not see [cp. 3 3] life, but the wrath of God abideth on him.	cp. 3 11; 11 3; 21 9; 23 39. cp. 3 17; 17 5. cp. 19 16, 29; 25 46.	cp. 11 9: also 1 7. cp. 1 11; 9 7; 12 6. cp. 10 17, 30.	cp. 7 19, 20; 13 35; 19 38; also 3 16. cp. 11 13. cp. 3 22; 20 13. cp. 10 25; 18 18, 30.

[1] Some ancient authorities read *he that cometh from heaven beareth witness of what he hath seen and heard.*　　[2] Or, *believeth not*

John 3 34: cp. Ezek. 4 11, 16.

(iii) In Samaria (§§ 14–16)

§ 14. Jesus and a Samaritan Woman

John 4 1-26	Matt. 4 12	Mark 1 14	Luke 4 14
1 When therefore the Lord [*cp.* 6 23; 11 2; 20 2, 18, 20, 25; 21 7, 12] knew how that the Pharisees had heard that Jesus was making and baptizing [*cp.* 3 22, 26] more disciples than John **2** (although Jesus himself baptized not, but his disciples), [*cp.* 3 24] **3** he left Judæa, and departed again	**12** Now when he heard that John was delivered up [*cp.* 11 2; 14 3], he withdrew	**14** Now after *cp.* 16 19, 20. that John was delivered up [*cp.* 6 17], Jesus came	**14** And *cp.* 7 13, 19; 10 1, 39, 41; 11 39; 12 42; 13 15; 17 5, 6; 18 6; 19 8; 22 61; 24 3, 34. *cp.* 3 19-20. Jesus returned in the power of the Spirit
into Galilee [*cp.* 4 47, 54: *also* 1 43; 6 1]. **4** And he must needs pass through Samaria. **5** So he cometh to a city of Samaria, called Sychar, near to the parcel of ground that Jacob gave to his son Joseph: **6** and Jacob's [1]well was there. Jesus therefore, being wearied with his journey, sat [2]thus [*cp.* 13 25] by the [1]well. It was about the sixth hour [*cp.* 1 39; 4 52; 19 14]. **7** There cometh a woman of Samaria to draw water: Jesus saith unto her, Give me to drink. **8** For his disciples were gone away into the city to buy food. **9** The Samaritan woman therefore saith unto him, How is it [*cp.* 6 60; 7 15: *also* 3 4, 9; 6 42, 52; 8 33; 12 34] that thou, being a Jew, askest drink of me, which am a Samaritan woman? ([3]For Jews have no dealings with Samaritans [*cp.* 8 48].) **10** Jesus answered and said unto her, If thou knewest the gift of God, and who it is that saith to thee, Give me to drink; thou wouldest have asked of him, and he would have given thee living water [*cp.* 7 38]. **11** The woman saith unto him, [4]Sir, thou hast nothing to draw with, and the well is deep: from whence then hast thou that living water? **12** Art thou greater than our father [*cp.* 8 53] Jacob, which gave us the well, and drank thereof himself, and his sons, and his cattle? **13** Jesus answered and said unto her, Every one that drinketh of this water shall thirst again: **14** but whosoever drinketh of the water that I shall give him shall never thirst [*cp.* 6 35: *also* 7 37]; but the water that I shall give him [*cp.* 6 27, 51] shall become in him a well of water springing up unto eternal life. **15** The woman saith unto him, [4]Sir, give me [*cp.* 6 34] this water, that I thirst not, neither come all the way hither to draw. **16** Jesus saith unto her, Go, call thy husband, and come hither. **17** The woman answered and said unto him, I have no husband. Jesus saith unto her, Thou saidst well, I have no husband: **18** for thou hast had five husbands; and he whom thou now hast is not thy husband: this hast thou said truly. **19** The woman saith unto him, [4]Sir, I perceive that thou art a prophet [*cp.* 1 48; 2 24, 25; 4 29; 5 6, 42; 6 61, 64; 11 14; 13 11, 18; 16 19, 30; 18 4; 21 17: *also* 4 44; 6 14; 7 40; 9 17]. **20** Our fathers worshipped in this mountain; and ye say, that in Jerusalem is the place [*cp.* 11 48] where men ought to worship. **21** Jesus saith unto her, Woman, believe me, the hour cometh [*cp.* 4 23; 5 25, 28; 16 2, 25, 32], when neither in this mountain, nor in Jerusalem, shall ye worship the Father. **22** Ye worship that which ye know not: we worship that which we know [*cp.* 3 11]: for salvation is from the Jews. **23** But the hour cometh [*cp. verse 21 above*], and now is [*cp.* 5 25; 16 32], when the true worshippers shall worship the Father in spirit and truth: [5]for such doth the Father seek to be his worshippers. **24** [6]God is a Spirit [*cp.* 3 6]: and they that worship him must worship in spirit and truth. **25** The woman saith unto him, I know that Messiah [*cp.* 1 41] cometh (which is called Christ [*cp.* 1 41]): when he is come [*cp.* 7 27, 31], he will declare unto us	into Galilee. *cp.* 10 5. *cp.* 9 4; 12 25; 16 8: *also* 13 57; 21 11, 46. *cp.* 2 4-6. *cp.* 1 16; 27 17, 22.	into Galilee. *cp.* 4 36. *cp.* 2 8; 8 17: *also* 6 4, 15.	into Galilee. *cp.* 17 11. *cp.* 9 52, 56; 10 38. *cp.* 9 52-53. *cp.* 5 22; 6 8; 9 47; 11 17: *also* 4 24; 7 16, 39; 13 33; 24 19. *cp.* 1 69, 71, 77; 2 30; 19 9: *also* 3 6.

all things [*cp.* 16 13-15]. **26** Jesus saith unto her, I that speak unto thee [*cp.* 9 37] am *he* [*cp.* 10 24–25: *also* 1 41; 4 29; 7 26, 41; 9 22; 11 27: *and* 4 42].

cp. 26 63-64: *also* 16 16: *and* 26 68; 27 17, 22.	*cp.* 14 61-62: *also* 8 29: *and* 15 32.	*cp.* 22 67-68: *also* 9 20: *and* 23 2, 35,39.

[1] Gr. *spring*: and so in ver. 14; but not in ver. 11, 12.   [2] Or, *as he was*
[3] Some ancient authorities omit *For Jews have no dealings with Samaritans.*
[4] Or, *Lord*   [5] Or, *for such the Father also seeketh*   [6] Or, *God is spirit*

John 4 5, 6, 12: *cp.* Gen. 33 19, 48 22; Josh. 24 32.

§ 15. Discourse with the Disciples

John 4 27-38

27 And upon this came his disciples; and they marvelled that he was speaking with a woman; yet no man said, What seekest thou [*cp.* 1 38; 18 4, 7; 20 15]? or, Why speakest thou with her [*cp.* 21 12]? **28** So the woman left her waterpot, and went away into the city, and saith to the men, **29** Come, see [*cp.* 1 39, 46; 11 34] a man, which told me all things that *ever* I did [*cp.* 4 17-19: *also* 4 39]: can this be the Christ [*cp.* 4 25]? **30** They went out of the city, and were coming to him. **31** In the mean while the disciples prayed him, saying, Rabbi [*cp.* 1 38, 49; 3 2; 6 25; 9 2; 11 8: *also* 20 16: *and* 3 26], eat. **32** But he said unto them, I have meat to eat that ye know not. **33** The disciples therefore said one to another, Hath any man brought him *aught* to eat [*cp.* 3 10; 8 27, 43; 10 6; 11 13; 12 16; 13 7, 28, 36; 14 5-10, 22; 16 17-18]? **34** Jesus saith unto them, My meat [*cp.* Matt. 4 4; Luke 4 4] is to do the will of him that sent me [*cp.* 5 30; 6 38: *also* 7 17; 9 31], and to accomplish his work [*cp.* 5 36; 17 4: *also* 19 28, 30: *and* 10 25, 32, 37; 14 10: *and* 3 21; 6 28-29; 9 3-4: *and* 5 17; 7 21]. **35** Say not ye, There are yet four months, and *then* cometh the harvest? behold, I say unto you, Lift up your eyes, and look on the fields, that they are [1]white already unto harvest. **36** He that reapeth receiveth wages, and gathereth fruit unto life eternal; that he that soweth and he that reapeth may rejoice together. **37** For herein is the saying true, One soweth, and another reapeth. **38** I sent you to reap that whereon ye have not laboured: others have laboured, and ye are entered into their labour.

cp. 26 25, 49: *also* 23 7, 8.	*cp.* 9 5; 11 21; 14 45: *also* 10 51.	
cp. 15 16; 16 8-12.	*cp.* 4 13; 6 52; 7 18; *etc.*	*cp.* 2 50; 9 45; 18 34.
cp. 7 21; 12 50; 21 31: *also* 6 10; 26 39, 42.	*cp.* 3 35: *also* 14 36.	*cp.* 22 42. *cp.* 12 50; 18 31; 22 37: *also* 13 32: *and* 2 49.
cp. 9 37. *cp.* 10 10. *cp.* 13 3, 18, 37.	*cp.* 4 3, 14.	*cp.* 10 2. *cp.* 10 7. *cp.* 8 5.
cp. 9 38.		*cp.* 10 2.

[1] Or, *white unto harvest. Already he that reapeth &c.*

John 4 36: *cp.* Ps. 126 5-6; Is. 9 3.   John 4 37: *cp.* Job 31 8; Mic. 6 15.

§ 16. Many of the Samaritans believe

John 4 39-42

39 And from that city many of the Samaritans believed on him [*cp.* 2 11, 23; 7 31; 8 30; 10 42; 11 45; 12 11, 42: *also* 7 48] because of the word of the woman [*cp.* 17 20], who testified, He told me all things that *ever* I did [*cp.* 4 29: *also* 4 17-19]. **40** So when the Samaritans came unto him, they besought him to abide with them: and he abode there two days [*cp.* 4 43]. **41** And many more believed because of his word [*cp.* 5 24; 8 31, 37, 43, 51, 52; 12 48; 14 23, 24; 15 3, 20: *also* 5 38; 8 55; 14 24; 17 6, 14, 17,20]; **42** and they said to the woman, Now we believe, not because of thy speaking: for we have heard for ourselves, and know [*cp.* 3 2; 9 24, 29, 31; 16 30; 21 24] that this is indeed the Saviour of the world [*cp.* 3 16-17; 5 34: 10 9; 12 47: *also* 1 29].

cp. 18 6.	*cp.* 9 42.	*cp.* 17 16: *also* 9 56; 10 33.
cp. 13 19-23.	*cp.* 2 2; 4 14-20, 33; 16 20.	*cp.* 4 32: *also* 1 2; 5 1; 8 11; *etc.*
cp. 22 16. *cp.* 1 21: *also* 18 11: *and* 20 28.	*cp.* 12 14. *cp.* 10 45.	*cp.* 20 21. *cp.* 2 11: *also* 9 55; 19 10.

(iv) In Galilee II (§§ 17-18)

§ 17. The Galilæans receive Jesus

John 4 43-45	Matt. 13 57; 4 12	Mark 6 4; 1 14	Luke 4 24; 4 14-15
43 And after the two days [*cp.* 4 40] he went forth from thence into Galilee. **44** For Jesus himself testified, that a prophet [*cp.* 4 19; 6 14; 7 40; 9 17] hath no honour in his own country [*cp.* 1 11; 5 43: *also* 3 11, 32]. **45** So when	**13 57** But Jesus said unto them, A prophet [*cp.* 21 11, 46] is not without honour, save in his own country,	**6 4** And Jesus said unto them, A prophet [*cp.* 6 15] is not without honour, save in his own country, and among his own kin, and in his own	**4 24** And he said, Verily I say unto you, No prophet [*cp.* 7 16, 39; 13 33; 24 19] is acceptable in his own country.
cp. 3 24. he came into Galilee, the Galilæans received him,	and in his own house. **4 12** Now when he heard that John was delivered up [*cp.* 11 2; 14 3], he withdrew into Galilee.	house. **1 14** Now ¦after that John was delivered up [*cp.* 6 17], Jesus came into Galilee.	**4 14** And *cp.* 3 19-20. Jesus returned in the power of the Spirit into Galilee: and a fame went out concerning him through all the region round about [*cp.* 4 37; 5 15; 7 17].
having seen all the things that he did in Jerusalem at the feast [*cp.* 2 23]: for they also went unto the feast. *cp.* 18 20.	*cp.* 4 24: *also* 9 26. *cp.* 4 23; 9 35.	*cp.* 1 28. *cp.* 1 39.	**15** And he taught in their synagogues [*cp.* 4 44], being glorified of all. *cp.* 11 16.

§ 18. The Healing of a Nobleman's Son

John 4 46-54	Matt. 8 5-13		Luke 7 1-10; 13 28-30
46 He came therefore again unto Cana [*cp.* 2 1: *also* 21 2] of Galilee, where he made the water wine [*cp.* 2 9]. And there was a certain ¹nobleman, whose son was sick at Capernaum.			**7 1** After he had ended all his sayings in the ears of the people,
	5 And when he was entered into Capernaum,		he entered into Capernaum. **2** And a certain centurion's ¹servant, who was ²dear unto him, was sick and at the point of death [*cp.* 8 42]. **3** And when he heard concerning Jesus,
verse 47 **47** When he heard that Jesus was come out of Judæa into Galilee [*cp.* 4 3, 54: *also* 1 43; 6 1], he went unto him, and besought *him* that he would come down, and heal his son: for he was at the point of death. **48** Jesus therefore said unto him, Except ye see signs and wonders, ye will in no wise believe [*cp.*	there came unto him a centurion, beseeching him, *cp.* 24 24. *cp.* 12 38; 16 1.		he sent unto him elders of the Jews, asking him that he would come and save his ¹servant. *verse* 2
		cp. 13 22. *cp.* 8 11.	*cp.* 11 16.

John

2 18; 6 30].
49 The ¹nobleman saith unto him, ²Sir, come down ere my child die [cp. 11 21, 32].

cp. 4 50; 5 8; 9 7; 11 43.

cp. 1 38.

cp. 10 16; 11 52.

cp. 12 36: *also* 1 12; 11 52.

cp. 19 30; 20 16.

50 Jesus saith unto him, Go thy way; thy son liveth. The man believed the word that Jesus spake unto him, and he went his way.
51 And as he was now going down, his ³servants met him, saying, that his son lived.
verse 53
52 So he inquired of them the hour when he began to amend. They said therefore unto him, Yesterday at the seventh hour [cp. 1 39; 4 6; 19 14] the fever

Matt.

6 and saying,
Lord, my ¹servant lieth in the house sick of the palsy [cp. 4 24; 9 2 ff.], grievously tormented [cp. 4 24].

7 And he saith unto him, I will come and heal him.
8 And the centurion answered and said, Lord, I am not ²worthy that thou shouldest come under my roof: but only say ³the word [cp. 8 16: also 8 3, 13, 32; 9 6, 22, 29; 12 13; 15 28; 17 7, 18], and my ¹servant shall be healed. 9 For I also am a man ⁴under authority, having under myself soldiers: and I say to this one, Go, and he goeth; and to another, Come, and he cometh; and to my ⁵servant, Do this, and he doeth it. 10 And when Jesus heard it, he marvelled, and said to them that followed, Verily I say unto you, ⁶I have not found so great faith, no, not in Israel. 11 And I say unto you, that many shall come from the east and the west, and shall ⁷sit down [cp. 26 29] with Abraham, and Isaac, and Jacob, in the kingdom of heaven [cp. 21 31, 41, 43; 22 7-10: also 10 18; 24 14; 26 13; 28 19]: 12 but the sons of the kingdom [cp. 13 38: also 5 9, 45] shall be cast forth into the outer darkness [cp. 22 13; 25 30]: there shall be the weeping and gnashing of teeth [cp. 13 42, 50; 22 13; 24 51; 25 30].

13 And Jesus said unto the centurion, Go thy way; as thou hast believed, *so* be it done unto thee [cp. 9 29; 15 28].

And the ¹servant was healed in that hour [cp. 9 22; 15 28; 17 18].

(centre references) *cp.* 5 35. — *cp.* 1 25, 41; 2 11; 3 5; 5 8, 34, 41; 7 29, 34; 9 25; 10 52. — *cp.* 5 30; 8 33. — *cp.* 14 25. — *cp.* 12 9; 13 10; 14 9; 16 15. — *cp.* 10 31. — *cp.* 7 29. — *cp.* 7 30.

Luke

cp. 2 3ff.   *cp.* 5 18ff.

4 And they, when they came to Jesus, besought him earnestly, saying, He is worthy that thou shouldest do this for him: 5 for he loveth our nation, and himself built us our synagogue.
6 And Jesus went with them. And when he was now not far from the house, the centurion sent friends to him, saying unto him, Lord, trouble [cp. 8 49] not thyself: for I am not ³worthy that thou shouldest come under my roof: 7 wherefore neither thought I myself worthy to come unto thee: but ⁴say the word [cp. 4 35, 39; 5 13, 24; 6 10; 7 14; 8 29, 32, 48, 54; 9 42; 13 12; 17 14; 18 42], and my ⁵servant shall be healed. 8 For I also am a man set under authority, having under myself soldiers: and I say to this one, Go, and he goeth; and to another, Come, and he cometh; and to my ¹servant, Do this, and he doeth it. 9 And when Jesus heard these things, he marvelled at him, and turned [cp. 7 44; 9 55; 10 23; 14 25; 22 61; 23 28] and said unto the multitude that followed him, I say unto you, I have not found so great faith, no, not in Israel.

cp. 14 15; 22 16, 18, 30.
13 28 There shall be the weeping and gnashing of teeth, when ye shall see Abraham, and Isaac, and Jacob, and all the prophets, in the kingdom of God [cp. 14 21-24; 20 16: also 2 30-32; 3 6; 24 47], and yourselves
cp. 6 35; 16 8; 20 36.
cast forth without.

29 And they shall come from the east and west, and from the north and south, and shall ⁶sit down in the kingdom of God. 30 And behold, there are last which shall be first, and there are first which shall be last.

7 10 And they that were sent, returning to the house, found the ¹servant whole.

left him. **53** So the father knew that *it was* at that hour in which Jesus said unto him, Thy son liveth: and himself believed, and his whole house. **54** This is again the second sign that Jesus did [*cp.* 2 11], having come out of Judæa into Galilee [*cp.* 4 3, 47: *also* 1 43; 6 1].

cp. 8 15.

verse 13

cp. 1 31.

cp. 4 39.

[1] Or, *king's officer* [2] Or, *Lord*
[3] Gr. *bondservants.*

[1] Or, *boy* [2] Gr. *sufficient.*
[3] Gr. *with a word.*
[4] Some ancient authorities insert *set*: as in Luke 7 8.
[5] Gr. *bondservant.*
[6] Many ancient authorities read *With no man in Israel have I found so great faith.*
[7] Gr. *recline.*

[1] Gr. *bondservant.*
[2] Or, *precious to him* Or, *honourable with him*
[3] Gr. *sufficient.*
[4] Gr. *say with a word.*
[5] Or, *boy* [6] Gr. *recline.*

(v) In Judæa II (§§ 19-23)

§ 19. **Jesus goes up to Jerusalem**

John 5 1

1 After these things there was [1]a feast of the Jews [*cp.* 6 4; 7 2: *also* 2 13; 11 55]; and Jesus went up to Jerusalem [*cp.* 2 13; 7 10: *also* 7 14].

[1] Many ancient authorities read *the feast.*

§ 20. **The Healing of a Sick Man at the Pool of Bethesda**

John 5 2-9a

2 Now there is in Jerusalem by the sheep *gate* a pool, which is called in Hebrew [1]Bethesda, having five porches. **3** In these lay a multitude of them that were sick, blind, halt, withered[2]. **5** And a certain man was there, which had been thirty and eight years in his infirmity. **6** When Jesus saw him lying, and knew [*cp.* 6 15: *also* 1 48; 2 24, 25; 4 19, 29; 5 42; 6 61, 64; 11 14; 13 11, 18; 16 19, 30; 18 4; 21 17] that he had been now a long time *in that case*, he saith unto him, Wouldest thou be made whole? **7** The sick man answered him, [3]Sir, I have no man, when the water is troubled [*cp. verse* 4], to put me into the pool: but while I am coming, another steppeth down before me.

cp. 14 35.

cp. 12 15; 16 8; 22 18; 26 10: *also* 9 4; 12 25.

cp. 6 55.

cp. 8 17: *also* 2 8.

cp. 13 11.

cp. 5 22; 6 8; 9 47; 11 17.

verse 8

cp. 5 27; 17 2.

8 Jesus saith unto him,
Arise,
take up thy bed, and walk.

	Matt. 9 5-7	Mark 2 9-12	Luke 5 23-25
	5 For whether is easier, to say, Thy sins are forgiven; or to say, Arise, and walk? **6** But that ye may know that the Son of man hath [1]power [*cp.* 7 29; 21 23 *ff.*; 28 18] on earth to forgive sins (then saith he to the sick of the palsy), Arise, and take up thy bed, and go	**9** Whether is easier, to say to the sick of the palsy, Thy sins are forgiven; or to say, Arise, and take up thy bed, and walk? **10** But that ye may know that the Son of man hath [1]power [*cp.* 1 22, 27; 11 28 *ff.*] on earth to forgive sins (he saith to the sick of the palsy), **11** I say unto thee, Arise [*cp.* 3 3; 5 41; 10 49], take up thy bed, and go	**23** Whether is easier, to say, Thy sins are forgiven thee; or to say, Arise and walk? **24** But that ye may know that the Son of man hath [1]power [*cp.* 4 32, 36; 20 2 *ff.*] on earth to forgive sins (he said unto him that was palsied), I say unto thee, Arise [*cp.* 6 8; 7 14; 8 54], and take up thy couch, and go

9 And straightway the man was made whole, and took up his bed and walked. *cp.* 9 24.	unto thy house. **7** And he arose, and departed to his house. *cp.* 5 16; 9 8; 15 31.	unto thy house. **12** And he arose, and straightway took up the bed, and went forth before them all. *cp.* 2 12.	unto thy house. **25** And immediately he rose up before them, and took up that whereon he lay, and departed to his house, glorifying God [*cp.* 2 20; 5 26; 7 16; 13 13; 17 15, 18; 18 43; 23 47].
[1] Some ancient authorities read *Bethsaida*, others, *Bethzatha*. [2] Many ancient authorities insert, wholly or in part, *waiting for the moving of the water: 4 for an angel of the Lord went down at certain seasons into the pool, and troubled the water: whosoever then first after the troubling of the water stepped in was made whole, with whatsoever disease he was holden.* [3] Or, *Lord*	[1] Or, *authority*	[1] Or, *authority*	[1] Or, *authority*

John 5 2: *cp.* Neh. 3 1, 32; 12 39.

§ 21. Consequent Controversy about Observance of the Sabbath

[*Cp.* Matt. 12 9-14 || Mark 3 1-6 || Luke 6 6-11; Luke 13 10-17, 14 1-6; John 7 21-24, 9 1-34: *also* Matt. 12 1-8 || Mark 2 23-28 || Luke 6 1-5]

John 5 9b-18

Now it was the sabbath on that day [*cp.* 9 14]. **10** So the Jews said unto him that was cured, It is the sabbath, and it is not lawful for thee to take up thy bed. **11** But he answered them, He that made me whole [*cp. verse* 15 *and* 7 23], the same said unto me, Take up thy bed, and walk. **12** They asked him, Who is the man [*cp.* 12 34] that said unto thee, Take up *thy bed*, and walk? **13** But he that was healed wist not who it was: for Jesus had conveyed himself away [*cp.* 6 15], a multitude being in the place. **14** Afterward Jesus findeth him in the temple, and said unto him, Behold, thou art made whole: sin no more [*cp.* 8 11], lest a worse thing befall thee. **15** The man went away, and told the Jews that it was Jesus which had made him whole [*cp. verse* 11 *and* 7 23]. **16** And for this cause did the Jews persecute Jesus [*cp. verse* 18: *also* 15 20], because he did these things on the sabbath [*cp. verse* 18: *also* 7 23; 9 16]. **17** But Jesus answered them, My Father worketh even until now, and I work [*cp.* 7 21: *also* 4 34; 5 36; 17 4: *and* 10 25, 32, 37; 14 10: *and* 3 21; 6 28-29; 9 3-4]. **18** For this cause therefore the Jews sought the more to kill him [*cp.* 7 1, 19, 25; 8 37, 40: *also* 11 53: *and* 7 30, 32, 44; 10 39; 11 57: *and* 5 16], because he not only brake the sabbath [*cp. verse* 16: *also* 7 23; 9 16], but also called God his own Father, making himself [*cp.* 8 53; 10 33; 19 7, 12] equal with God [*cp.* 10 33, 36; 19 7].	*cp.* 12 2: *also* 12 10, 12. *cp.* 8 27; 21 10. *cp.* 12 14; 26 4; 27 1: *also* 21 46. *cp.* 26 63-64.	*cp.* 2 24: *also* 3 4. *cp.* 1 27; 2 7; 4 41. *cp.* 11 18: *also* 3 6; 14 1: *and* 12 12. *cp.* 14 61-62.	*cp.* 6 2: *also* 6 9; 14 3. *cp.* 4 36; 5 21; 7 49; 8 25; 9 9. *cp.* 19 47: *also* 22 2: *and* 20 19: *and* 6 11. *cp.* 22 70.

John 5 18: *cp* Wisd. 2 16-20.

§ 22. A Discourse of Jesus (i)

John 5 19-29

19 Jesus therefore answered and said unto them,
    Verily, verily, I say unto you, The Son can do nothing of himself [*cp.* 5 30; 8 28: *also* 5 31; 7 17, 28; 8 13, 14, 18, 42, 54; 10 18; 12 49; 14 10: *and* 16 13], but what he seeth the Father doing: for what things soever he doeth, these the Son also doeth in like manner [*cp.* 12 45; 14 9-11; 15 24: *also* 10 30; 17 11, 22]. **20** For

the Father loveth the Son [*cp.* 3 35; 10 17; 15 9-10; 17 23, 24, 26], and sheweth him all things that himself doeth: and greater works than these [*cp.* 1 50; 14 12] will he shew him, that ye may marvel. **21** For as the Father raiseth the dead and quickeneth them, even so the Son also quickeneth whom he will [*cp.* 6 39, 40, 44, 54; 11 25-26]. **22** For neither doth the Father judge any man, but he hath given all judgement unto the Son [*cp.* 5 27; 9 39: *also* 8 26: *and* 3 17; 12 47]; **23** that all may honour the Son, even as they honour the Father [*cp.* 8 49]. He that honoureth not the Son honoureth not the Father which sent him [*cp.* 12 44-45; 13 20: *also* 15 23]. **24** Verily, verily, I say unto you, He that heareth my word [*cp.* 8 43: *also* 4 41; 8 31, 37, 51, 52; 12 48; 14 23, 24; 15 3, 20: *and* 5 38; 8 55; 14 24; 17 6, 14, 17, 20], and believeth him that sent me, hath eternal life [*cp.* 3 15, 16, 36; 6 40, 47: *also* 11 25-26; 20 31: *and* 4 14, 36; *etc.*: Matt. 19 16, 29; 25 46: Mark 10 17, 30: Luke 10 25; 18 18, 30], and cometh not into judgement [*cp.* 3 18-19: *also* 12 31; 16 11: *and* 5 29; 12 48], but hath passed out of death into life [*cp.* 6 50, 51, 58; 8 51; 10 28; 11 25-26]. **25** Verily, verily, I say unto you, The hour cometh [*cp.* 4 21, 23; 5 28; 16 2, 25, 32], and now is [*cp.* 4 23; 16 32], when the dead shall hear the voice of the Son of God [*cp.* 5 28; 10 16, 27; 18 37: *also* 11 43-44]; and they that hear shall live. **26** For as the Father hath life in himself [*cp.* 6 57], even so gave he to the Son also to have life in himself [*cp.* 1 4; 6 57; 11 25; 14 6: *also* 3 15; *etc*: *and* 10 18]: **27** and he gave him authority [*cp.* 3 35; 13 3; 17 2: *also* 10 18] to execute judgement, because he is [1]the Son of man [*cp.* 5 22; 9 39: *also* 8 26: *and* 3 17; 12 47]. **28** Marvel not [*cp.* 3 7] at this: for the hour cometh [*cp. verse* 25], in which all that are in the tombs shall hear his voice [*cp. verse* 25], **29** and shall come forth [*cp.* 11 43-44]; they that have done good, unto the resurrection of life; and they that have [2]done ill, unto the resurrection of judgement [*cp.* 12 48].

cp. 3 17; 17 5.	*cp.* 1 11; 9 7; 12 6.	*cp.* 3 22; 20 13.
cp. 16 27; 25 31-46.		
cp. 10 40.	*cp.* 9 37.	*cp.* 9 48; 10 16.
cp. 13 19-23.	*cp.* 2 2; 4 14-20,33; 16 20.	*cp.* 4 32: *also* 1 2; 8 12-15: *and* 5 1; 8 11, 21; 11 28.
cp. 16 16; 26 63.		
cp. 9 6, 8; 11 27; 28 18.	*cp.* 2 10.	*cp.* 5 24; 10 22.
cp. 16 27; 25 31-46.		
cp. 25 46.		

[1] Or, *a son of man*   [2] Or, *practised*

John 5 29: *cp.* Is. 26 19; Dan. 12 2.

§ 23. **A Discourse of Jesus** (ii)

John 5 30-47

30 I can of myself do nothing [*cp.* 5 19; 8 28: *also* 5 31; 7 17, 28; 8 13, 14, 18, 42, 54; 10 18; 12 49; 14 10: *and* 16 13]: as I hear, I judge: and my judgement is righteous [*cp.* 8 16: *also* 7 24]; because I seek not mine own will [*cp.* 6 38], but the will of him that sent me [*cp.* 4 34; 6 38: *also* 7 17; 9 31]. **31** If I bear witness of myself [*cp.* 8 13, 14, 18: *also* 5 19, 30; 7 17; *etc.*], my witness is not true [*cp.* 8 13, 14: *also* 19 35; 21 24]. **32** It is another that beareth witness of me [*cp. verse* 37 *and* 8 18]; and I know that the witness which he witnesseth of me is true. **33** Ye have sent unto John [*cp.* 1 19, 24], and he hath borne witness unto the truth [*cp.* 1 7, 8, 15, 19-36; 3 26-36; 10 41: *also* 18 37]. **34** But the witness which I receive is not from man [*cp. verse* 41]: howbeit I say these things, that ye may be saved [*cp.* 3 16-17; 10 9; 12 47: *also* 4 42]. **35** He was the lamp [*cp.* 1 8] that burneth and shineth: and ye were willing to rejoice for a season in his light. **36** But the witness which I have is greater than *that of* John: for the works which the Father hath given me to accomplish [*cp.* 4 34; 17 4: *also* 19 28, 30: *and* 10 25, 32, 37; 14 10: *and* 3 21; 6 28-29; 9 3-4: *and* 5 17; 7 21], the very works that I do, bear witness of me [*cp.* 10 25: *also* 3 2; 9 16, 33; 10 21], that the Father hath sent me. **37** And the Father which sent me, he hath borne witness of me [*cp.* 8 18: *also* 5 32]. Ye have neither heard his voice at any time, nor seen his form [*cp.* 1 18; 6 46: *also* 14 7-9]. **38** And ye have not his word [*cp.* 8 55; 14 24; 17 6, 14, 17, 20: *also* 5 24; 8 31; *etc.*] abiding in you: for whom he sent [*cp.* 3 34; 6 29; 10 36; 17 3: *also* 3 17; *etc.*], him ye believe not. **39** [1]Ye search the

cp. 7 21; 12 50; 21 31: *also* 6 10; 26 39, 42.	*cp.* 3 35: *also* 14 36.	*cp.* 22 42.
cp. 1 21: *also* 18 11: *and* 20 28.	*cp.* 10 45.	*cp.* 2 11: *also* 9 55; 19 10.
		cp. 12 50; 18 31; 22 37: *also* 13 32: *and* 2 49 *mg.*
		cp. 5 1; 8 11, 21; 11 28.

	cp. 21 42; etc.	cp. 9 12; etc.	cp. 18 31; etc.
scriptures, because ye think that in them ye have eternal life; and these are they which bear witness [cp. 13 18; 15 25; 17 12] of me; **40** and ye will not come to me [cp. 6 35, 37, 44, 45, 65; 7 37], that ye may have life [cp. 1 4; 10 10; etc.]. **41** I receive not glory from men [cp. verse 34]. **42** But I know you [cp. 1 48; 2 24, 25; 5 6; 6 15, 61, 64; 13 11, 18; 16 19, 30; 18 4; 21 17: also 4 19, 29; 11 14], that ye have not the love of God [cp. Luke 11 42: also Matt. 22 37; Mark 12 30, 33; Luke 10 27] in yourselves. **43** I am come in my Father's name[cp. 10 25: also 12 13: and 17 12], and ye receive me not [cp. 1 11: also 3 11, 32: and 4 44]: if another shall come in his own name, him ye will receive. **44** How can ye believe [cp. 12 39], which receive glory one of another, and the glory that cometh from ²the only [cp. 17 3] God ye seek not [cp. 12 43: also 1 14; 6 46; 7 29; 9 16, 33; 16 27, 28; 17 8]? **45** Think not that I will accuse you to the Father: there is one that accuseth you, even Moses, on whom ye have set your hope [cp. 9 28-29]. **46** For if ye believed Moses, ye would believe me; for he wrote of me [cp. 1 45]. **47** But if ye believe not his writings, how shall ye believe my words?	cp. 11 28. cp. 9 4; 12 15, 25; 16 8; 22 18; 26 10. cp. 21 9; 23 39. cp. 24 4-5, 24. cp. 24 27, 44. cp. 16 31.	cp. 2 8; 8 17. cp. 11 9. cp. 13 5-6, 22.	cp. 5 22; 6 8; 9 47; 11 17. cp. 13 35; 19 38. cp. 21 8.

¹ Or, *Search the scriptures*   ² Some ancient authorities read *the only* one.

John 5 35: *cp.* Ecclus. 48 1.   John 5 37: *cp.* Deut. 4 12, 15.

(vi) In Galilee III (§§ 24-31)

§ 24. **The Feeding of the Five Thousand**

[*Cp.* Matt. 15 32-39: Mark 8 1-10]

John 6 1-14	Matt. 14 13-21	Mark 6 30-44	Luke 9 10-17
		30 And the apostles gather themselves together unto Jesus; and they told him all things, whatsoever they had done, and whatsoever they had taught.	**10** And the apostles, when they were returned, declared unto him what things they had done.
1 After these things Jesus	**13** Now when Jesus heard *it*,	**31** And he saith unto them, Come ye yourselves apart [cp. 4 10, 34; 9 2, 28; 13 3] into a desert place, and rest a while. For there were many coming and going, and they had no leisure so much as to eat [cp. 3 20].	And he took them, cp. 10 23.
	cp. 17 1, 19; 20 17; 24 3.		
went away	he withdrew [cp. 8 18] from thence in a boat, to a desert place apart [see above]:	**32** And they went away [cp. 1 35, 45] in the boat to a desert place apart [see above]. cp. 6 45; 8 22.	and withdrew [cp. 4 42; 5 16] apart [see above] to a city called Bethsaida.
cp. 1 44; 12 21. to the other side of the sea [cp. 6 16, etc.] of Galilee, which is *the sea* of Tiberias [cp. 21 1]. **2** And a great multitude	cp. 4 18; 15 29: also 8 24; etc. and when the multitudes heard thereof,	cp. 1 16; 7 31: also 2 13; etc. **33** And *the people* saw them going, and many knew *them*, and they ran there together	cp. 5 1, 2; 8 22, 23, 33. **11** But the multitudes perceiving it
followed him,	they followed him ¹on foot from the cities. **14** And he came forth, and saw a great multitude, and he had compassion on them [cp. 9 36; 15 32: also 20 34],	¹on foot from all the cities, and outwent them. **34** And he came forth and saw a great multitude, and he had compassion on them [cp. 8 2: also 1 41], because	followed him: and he welcomed them [cp. 7 13: and 10 33; 15 20],

John (column 1)

cp. 10 11-16.

because they beheld [cp. 2 23; 7 3; 11 45] the signs [cp. 2 11, 23; 3 2; 4 54; 6 14, 26; 7 31; 9 16; 11 47; 12 18, 37; 20 30] which he did on them that were sick. **3** And Jesus went up into the mountain [cp. 6 15], and there he sat with his disciples. **4** Now the passover, the feast of the Jews [cp. 5 1; 7 2: also 2 13; 11 55], was at hand. **5** Jesus therefore lifting up his eyes, and seeing that a great multitude cometh unto him, saith unto Philip [cp. 1 43-48; 12 21-22; 14 8-9],

Whence are we to buy ¹bread, that these may eat? **6** And this he said to prove him: for he himself knew what he would do.

7 Philip answered him, Two hundred ²pennyworth of ¹bread is not sufficient [cp. 14 8] for them, that every one may take a little.

8 One of his disciples, Andrew [cp. 1 40, 44; 12 22] Simon Peter's [cp. 1 40; 6 68; etc.] brother, saith unto him, **9** There is a lad here, which hath
five barley loaves, and two fishes [cp. verse 11; and 21 9, 10, 13]: but what are these among so many?

Matthew (column 2)

cp. 9 36: also 10 6; 15 24; 26 31.

and healed

their sick.
cp. 5 1; 14 23; 15 29; 17 1; 28 16.
cp. 15 29: also 5 1; 24 3.

cp. 3 7; 5 1; 8 18; 9 36.

cp. 10 3.

15 And when even was come, the disciples came to him, saying, The place is desert, and the time is already past; send the multitudes away [cp. 15 23], that they may go into the villages,

and buy themselves food.

16 But Jesus said unto them, They have no need to go away; give ye them to eat. **17** And they say unto him,

cp. 15 34.

cp. 14 18; 10 2.
cp. 16 16.

We have here but five loaves, and two fishes.

Mark (column 3)

they were as sheep not having a shepherd [cp. 14 27]: and he began to teach them many things.

cp. 3 13; 6 46; 9 2.

cp. 13 3.

cp. 3 18.

35 And when the day was now far spent, his disciples came unto him, and said, The place is desert, and the day is now far spent: **36** send them away, that they may go into the country and villages round about, and buy themselves somewhat to eat.

37 But he answered and said unto them,

Give ye them to eat. And they say unto him, Shall we go and buy two hundred ²pennyworth of bread,

and give them to eat? **38** And he saith unto them, How many loaves have ye [cp. 8 5]? go and see. And when they knew,

cp. 1 16, 29; 3 18; 13 3.

they say,

Five, and two fishes.

Luke (column 4)

and spake to them of the kingdom of God, and them that had need of healing he healed [cp. 6 19; 9 2, 42; 14 4; 22 51].

cp. 6 12; 9 28.

cp. 6 20.

cp. 6 14.

12 And the day began to wear away; and the twelve came, and said unto him,

Send the multitude away, that they may go into the villages and country round about, and lodge, and get victuals:

for we are here in a desert place. **13** But he said unto them,

Give ye them to eat. And they said,

cp. 6 14.
cp. 5 8.

We have no more than five loaves and two fishes;

except we should go and buy food for all this people.

verse 10

10 Jesus said,

Make the people
sit down.

Now there was
much   grass
in the place.
So the men
sat down,
in number
about   five   thousand.
11 Jesus therefore took
the   loaves;
and
cp. 11 41; 17 1.

having given thanks [*cp.* 6
23],
he distributed

to them that were set
down; likewise [*cp.* 21 13]
also of the fishes [*cp. verse*
9: *and* 21 9, 10, 13] as much
as they would. **12** And
when they   were
filled, he saith unto his
disciples, Gather up the
broken pieces which re-
main over, that nothing be
lost. **13** So they gathered
them up, and filled twelve
baskets with broken pieces
from   the   five   barley
loaves,   which re-
mained over unto them

that
had eaten.
verse 10

14 When therefore the
people saw the ³sign [*cp.*
6 2] which he did, they
said, This is [*cp.* 1 34; 4 29,
42; 7 41] of a truth the
prophet [*cp.* 7 40: *also* 1 21,
25: *and* 4 19, 44; 9 17] that
cometh [*cp.* 1 15, 27; 3 31;
11 27; 12 13: *also* 1 30] into
the world [*cp.* 11 27: *also*
1 9; 3 19; 9 39; 10 36; 12
46; 16 28; 17 18; 18 37].

¹ Gr. *loaves.*
² See marginal note on Matt. 18 28.
³ Some ancient authorities read
signs.

---

verse 21
18 And he said,
Bring them hither to
me [*cp.* 17 17]. **19** And
he commanded the multi-
tudes   to ²sit down

on the   grass;

verse 21
and he   took
the five loaves, and the
two fishes, and looking
up to heaven,
he blessed [*cp.* 26 26:
also 15 36; 26 27],
and brake
and   gave the loaves to
the   disciples, and the
disciples to   the
multitudes.

20 And
they did all eat, and were
filled:

and they took
up

that which re-
mained over   of
the broken pieces, twelve
baskets full.
21 And they that
did eat   were about
five thousand men, beside
women and children [*cp.*
15 38].
cp. 12 23; 14 2; 21 11; 27 54:
also 8 27; 21 10.

cp. 13 57; 21 11, 46.

cp. 3 11; 11 3; 21 9; 23 39.

¹ Or, *by land*
² Gr. *recline.*

---

verse 44

39 And
he   commanded   them
that all should ³sit down
by companies

upon the green grass.
40 And they

sat down in ranks, by
hundreds, and by fifties.
verse 44
41 And he   took
the five loaves and the
two fishes, and looking
up to heaven [*cp.* 7 34],
he blessed [*cp.* 8 7; 14 22:
also 8 6; 14 23],
and brake the loaves;
and he gave   to
the disciples
to set before them;

and the two fishes divided
he among
them all.   **42** And
they did all eat, and were
filled.

43 And they took
up

broken   pieces, twelve
basketfuls, and also of the
fishes. **44** And they that
ate the loaves were
five thousand men.

cp. 6 15; 15 39: *also* 2 7;
4 41: *and* 1 27.

cp. 6 4, 15.

cp. 11 9: *also* 1 7.

¹ Or, *by land*
² See marginal note on Matt.
18 28.
³ Gr. *recline.*

---

14 For they were about
five   thousand   men.
And he said unto his
disciples,

Make them
¹sit down
in companies, about fifty
each.

15 And they did
so, and made them all
¹sit down.

verse 14
16 And he   took
the five loaves and the
two fishes, and looking
up to heaven,
he blessed [*cp.* 24 30:
also 22 17, 19] them,
and brake;
and   gave   to
the disciples
to set before the
multitude.

17 And
they did   eat, and were
all filled:

and there was taken
up

that which re-
mained over to them of
broken pieces, twelve
baskets.

verse 14

cp. 23 47: *also* 5 21; 7 49;
8 25; 9 9: *and* 4 36.

cp. 4 24; 7 16, 39; 13 33;
24 19.
cp. 7 19, 20; 13 35; 19 38:
also 3 16.

¹ Gr. *recline.*

John 6 14: *cp.* Deut. 18 15.

§ 25. **Jesus walks on the Water**

[*Cp.* Matt. 8 23-27: Mark 4 35-41: Luke 8 22-25]

John 6 15-21	Matt. 14 22-33	Mark 6 45-52	
15 Jesus therefore perceiving [*cp.* 5 6] that they were about to come and take him by force, to make him king [*cp.* 12 12-15],	*cp.* 12 15; 16 8; 22 18; 26 10.	*cp.* 8 17.	
	cp. 21 9.	*cp.* 11 9-10.	*cp.* 19 37-38.
	22 And straightway he constrained the disciples to enter into the boat, and to go before him unto the other side [*cp.* 8 18],	**45** And straightway he constrained his disciples to enter into the boat, and to go before *him* unto the other side [*cp.* 4 35] to Bethsaida [*cp.* 8 22], while he himself sendeth the multitude away. **46** And after he had taken leave of them,	*cp.* 8 22. *cp.* 9 10.
with-drew again into the mountain [*cp.* 6 3: *also* 5 13] himself alone. *cp.* 11 41; 12 27-28; 17 1 *ff.*	till he should send the multitudes away. **23** And after he had sent the multitudes away, he went up into the mountain [*cp.* 5 1; 15 29; 17 1; 28 16] apart to pray [*cp.* 19 13; 26 36, 39, 42, 44: *and* 11 25]: and when even was come,	he departed into the mountain [*cp.* 3 13; 9 2] to pray [*cp.* 1 35; 14 32, 35, 39].	*cp.* 6 12; 9 28: *also* 3 21; 5 16; 9 18, 29; 11 1; 22 41, 44: *and* 10 21.
16 And when evening came, his disciples went down unto the sea; **17** and they entered into a boat, and were going over the sea into Capernaum.		**47** And when even was come,	
		the boat was in the midst of the sea, and he alone on the land.	
And it was now dark, and Jesus had not yet come to them. **18** And the sea was rising by reason of a great wind that blew. **19** When therefore they had rowed about five and twenty or thirty furlongs,	**24** But the boat ¹was now in the midst of the sea, distressed by the waves; for the wind was contrary. **25** And	**48** And seeing them distressed in rowing, for the wind was contrary unto them,	
	in the fourth watch of the night he came unto them, walking upon the sea.	about the fourth watch of the night he cometh unto them, walking on the sea; and he would have passed by them: **49** but they, when they saw him walking on the sea,	
they behold Jesus walking on the sea, and drawing nigh unto the boat:	**26** And when the disciples saw him walking on the sea, they were troubled, saying, It is an apparition; and they cried out	supposed that it was an apparition, and cried out: **50** for they all saw him, and were troubled. But	*cp.* 24 37.
and they were afraid. **20** But he saith unto them, *cp.* 16 33. It is I; be not afraid. *cp.* 13 36, 37; 21 21: *also* 6 68.	for fear. **27** But straightway Jesus spake unto them, saying, Be of good cheer [*cp.* 9 2, 22]; it is I; be not afraid [*cp.* 17 7; 28 10]. **28** And Peter [*cp.* 15 15; 16 22; 17 4; 18 21; 19 27; 26 33: *also* 16 16; 17 24] answered him and said, Lord, if it be thou, bid me come unto thee upon the waters. **29** And he said, Come. And Peter went down from the boat, and walked upon the waters, ²to come to Jesus. **30** But	he straightway spake with them, and saith unto them, Be of good cheer [*cp.* 10 49]: it is I; be not afraid. *cp.* 8 32; 9 5; 10 28; 11 21; 14 29: *also* 8 29.	*cp.* 8 45; 9 33; 12 41; 18 28: *also* 5 8; 9 20.
cp. 21 7.	when he saw the wind³, he was afraid; and beginning to sink, he cried out, saying, Lord, save me [*cp.* 8 25]. **31** And immediately Jesus stretched forth his hand, and		

cp. 3 12; 6 64; 14 10; 20 27.

21 They were willing therefor to receive   him into the boat: and straightway   the boat was at the land whither they were going.

took hold of him, and saith unto him, O thou of little faith [cp. 6 30; 8 26; 16 8: also 17 20], wherefore didst thou doubt [cp. 21 21; 28 17]? **32** And when they were
    gone up   into the boat,   the wind ceased.

cp. 14 34.

33 And they that were in the boat worshipped him, saying, Of a truth thou art the Son of God.

cp. 4 40; 11 22; 16 14.

cp. 11 23; 16 14.   **51** And

he went up unto them into the boat; and   the wind ceased [cp. 4 39]:

cp. 6 53.

and they   were

sore amazed in themselves; **52** for they understood not concerning the loaves, but their heart was hardened.

cp. 12 28: also 8 25; 17 5, 6; 22 32; 24 25, 38.

---

[1] Some ancient authorities read *was many furlongs distant from the land.*
[2] Some ancient authorities read *and came.*
[3] Many ancient authorities add *strong.*

---

§ 26. **Jesus the Bread of Life** (i)

John 6 22-40

22 On the morrow [cp. 1 29, 35, 43; 12 12] the multitude which stood on the other side of the sea saw that there was none other [1]boat [cp. 21 8] there, save one, and that Jesus entered not with his disciples into the boat, but *that* his disciples went away alone **23** (howbeit there came [2]boats from Tiberias nigh unto the place where they ate the bread after the Lord [cp. 4 1; 11 2; 20 2, 18, 20, 25; 21 7, 12] had given thanks [cp. 6 11]): **24** when the multitude therefore saw that Jesus was not there, neither his disciples, they themselves got into the [2]boats, and came to Capernaum, seeking Jesus. **25** And when they found him on the other side of the sea, they said unto him, Rabbi [cp. 1 38, 49; 3 2; 4 31; 9 2; 11 8: also 20 16: and 3 26], when camest thou hither? **26** Jesus answered them and said, Verily, verily I say unto you, Ye seek me, not because ye saw signs [cp. 2 11, 23; 3 2; 4 54; 6 2, 14; etc.], but because ye ate of the loaves, and were filled. **27** Work not for the meat which perisheth, but for the meat which abideth unto eternal life, which the Son of man shall give unto you [cp. 4 14; 6 51]: for him the Father, *even* God, hath sealed [cp. 3 33]. **28** They said therefore unto him, What must we do, that we may work the works of God [cp. 3 21; 9 3-4: also 10 25, 32, 37; 14 10: and 4 34; 5 36; 17 4: and 5 17; 7 21]? **29** Jesus answered and said unto them, This is the work of God, that ye believe on him whom [3]he hath sent [cp. 3 34; 5 38; 10 36; 17 3: also 3 17; etc.]. **30** They said therefore unto him, What then doest thou for a sign [cp. 2 18: also 4 48], that we may see, and believe thee? what workest thou? **31** Our fathers ate the manna in the wilderness [cp. 6 49]; as it is written, He gave them bread out of heaven to eat. **32** Jesus therefore said unto them, Verily, verily, I say unto you, It was not Moses that gave you the bread out of heaven; but my Father giveth you the true [cp. 6 55: also 1 9; 15 1: and 17 3] bread out of heaven. **33** For the bread of God is that which cometh down out of heaven [cp. verse 38 below], and giveth life unto the world. **34** They said therefore unto him, Lord, evermore give us [cp. 4 15] this bread. **35** Jesus said unto them, I am the bread of life [cp. 6 48: also 6 51: and 6 41, 51, 58]: he that cometh to me [cp. 5 40; 6 37, 44, 45, 65; 7 37] shall not hunger, and he that believeth on me shall never thirst [cp. 4 14: also 7 37]. **36** But I said unto you, that ye have seen me, and yet believe not [cp. 10 25; 12 37: also 1 11; 3 11, 32; 5 43]. **37** All that which the Father giveth me [cp. 10 29; 17 2, 6, 9, 11, 12, 24; 18 9] shall come unto

cp. 27 62.

cp. 26 25, 49: also 23 7, 8.

cp. 19 16.

cp. 12 38; 16 1.

cp. 11 28.

cp. 11 12.

cp. 3 9.

cp. 16 19, 20.

cp. 9 5; 11 21; 14 45: also 10 51.

cp. 10 17.

cp. 8 11.

cp. 7 13, 19; 10 1, 39, 41; etc.

cp. 3 10, 12, 14; 10 25; 18 18.

cp. 11 16.

me [*cp. verse* 35 *above*]; and him that cometh to me I will in no wise cast out. **38** For I am come down from heaven [*cp.* 3 13, 31; 6 42; 8 23: *also* 6 32-33, 41, 50, 58], not to do mine own will [*cp.* 5 30], but the will of him that sent me [*cp.* 4 34; 5 30: *also* 7 17; 9 31]. **39** And this is the will of him that sent me, that of all that which he hath given me [*cp. verse* 37 *above*] I should lose nothing [*cp.* 17 12; 18 9: *also* 3 16; 10 28], but should raise it up at the last day [*cp.* 6 40, 44, 54: *also* 11 24: *and* 5 21; 11 25: *and* 12 48]. **40** For this is the will of my Father, that every one that beholdeth the Son [*cp.* 6 62: *also* 12 45; 14 19; 16 10, 16, 17, 19: *and* 14 17], and believeth on him, should have eternal life [*cp.* 3 15, 16, 36; 5 24; 6 47: *also* 11 25-26; 20 31: *and* 4 14, 36; *etc.*]; and [4]I will raise him up at the last day [*cp. verse* 39 *above*].

cp. 11 28.			
cp. 7 21; 12 50; 21 31: *also* 6 10; 26 39, 42.	*cp.* 3 35: *also* 14 36.	*cp.* 22 42.	
			cp. 15 6.
cp. 18 14.			
cp. 19 16, 29; 25 46.	*cp.* 10 17, 30.	*cp.* 10 25; 18 18, 30.	

[1] Gr. *little boat*.   [2] Gr. *little boats*.   [3] Or, *he sent*   [4] Or, *that I should raise him up*

John 6 27: *cp.* Is. 55 2: *and* Ezek. 9 4.   John 6 31: Neh. 9 15; Ps. 78 24; Ps. 105 40: *cp.* Exod. 16 15: *also* Num. 11 7-9.

§ 27. **Jesus the Bread of Life** (ii)

John 6 41-51	Matt. 13 53-57	Mark 6 1-3	Luke 4 16, 21-22, 28
41 The Jews therefore murmured [*cp.* 6 43, 61; 7 12, 32] concerning him,			
	53 And it came to pass, when Jesus had finished these parables, he departed thence. **54** And	**1** And	
cp. 1 11.	coming into his own country [*cp.* 9 1: *also* 4 13]	he went out from thence; and he cometh into his own country; and his disciples follow him. **2** And when the sabbath was come, he	**16** And he came to Nazareth, where he had been brought up: and
cp. 6 59: *also* 18 20.	he taught them in their synagogue,	began to teach in the synagogue:	he entered, as his custom was, into the synagogue on the sabbath day, and stood up to read. . . . **21** And he began to say unto them, To-day hath this scripture been fulfilled in your ears. **22** And
	cp. 4 17.	*cp.* 1 15.	
cp. 7 15, 21, 46.	insomuch that they were astonished [*cp.* 7 28; 19 25; 22 22, 33: *also* 8 27; 9 33; 12 23; 15 31; 21 20; 27 14],	[1]many hearing him were astonished [*cp.* 1 22, 27; 10 24, 26; 11 18; 12 17: *also* 2 12; 5 20, 42; 6 51; 7 37; 10 32; 15 5; 16 8],	all bare him witness, and wondered [*cp.* 2 47, 48; 4 32, 36; 20 26: *also* 5 9, 26; 8 25, 56; 9 43; 11 14; 24 12, 41] at the words of grace which proceeded out of his mouth:
because he said, I am the bread which came down out of heaven [*cp. verses* 50, 51, *and* 58: *also* 6 35, 48, 51: *and* 3 13, 31; 6 38, 42; 8 23]. **42** And they said,	and said, Whence hath this man [*cp. verse* 56] this wisdom,	saying, Whence hath this man these things? and, What is the wisdom that is given unto this man, and *what mean* such [2]mighty works wrought by his hands [*cp.* 1 31, 41; 5 23, 41; 6 5; 7 33; 8 22, 23, 25; 9 27: *and* 10 13, 16]?	and they said,
cp. 9 6.	and these [1]mighty works? *cp.* 8 3, 15; 9 18, 25, 29; 20 34: *also* 14 31; 17 7; 19 13, 15.		*cp.* 4 40; 5 13; 7 14; 8 54; 13 13; 14 4; 22 51: *also* 18 15.
Is not this Jesus, the son of Joseph [*cp.* 1 45], whose father and mother we know [*cp.* 7 27, 28: *also* 8 14, 19; 9 29, 30]?	**55** Is not this the carpenter's son? is not his mother called	**3** Is not this the carpenter, the son of	Is not this Joseph's son [*cp.* 3 23]?

	Matt.	Mark	Luke
how doth he now say [*cp.* 3 4, 9; 6 52; 8 33; 12 34: *also* 4 9; 6 60; 7 15], I am come down out of heaven [*cp.* 6 38]? *cp.* 6 61: *also* 16 1.	Mary? and his brethren, James, and Joseph, and Simon, and Judas? **56** And his sisters, are they not all with us? Whence then hath this man all these things?	Mary, and brother of James, and Joses, and Judas, and Simon? and are not his sisters here with us? *verse* 2	
	57 And they were ²offended [*cp.* 11 6; 15 12; 26 31, 33: *also* 13 21; 24 10] in him.	³offended [*cp.* 14 27, 29: *also* 4 17] in him.	**28** And they were *cp.* 7 23. all filled with wrath in the synagogue, as they heard these things. . . .

¹ Gr. *powers.*
² Gr. *caused to stumble.*

¹ Some ancient authorities insert *the.*
² Gr. *powers.*
³ Gr. *caused to stumble.*

John	Matt.	Mark	Luke
43 Jesus answered and said unto them, Murmur [*cp. verse* 41 *above*] not among yourselves. **44** No man can come to me [*cp.* 5 40; 6 35, 37, 45, 65; 7 37], except the Father which sent me draw him [*cp.* 6 65: *also* 12 32]: and I will raise him up in the last day [*cp.* 6 39, 40, 54: *also* 11 24: *and* 5 21; 11 25: *and* 12 48]. **45** It is written in the prophets, And they shall all be taught of God. Every one that hath heard from the Father, and hath learned, cometh unto me [*cp. verse* 44 *above*].	*cp.* 11 28.		
46 Not that any man hath seen the Father [*cp.* 1 18; 5 37: *also* 14 7-9], save he which is from God [*cp.* 1 14; 5 44; 7 29; 9 16, 33; 16 27, 28; 17 8], he hath seen the Father [*cp.* 1 18; 7 29; 8 19; 10 15; 17 25-26].	*cp.* 11 28.		
47 Verily, verily, I say unto you, He that believth hath eternal life [*cp.* 3 15, 16, 36; 5 24; 6 40: *also* 11 25-26; 20 31: *and* 4 14, 36; *etc.*]. **48** I am the bread of life [*cp.* 6 35: *also* 6 51: *and* 6 41, 51, 58]. **49** Your fathers did eat the manna in the wilderness [*cp.* 6 31], and they died. **50** This is the bread which cometh down out of heaven [*cp.* 6 58], that a man may eat thereof, and not die [*cp.* 6 51, 58: *also* 5 24; 8 51; 10 28; 11 25-26]. **51** I am the living bread [*cp.* 6 35, 48] which came down out of heaven [*cp.* 6 41, 50, 58: *also* 3 13, 31; 6 38, 42; 8 23]: if any man eat of this bread, he shall live for ever [*cp. verse* 50 *above*]: yea and the bread which I will give [*cp.* 4 14; 6 27] is my flesh, for the life of the world.	*cp.* 11 27. *cp.* 19 16, 29; 25 46.	*cp.* 10 17, 30.	*cp.* 10 22. *cp.* 10 25; 18 18, 30.

John 6 45: Is. 54 13.

§ 28. **Jesus the Bread of Life** (iii)

John 6 52-59

John	Matt.	Mark	Luke
52 The Jews therefore strove one with another [*cp.* 7 12, 40-43; 9 16; 10 19-21], saying, How can this man give us his flesh [*cp.* 1 14] to eat [*cp.* 3 4, 9; 6 42; 8 33; 12 34: *also* 4 9; 6 60; 7 15]? **53** Jesus therefore said unto them, Verily, verily, I say unto you, Except ye [*cp.* 3 3, 5; 8 24: *also* 13 8] eat the flesh of the Son of man and drink his blood, ye have not life in yourselves. **54** He that eateth my flesh and drinketh my blood hath eternal life; and I will raise him up at the last day [*cp.* 6 39, 40, 44: *also* 11 24: *and* 5 21; 11 25: *and* 12 48]. **55** For my flesh is ¹meat indeed [*cp.* 6 32: *also* 1 9; 15 1: *and* 17 3], and my blood is ²drink indeed. **56** He that eateth my flesh and drinketh my blood abideth in me [*cp.* 15 4, 5, 7: *also* 8 31: *and* 14 20; 17 21, 23, 26], and I in him. **57** As the living Father [*cp.* 5 26] sent me, and I live because of the Father [*cp.* 5 26]; so he that eateth me, he also shall live because of me [*cp.* 1 4; 11 25; 14 6: *also* 3 15; *etc.*]. **58** This is the bread which came down out of heaven [*cp.* 6 50]: not as the		*cp.* 16 16; 26 63.	

	cp. 13 54.	cp. 6 2.	cp. 4 16.
fathers did eat, and died: he that eateth this bread shall live for ever [cp. 6 50, 51: also 5 24; 8 51; 10 28; 11 25-26]. **59** These things said he in ³the synagogue [cp. 18 20], as he taught in Capernaum.			

¹ Gr. *true meat.*   ² Gr. *true drink.*   ³ Or, *a synagogue*

§ 29. **Many Disciples hesitate**

John 6 60-65

John 6 60-65			
60 Many therefore of his disciples, when they heard *this*, said, This is a hard saying; who can [cp. 4 9; 7 15: also 3 4, 9; 6 42, 52; 8 33; 12 34] hear ¹it [cp. 16 12, 25]? **61** But Jesus knowing in himself [cp. 1 48; 2 24, 25; 5 6, 42; 6 64; 13 11, 18; 16 19, 30; 18 4; 21 17: also 4 19, 29; 11 14] that his disciples murmured [cp. 6 41, 43; 7 12, 32] at this, said unto them, Doth this cause you to stumble [cp. 16 1]?	cp. 11 15; 13 9, 43: also 19 11, 12: and 13 34. cp. 9 4; 12 25; 16 8.	cp. 4 33: also 4 9, 23; 7 16: and 4 34. cp. 2 8; 8 17.	cp. 8 8; 14 35. cp. 5 22; 6 8; 9 47; 11 17.
62 *What* then if ye should behold the Son of man [cp. 6 40: also 12 45; 14 19; 16 10, 16, 17, 19: and 14 17] ascending where he was before [cp. 3 13: also 20 17: and 1 51]?	cp. 11 6; 13 57; 15 12; 26 31, 33: also 13 21; 24 10.	cp. 6 3; 14 27, 29; also 4 17.	cp. 7 23.
63 It is the spirit that quickeneth; the flesh profiteth nothing [cp. 3 6]: the words that I have spoken unto you are spirit, and are life [cp. 6 68; 12 50: also 3 34; 8 26, 47; 12 47-50; 14 10; 17 8, 14].	cp. 26 64.	cp. 14 62.	cp. 22 69.
64 But there are some of you that believe not. For Jesus knew [cp. verse 61] from the beginning [cp. 15 27; 16 4: also 8 44] who they were that believed not [cp. 3 12; 14 10; 20 27], and who it was that should betray him [cp. 13 11, 21: also 6 71; 12 4; 18 2, 5: and 13 2].			cp. 1 2.
	cp. 8 26; 14 31; 16 8; 17 20; 21 21; 28 17. cp. 26 21: also 10 4; 26 25, 46, 48; 27 3: and 26 23, 24.	cp. 4 40; 11 22; 16 14. cp. 14 18: also 3 19; 14 42, 44: and 14 21.	cp. 8 25; 12 28; 17 5-6; 22 32; 24 25, 38. cp. 22 21: and 22 22.
65 And he said, For this cause have I said unto you [cp. 6 44], that no man can come unto me [cp. 5 40; 6 35, 37, 44, 45; 7 37], except it be given unto him [cp. 3 27; 19 11] of the Father.	cp. 11 28.		

¹ Or, *him*

§ 30. Some go back: Peter's Confession

John 6 66-71	Matt. 16 13-16	Mark 8 27-29	Luke 9 18-20
66 Upon this many of his disciples went back [*cp.* 6 60, 64], and walked no more with him. **67** Jesus said therefore unto the twelve, Would ye also go away?	**13** Now when Jesus came into the parts of Cæsarea Philippi,	**27** And Jesus went forth, and his disciples, into the villages of Cæsarea Philippi: and in the way	**18** And it came to pass, as he was praying [*cp.* 3 21; 5 16; 6 12; 9 28, 29; 11 1; 22 41, 44: *also* 10 21] alone, the disciples were with him: and he asked
cp. 11 41; 12 27-28; 17 1-26.	*cp.* 14 23; 19 13; 26 36, 39, 42, 44: *also* 11 25.	*cp.* 1 35; 6 46, 47; 14 32, 35, 39.	
	he asked his disciples, saying, Who do men say [1]that the Son of man is? **14** And they said [*cp.* 14 2], Some *say* John the Baptist; some, Elijah: and others, Jeremiah, or one of the prophets. **15** He saith unto them, But who say ye that I am? **16** And Simon	he asked his disciples, saying unto them, Who do men say that I am? **28** And they told him, saying [*cp.* 6 14, 15], John the Baptist: and others, Elijah; but others, One of the prophets. **29** And he asked them, But who say ye that I am?	them, saying, Who do the multitudes say that I am? **19** And they answering said [*cp.* 9 7, 8], John the Baptist; but others *say*, Elijah; and others, that one of the old prophets is risen again. **20** And he said unto them, But who say ye that I am? And
68 Simon [*cp.* 1 40; 6 8; 13 6, 36; *etc.*] Peter [*cp.* 13 36-37; 21 21] answered him, Lord, to whom shall we go? thou [1]hast the words of eternal life [*cp.* 6 63; 12 50: *also* 3 34; 8 26, 47; 12 47-50; 14 10; 17 8, 14]. **69** And we have believed and know [*cp.* 9 38; 11 27; 16 30: *also* 16 27; 17 8: *and* 20 31] that thou art the Holy One *cp.* 1 41; 4 25, 26, 29; 7 26, 41; 9 22; 10 24; 11 27. *cp.* 1 34; *etc.*	**16** And Simon [*cp.* 4 18; 10 2] Peter [*cp.* 14 28; 15 15; 16 22; 17 4; 18 21; 19 27; 26 33: *also* 17 24] answered and said,	Peter [*cp.* 8 32; 9 5; 10 28; 11 21; 14 29] answereth and saith unto him,	*cp.* 5 8. Peter [*cp.* 8 45; 9 33; 12 41; 18 28] answering said,
of [*cp.* 6 57: *also* 5 26] God.	*cp.* 1 24. Thou art the Christ [*cp.* 26 63: *also* 26 68; 27 17, 22], the Son [*cp.* 4 3, 6; 8 29; 14 33; 26 63; 27 40, 43, 54: *also* 3 17; 17 5] of the living [*cp.* 26 63] God.	*cp.* 1 24. Thou art the Christ [*cp.* 14 61: *also* 15 32]. *cp.* 1 1; 3 11; 5 7; 15 39: *also* 1 11; 9 7.	*cp.* 4 34. The Christ [*cp.* 22 67: *also* 23 2, 35, 39] *cp.* 1 35; 4 3, 9, 41; 8 28; 22 70: *also* 3 22; 9 35. of God [*cp.* 23 35].
70 Jesus answered them, Did not I choose you [*cp.* 13 18; 15 16, 19] the twelve, and one of you is a devil [*cp.* 13 2, 27]? **71** Now he spake of Judas *the son* of Simon Iscariot [*cp.* 13 26: *also* 13 2: *and* 12 4; 14 22], for he it was that should betray him [*cp.* 6 64; 12 4; 13 11; 18 2, 5: *also* 13 2, 21], being one of the twelve [*cp.* 20 24].	*cp.* 10 4; 26 14. *cp.* 10 4; 26 25, 46, 48; 27 3: *also* 26 21, 23, 24. *cp.* 26 14, 47.	*cp.* 3 14. *cp.* 3 19; 14 10. *cp.* 3 19; 14 42, 44: *also* 14 18, 21. *cp.* 14 10, 20, 43.	*cp.* 6 13. *cp.* 22 3. *cp.* 6 16; 22 3. *cp.* 22 21, 22. *cp.* 22 47.
[1] Or, *hast words*	[1] Many ancient authorities read *that I the Son of man am.* See Mark 8 27; Luke 9 18.		

§ 31. Jesus remains in Galilee

John 7 1-9

1 And after these things Jesus walked in Galilee: for he would not walk in Judæa, because the Jews sought to kill him [*cp.* 5 18; 7 19, 25; 8 37, 40: *also* 11 53: *and* 7 30, 32, 44; 10 39; 11 57: *and* 5 16]. **2** Now the feast of the Jews [*cp.* 5 1; 6 4: *also* 2 13; 11 55], the feast of tabernacles, was at hand. **3** His brethren [*cp.* 2 12; 7 5, 10] therefore said unto him, Depart hence, and go into Judæa, that thy disciples also may behold [*cp.* 2 23; 6 2; 11 45] thy works which thou doest. **4** For no man doeth anything in secret [*cp.* 7 10: *also* 18 20], [1]and himself seeketh to be known openly [*cp.* 7 13, 26; 10 24: *also* 11 14, 54; 16 25, 29; 18 20]. If thou doest these things, manifest thyself [*cp.* 1 31; 2 11; 3 21; 9 3; 17 6; 21 1, 14: *also* 14 21, 22] to the world [*cp.* 14 22]. **5** For even his brethren [*see verse 3 above*] did not believe on him. **6** Jesus therefore saith unto them, My time is not yet come [*cp. verse* 8: *also* 2 4; 7 30; 8 20: *and* 12 23, 27; 13 1; 17 1]; but your time is alway ready. **7** The world cannot hate you [*cp.* 15 18, 19; 17 14]; but me it hateth [*cp.* 15 18, 24], because I testify of it, that its works are evil [*cp.* 3 19]. **8** Go ye up unto the feast: I go not up [2]yet unto this feast; because my time is not yet fulfilled [*cp. verse* 6]. **9** And having said these things unto them, he abode *still* in Galilee.	*cp.* 12 14; 21 46; 26 4; 27 1. *cp.* 12 46-50; 13 55. *cp.* 13 57-58. *cp.* 26 18: *also* 26 45. *cp.* 10 22; 24 9.	*cp.* 36; 11 18; 12 12; 14 1. *cp.* 3 31-35; 6 3. *cp.* 8 32. *cp.* 16 12, 14. *cp.* 6 3-6. *cp.* 14 35, 41. *cp.* 13 13.	*cp.* 6 11; 19 47; 20 19; 22 2. *cp.* 8 19-21. *cp.* 22 14: *also* 22 53. *cp.* 1 71; 6 22, 27; 21 17.

[1] Some ancient authorities read *and seeketh it to be known openly.*
[2] Many ancient authorities omit *yet.*

(vii) In Judæa III (§§ 32-47)

§ 32. Jesus goes up to Jerusalem for the Feast of Tabernacles

John 7 10-13

10 But when his brethren [*cp.* 2 12; 7 3, 5] were gone up unto the feast, then went he also up [*cp.* 2 13; 5 1: *also* 7 14], not publicly, but as it were in secret [*cp.* 7 4: *also* 18 20]. **11** The Jews therefore sought him [*cp.* 11 56] at the feast, and said, Where is he [*cp.* 9 12: *also* 8 10]? **12** And there was much murmuring [*cp.* 6 41, 43, 61; 7 32] among the multitudes concerning him [*cp.* 6 52; 7 40-43; 9 16; 10 19-21]: some said, He is a good man; others said, Not so, but he leadeth the multitude astray [*cp.* 7 47]. **13** Howbeit no man spake openly [*cp.* 7 4, 26; 10 24: *also* 11 14, 54; 16 25, 29; 18 20] of him for fear of the Jews [*cp.* 19 38; 20 19: *also* 9 22: *and* 12 42].	*cp.* 12 46-50; 13 55.	*cp.* 3 31-35; 6 3. *cp.* 8 32.	*cp.* 8 19-21. *cp.* 23 2, 14.

§ 33. Jesus teaches in the Temple during the Feast

John 7 14-24

14 But when it was now the midst of the feast Jesus went up into the temple [*cp.* 2 13-14: *also* 5 14; 10 23], and taught [*cp.* 7 28; 8 2, 20; 18 20]. **15** The Jews therefore marvelled [*cp. verse* 21: *also* 7 46], saying, How knoweth [*cp.* 4 9; 6 60: *also* 3 4, 9; 6 42, 52; 8 33; 12 34] this man letters, having never learned? **16** Jesus therefore answered them, and said, My teaching is not mine [*cp.* 14 24: *also* 3 34; 8 26, 28, 38, 40; 12 49; 14 10; 15 15], but his that sent me. **17** If any man willeth to do his will [*cp.* 9 31: *also* 4 34; 5 30; 6 38], he shall know of the teaching, whether it be of God, or *whether* I speak from myself [*cp.* 12 49; 14 10: *also* 5 19, 30; 8 28: *and* 7 28; 8 42: *and* 16 13]. **18** He that speaketh from	*cp.* 21 12: *also* 21 23; 26 55. *cp.* 7 28; 13 54; 19 25; 22 22, 33: *also* 8 27; *etc.* *cp.* 7 21; 12 50; 21 31: *also* 6 10; 26 39, 42.	*cp.* 11 11, 15: *also* 11 27; 12 35; 14 49. *cp.* 1 22, 27; 6 2; 10 24, 26; 11 18; 12 17: *also* 2 12; *etc.* *cp.* 3 35: *also* 14 36.	*cp.* 19 45: *also* 19 47; 20 1; 21 37; 22 53. *cp.* 2 47; 4 22, 32, 36; 20 26; *also* 5 9; *etc.* *cp.* 22 42.

himself seeketh his own glory [*cp.* 8 50: *also* 5 44]: but he that seeketh the glory of him that sent him, the same is true, and no unrighteousness is in him. **19** Did not Moses give you the law [*cp.* 1 17: *also* 1 45; 7 23; 8 5], and *yet* none of you doeth the law? Why seek ye to kill me [*cp.* 5 18; 7 1, 25; *etc.*]? **20** The multitude answered, Thou hast a ¹devil [*cp.* 8 48, 52; 10 20]: who seeketh to kill thee? **21** Jesus answered and said unto them, I did one work [*cp.* 5 17: *also* 4 34; 5 36; 17 4: *and* 10 25, 32, 37; 14 10: *and* 3 21; 6 28-29; 9 3-4], and ye all ²marvel [*cp. verse* 15]. **22** For this cause hath Moses given you circumcision (not that it is of Moses, but of the fathers); and on the sabbath ye circumcise a man. **23** If a man receiveth circumcision on the sabbath, that the law of Moses may not be broken; are ye wroth with me, because I made a man every whit whole [*cp.* 5 11, 15] on the sabbath [*cp.* 5 16, 18; 9 16]? **24** Judge not according to appearance, but judge righteous judgement [*cp.* 5 30: *also* 8 16].

cp. 12 14; *etc.*	*cp.* 11 18; *etc.*	*cp.* 19 47; *etc.*
cp. 9 34; 10 25; 12 24.	*cp.* 3 22.	*cp.* 11 15, 18.
cp. 12 5.		
cp. 12 11-12.	*cp.* 3 4.	*cp.* 6 9; 13 15-16; 14 5.
		cp. 12 57.

¹ Gr. *demon.*   ² Or, *marvel because of this. Moses hath given you circumcision*

John 7 22: *cp.* Lev. 12 3 *and* Gen. 17 9-14.   John 7 24: *cp.* Deut. 1 16-17; 16 18-19.

§ 34. Questioning among the People about who Jesus is provokes an Attempt by the Chief Priests and Pharisees to arrest Him

John 7 25-36

25 Some therefore of them of Jerusalem said, Is not this he whom they seek to kill [*cp.* 5 18; 7 1, 19; *etc.*]? **26** And lo, he speaketh openly [*cp.* 7 4, 13; 10 24: *also* 11 14, 54; 16 25, 29; 18 20], and they say nothing unto him. Can it be that the rulers [*cp.* 3 1; 7 48; 12 42] indeed know that this is the Christ [*cp.* 1 41; 4 25, 29; 7 41; 9 22; 10 24; 11 27: *also* 4 26, 42: Matt. 16 16; 26 63: *also* 26 68; 27 17, 22: Mark 8 29; 14 61: *also* 15 32: Luke 9 20; 22 67: *also* 23 2, 35, 39]? **27** Howbeit we know this man whence he is [*cp.* 6 42: *also* 8 14, 19; 9 29, 30: *and* 19 9]: but when the Christ cometh [*cp.* 4 25; 7 31], no one knoweth whence he is. **28** Jesus therefore cried in the temple, teaching [*cp.* 7 14; 8 2, 20; 18 20] and saying, Ye both know me, and know whence I am; and I am not come of myself [*cp.* 8 42: *also* 5 19, 30; 8 28: *and* 7 17; 12 49; 14 10; *etc.*: *and* 16 13], but he that sent me is true [*cp.* 8 26: *also* 3 33: *and* 17 17], whom ye know not [*cp.* 8 19, 55; 15 21; 16 3; 17 25: *also* 4 22]. **29** I know him [*cp.* 8 55; 10 15; 17 25: *also* 1 18; 6 46; 8 19], because I am from him [*cp.* 1 14; 5 44; 6 46; 9 16, 33; 16 27, 28; 17 8], and he sent me. **30** They sought therefore to take him [*cp. verse* 32; 7 44; 10 39; 11 57: *also* 5 18; 7 1, 19, 25; 8 37, 40; 11 53: *and* 5 16]: and no man laid his hand on him [*cp.* 7 44; 8 20], because his hour was not yet come [*cp.* 2 4; 7 6, 8; 8 20: *also* 12 23; 13 1; 17 1: *and* 12 27]. **31** But of the multitude many believed on him [*cp.* 2 11, 23; 4 39, 41; 8 30; 10 42; 11 45; 12 11, 42: *also* 7 48]; and they said, When the Christ shall come [*cp.* 4 25; 7 27], will he do more signs [*cp.* 2 11, 23; 3 2; *etc.*] than those which this man hath done? **32** The Pharisees heard the multitude murmuring these things concerning him [*cp.* 7 12: *also* 6 41, 43, 61: *and* 6 52; 7 40-43; 9 16; 10 19-21]; and the chief priests and the Pharisees sent officers [*cp.* 7 45, 46] to take him [*cp. verse* 30]. **33** Jesus therefore said, Yet a little while [*cp.* 12 35; 13 33; 14 19; 16 16-19] am I with you, and I go unto him that sent me [*cp.* 16 5: *also* 14 12, 28; 16 10, 17, 28: *and* 17 11, 13: *and* 20 17: *and* 13 1, 3]. **34** Ye shall seek me [*cp.* 7 36; 8 21; 13 33], and shall not find me: and where I am [*cp.* 7 36; 12 26; 14 3; 17 24], ye cannot come [*cp.* 7 36; 8 21, 22; 13 33: *also* 13 36]. **35** The Jews therefore said among themselves, Whither will this man go [*cp.* 8 14; *etc.*] that we shall not find him [*cp.* 8 22]? will he go unto the Dispersion ¹among the Greeks [*cp.* 12 20], and teach the Greeks? **36** What is this word that he said, Ye shall seek me, and shall not find me: and where I am, ye cannot come?

cp. 12 14; *etc.*	*cp.* 11 18; *etc.*	*cp.* 19 47; *etc.*
	cp. 8 32.	
cp. 9 18.	*cp.* 5 22.	*cp.* 14 1; 18 18; 23 13, 35; 24 20: *also* 8 41; 13 14.
cp. 13 55-56.	*cp.* 6 3.	*cp.* 4 22: *also* 13 25, 27.
cp. 21 23; 26 55.	*cp.* 11 27; 12 35; 14 49.	*cp.* 19 47; 20 1; 21 37; 22 53.
cp. 11 27.		*cp.* 10 22.
cp. 21 46; *etc.*	*cp.* 12 12; *etc.*	*cp.* 20 19; *etc.*
cp. 26 18, 45.	*cp.* 14 35, 41.	*cp.* 22 14, 53.
cp. 18 6.	*cp.* 9 42.	
cp. 21 46: *also* 12 14; 26 4; 27 1.	*cp.* 12 12: *also* 3 6; 11 18; 14 1.	*cp.* 20 19: *also* 19 47; 22 2: *and* 6 11.
	cp. 7 26.	

¹ Gr. *of.*

§ 35. Jesus's Teaching on the Last Day of the Feast leads to a Division among the People

John 7 37-44

John 7 37-44			
37 Now on the last day, the great *day* of the feast, Jesus stood and cried, saying, If any man thirst [*cp.* 4 14; 6 35], let him come unto me [*cp.* 5 40; 6 35, 37, 44, 45, 65], and drink. **38** He that believeth on me, as the scripture hath said, out of his belly shall flow rivers of living water [*cp.* 4 10: *also* 19 34]. **39** But this spake he of the Spirit, which they that believed on him were to receive [*cp.* 20 22: *also* 14 17, 26; 15 26; 16 13: *and* 14 16; 16 7: *and* 1 33; 3 34]: [1]for the Spirit was not yet *given*; because Jesus was not yet glorified [*cp.* 12 16, 23; 13 31: *also* 11 4; 17 10: *and* 17 1 *ff.*]. **40** *Some* of the multitude therefore, when they heard these words, said, This is of a truth the prophet [*cp.* 6 14: *also* 1 21, 25: *and* 4 19, 44; 9 17]. **41** Others said, This is the Christ [*cp.* 1 41; 4 25, 29; 7 26; 9 22; 10 24; 11 27: *also* 4 26, 42: Matt. 16 16; 26 63: *also* 26 68; 27 17, 22: Mark 8 29; 14 61: *also* 15 32: Luke 9 20; 22 67: *also* 23 2, 35, 39]. But some said, What, doth the Christ come out of Galilee [*cp.* 7 52: *also* 1 46]? **42** Hath not the scripture said that the Christ cometh of the seed of David, and from Bethlehem, the village where David was? **43** So there arose a division in the multitude because of him [*cp.* 9 16; 10 19-21: *also* 6 52; 7 12]. **44** And some of them would have taken him [*cp.* 7 30, 32; 10 39; 11 57: *also* 5 18; 7 1, 19, 25; 8 37, 40; 11 53: *and* 5 16]; but no man laid hands on him [*cp.* 7 30; 8 20].	*cp.* 5 6. *cp.* 11 28. *cp.* 13 57; 21 11, 46. *cp.* 1 1; 22 42. *cp.* 2 4-6. *cp.* 21 46: *also* 12 14; 26 4; 27 1.	 *cp.* 6 4, 15. *cp.* 12 35. *cp.* 12 12: *also* 3 6; 11 18; 14 1.	*cp.* 24 49: *also* 11 13. *cp.* 4 24; 7 16, 39; 13 33; 24 19. *cp.* 20 41. *cp.* 2 4. *cp.* 20 19: *also* 19 47; 22 2: *and* 6 11.

[1] Some ancient authorities read *for the Holy Spirit was not yet given.*

John 7 37: *cp.* Lev. 23 36; Num. 29 35: *also* Neh. 8 18: *and* Is. 55 1.   John 7 38: *cp.* Is. 12 3; Ezek. 47 1? John 7 40: *cp.* Deut. 18 15.   John 7 42: *cp.* Is. 11 1: *also* Mic. 5 2: *and* 1 Sam. 16 1.

§ 36. The Attempt at Arrest fails

John 7 45-52

John 7 45-52			
45 The officers [*cp.* 7 32] therefore came to the chief priests and Pharisees; and they said unto them, Why did ye not bring him? **46** The officers answered, Never man so spake [*cp.* 7 15, 21]. **47** The Pharisees therefore answered them, Are ye also led astray [*cp.* 7 12]? **48** Hath any of the rulers [*cp.* 3 1; 7 26; 12 42] believed on him, or of the Pharisees? **49** But this multitude which knoweth not the law are accursed. **50** Nicodemus saith unto them (he that came to him before [*cp.* 3 1 *ff.*; 19 39], being one of them), **51** Doth our law [*cp.* 19 7: *also* 8 17; 10 34; 15 25; 18 31] judge a man, except it first hear from himself and know what he doeth? **52** They answered and said unto him, Art thou also of Galilee? Search, and [1]see that out of Galilee [*cp.* 7 41: *also* 1 46] ariseth no prophet.	*cp.* 7 28; 13 54; *etc.* *cp.* 9 18.	*cp.* 1 22, 27; *etc.* *cp.* 5 22.	*cp.* 2 47; 4 22; *etc.* *cp.* 14 1; 18 18; 23 13, 35; 24 20; *also* 8 41; 13 14.

[1] Or, *see: for out of Galilee &c.*

John 7 51: *cp.* Deut. 1 16: *also* 17 6; 19 15.

§ 37. Jesus is questioned about a Woman taken in Adultery

John 7 53 - 8 11

John 7 53 - 8 11			
53 [1][And they went every man unto his own house: **8 1** but Jesus went [*cp.* 18 1] unto the mount of Olives. **2** And early in the morning he came again into the temple, and all the people came	*cp.* 26 30: *also* 21 17: *and* 24 3.	*cp.* 14 26: *also* 11 11, 19: *and* 13 3.	*cp.* 21 37; 22 39. *cp.* 21 38.

unto him; and he sat down, and taught them [*cp.* 7 14, 28; 8 20; 18 20]. **3** And the scribes and the Pharisees bring a woman taken in adultery; and having set her in the midst, **4** they say unto him, [2]Master, this woman hath been taken in adultery, in the very act. **5** Now in the law [*cp.* 1 17, 45; 7 19, 23] Moses commanded us to stone such: what then sayest thou of her? **6** And this they said,[3] tempting him, that they might have *whereof* to accuse him. But Jesus stooped down, and with his finger wrote on the ground. **7** But when they continued asking him, he lifted up himself, and said unto them, He that is without sin among you, let him first cast a stone at her. **8** And again he stooped down, and with his finger wrote on the ground. **9** And they, when they heard it, went out one by one, beginning from the eldest, *even* unto the last: and Jesus was left alone, and the woman, where she was, in the midst. **10** And Jesus lifted up himself, and said unto her, Woman, where are they [*cp.* 7 11; 9 12]? did no man condemn thee? **11** And she said, No man, Lord. And Jesus said, Neither do I condemn thee: go thy way; from henceforth sin no more [*cp.* 5 14].]

	cp. 21 23; 26 55.	*cp.* 11 27; 12 35; 14 49.	*cp.* 19 47; 20 1; 21 37; 22 53.
	cp. 16 1; *etc.* *cp.* 12 10; 22 15.	*cp.* 8 11; *etc.* *cp.* 3 2; 12 13.	*cp.* 10 25; *etc.* *cp.* 6 7; 11 53-54; 20 20.
	cp. 7 3-4.		*cp.* 6 41-42.

[1] Most of the ancient authorities omit John 7 53-8 11. Those which contain it vary much from each other.   [2] Or, *Teacher*   [3] Or, *trying*

John 8 5: Lev. 20 10; Deut. 22 22-24: *cp.* Ezek. 16 38, 40.   John 8 7: *cp.* Deut. 17 7.

§ 38. Jesus the Light of the World

John 8 12-20

12 Again therefore Jesus spake unto them, saying, I am the light of the world [*cp.* 9 5; 12 46: *also* 1 4, 5, 9; 3 19; 12 35-36]: he that followeth me [*cp.* 10 27: *also* 10 4: *and* 1 43; 12 26; 21 19, 22] shall not walk in the darkness [*cp.* 12 35: *also* 1 5; 12 46: *and* 11 10], but shall have the light of life [*cp.* 1 4]. **13** The Pharisees therefore said unto him, Thou bearest witness of thyself [*cp.* 5 31; 8 14, 18: *also* 5 19, 30; 7 17; *etc.*]; thy witness is not true [*cp.* 5 31, 32; 8 14: *also* 19 35; 21 24]. **14** Jesus answered and said unto them, Even if I bear witness of myself, my witness is true [*cp. verse* 13 *above*]; for I know whence I came [*cp.* 7 27, 28; 9 29, 30; 19 9: *also* 3 8], and whither I go [*cp.* 8 21, 22; 13 33, 36; 14 4: *also* 7 35; 13 36; 14 5; 16 5: *and* 3 8; 12 35]; but ye know not whence I come, or whither I go [*cp.* 9 29, 30; 19 9: *also* 6 42; 7 27, 28: *and* 3 8]. **15** Ye judge after the flesh; I judge no man [*cp.* 12 47: *also* 3 17]. **16** Yea and if I judge, my judgement is true [*cp.* 5 30: *also* 7 24]; for I am not alone [*cp.* 8 29; 16 32], but I and the Father that sent me. **17** Yea and in your law [*cp.* 10 34; 18 31: *also* 15 25: *and* 7 51; 19 7] it is written, that the witness of two men is true. **18** I am he that beareth witness of myself [*cp. verse* 13 *above*], and the Father that sent me beareth witness of me [*cp.* 5 37: *also* 5 32]. **19** They said therefore unto him, Where is thy Father? Jesus answered, Ye know neither me [*cp.* 16 3 *and verse* 14 *above*], nor my Father [*cp.* 7 28; 8 55; 15 21; 16 3; 17 25: *also* 4 22]: if ye knew me, ye would know my Father also [*cp.* 14 7]. **20** These words spake he in the treasury, as he taught in the temple [*cp.* 7 14, 28; 8 2; 18 20]: and no man took him [*cp.* 7 30, 44]; because his hour was not yet come [*cp.* 2 4; 7 6, 8, 30: *also* 12 23; 13 1; 17 1: *and* 12 27].

	cp. 5 14. *cp.* 16 24; *etc.*	*cp.* 8 34; *etc.*	*cp.* 9 23; *etc.*
			cp. 13 25, 27.
	cp. 26 56. *cp.* 18 16.	*cp.* 14 50.	
	cp. 21 23; 26 55. *cp.* 26 18, 45.	*cp.* 11 27; 12 35; 14 49. *cp.* 14 35, 41.	*cp.* 19 47; 20 1; *etc.* *cp.* 22 14, 53.

John 8 17: Deut. 19 15; *cp.* Deut. 17 6 *and* Num. 35 30.

§ 39. Further Teaching of Jesus about who He is

John 8 21-30

21 He said therefore again unto them, I go away [*cp.* 14 28: *also* 7 33; 14 2, 3; *etc.*], and ye shall seek me [*cp.* 7 34, 36; 13 33], and shall die in your sin: whither I go [*cp.* 8 14, 22; 13 33, 36; 14 4: *also* 7 35; 13 36; 14 5; 16 5: *and* 3 8; 12 35], ye cannot come [*cp.* 7 34, 36; 8 22; 13 33: *also* 13 36]. **22** The Jews therefore said, Will he kill himself, that he saith, Whither I go, and ye cannot come [*cp.* 7 35]? **23** And he said unto them, Ye are from beneath; I am from above [*cp.* 3 31: *also* 3 13; 6 32-33, 38, 41-42, 50-51, 58]: ye are of this world; I am not of this world [*cp.* 17 14, 16: *also* 18 36: *and* 15 19]. **24** I said therefore unto you, that ye shall die in your sins [*cp. verse* 21 *above*]: for except ye [*cp.* 3 3, 5; 6 53: *also* 13 8] believe that [1]I am *he* [*cp. verse* 28 *below and* 13 19: *also* 8 58], ye shall die in your sins [*cp.* 16 9]. **25** They said therefore unto him, Who art thou [*cp.* 1 19; 21 12]? Jesus said unto them, [2]Even that which I have also spoken unto you from the beginning. **26** I have many things to speak [*cp.* 16 12: *also* 14 30] and to judge concerning you [*cp.* 5 22, 27: *also* 9 39: *and* 3 17; 12 47]: howbeit he that sent me is true [*cp.* 7 28: *also* 3 33: *and* 17 17]; and the things which I heard from him [*cp.* 3 34; 7 16; 8 28, 38, 40; 12 49, 50; 14 10, 24; 15 15], these speak I [3]unto the world [*cp.* 3 34; 8 47; 12 47-50; 14 10; 17 8, 14: *also* 6 63, 68: *and* 18 20]. **27** They perceived not [*cp.* 3 10; 4 33; 8 43; 10 6; 11 13; 12 16; 13 7, 28, 36; 14 5-10, 22; 16 17-18] that he spake to them of the Father. **28** Jesus therefore said, When ye have lifted up the Son of man [*cp.* 3 14; 12 32-34: *also* 2 19-22], then shall ye know that [4]I am *he* [*cp. verse* 24 *above and* 13 19: *also* 8 58], and *that* I do nothing of myself [*cp.* 5 19, 30: *also* 5 31; 7 17, 28; 8 13, 14, 18, 42, 54; 10 18; 12 49; 14 10: *and* 16 13], but as the Father taught me [*cp.* 3 34; 7 16; 8 26, 38, 40; 12 49, 50; 14 10, 24; 15 15], I speak these things. **29** And he that sent me is with me; he hath not left me alone [*cp.* 8 16; 16 32]; for I do always the things that are pleasing to him. **30** As he spake these things, many believed on him [*cp.* 2 11, 23; 4 39, 41; 7 31; 10 42; 11 45; 12 11, 42: *also* 7 48].

[1] Or, *I am*　　[2] Or, How is it *that I even speak to you at all?*　　[3] Gr. *into.*　　[4] Or, *I am*
Or, *I am* he: *and I do*

		cp. 13 6; 14 62.	*cp.* 21 8; 22 70.
cp. 15 16; 16 8-12.	*cp.* 4 13; 6 52; 7 18; 8 17-21; *etc.*	*cp.* 2 50; 9 45; 18 34.
cp. 16 21-23; *etc.*	*cp.* 8 31-33; *etc.*: *and* 13 6; 14 62.	*cp.* 9 22; *etc.*: *and* 21 8; 22 70.
cp. 26 56.	*cp.* 14 50.	
cp. 18 6.	*cp.* 9 42.	

§ 40. Jesus, Abraham, and Abraham's Seed

John 8 31-59

31 Jesus therefore said to those Jews which had believed him [*cp.* 8 30], If ye abide in [*cp.* 6 56; 15 4, 5, 7: *also* 17 21] my word [*cp.* 4 41; 5 24; 8 37, 43, 51, 52; 12 48; 14 23, 24; 15 3, 20: *also* 5 38; 8 55; 14 24; 17 6, 14, 17, 20], *then* are ye truly my disciples [*cp.* 13 35; 15 8]; **32** and ye shall know the truth [*cp.* 1 14, 17; 5 33; 14 6; 18 37], and the truth shall make you free. **33** They answered unto him, We be Abraham's seed [*cp. vv.* 37, 39, 53, *below*], and have never yet been in bondage to any man: how sayest thou [*cp.* 12 34: *also* 14 9: *and* 3 4, 9; 6 42, 52, 60: *and* 4 9; 7 15], Ye shall be made free? **34** Jesus answered them, Verily, verily, I say unto you, Every one that committeth sin is the bond-servant of sin. **35** And the bondservant abideth not in the house for ever: the son abideth for ever. **36** If therefore the Son shall make you free, ye shall be free indeed. **37** I know that ye are Abraham's seed [*cp. verse* 33 *above*]; yet ye seek to kill me [*cp.* 5 18; 7 1, 19, 25; 8 40: *also* 11 53: *and* 7 30, 32, 44; 10 39; 11 57: *and* 5 16], because my word [*cp. verse* 31 *above*] [1]hath not free course in you. **38** I speak the things which I have seen with [2]*my* Father [*cp.* 3 34; 7 16; 8 26, 28, 40; 12 49, 50; 14 10, 24; 15 15]: and ye also do the things which ye heard from *your* father. **39** They answered and said unto him, Our father is Abraham [*cp. verse*

cp. 13 19-23.	*cp.* 2 2; 4 14-20, 33; 16 20.	*cp.* 4 32; *etc.*
		cp. 14 26, 27, 33.
cp. 3 9.		*cp.* 3 8; 13 16; 16 24, 30; 19 9.
cp. 3 9.		*cp.* 3 8; *etc.*
cp. 12 14; *etc.*	*cp.* 11 18; *etc.*	*cp.* 19 47; *etc.*
cp. 19 11, 12.		
cp. 3 9.		*cp.* 3 8; *etc.*

33 *above*]. Jesus saith unto them, If ye [3]were Abraham's children, [4]ye would do the works of Abraham. **40** But now ye seek to kill me [*cp. verse 37 above*], a man that hath told you the truth, which I heard from God [*cp. verse 38 above*]: this did not Abraham. **41** Ye do the works of your father. They said unto him, We were not born of fornication; we have one Father, *even* God. **42** Jesus said unto them, If God were your Father, ye would love me: for I came forth and am come from God [*cp.* 16 28: *also* 13 3; 16 27, 30; 17 8]; for neither have I come of myself [*cp.* 7 28: *also* 5 19, 30; 8 28: *and* 7 17; 12 49; 14 10; *etc.*: *and* 16 13], but he sent me. **43** Why do ye not [5]understand my speech [*cp.* 3 10; 4 33; 8 27; 10 6; 11 13; 12 16; 13 7, 28, 36; 14 5-10, 22; 16 17-18]? *Even* because ye cannot hear my word [*cp.* 5 24 *and verse 31 above*]. **44** Ye are of *your* father the devil, and the lusts of your father it is your will to do. He was a murderer from the beginning, and [6]stood not in the truth, because there is no truth in him. [7]When he speaketh a lie, he speaketh of his own [*cp.* 1 11; 13 1; 15 19; 16 32; 19 27]: for he is a liar, and the father thereof. **45** But because I say the truth, ye believe me not. **46** Which of you convicteth me of sin [*cp.* 16 8]? If I say truth, why do ye not believe me? **47** He that is of God heareth the words of God [*cp.* 3 34; 8 26; 12 47-50; 14 10; 17 8, 14: *also* 6 63, 68]: for this cause ye hear *them* not, because ye are not of God. **48** The Jews answered and said unto him, Say we not well that thou art a Samaritan [*cp.* 4 9], and hast a [8]devil [*cp.* 7 20; 8 52; 10 20]? **49** Jesus answered, I have not a [8]devil; but I honour my Father [*cp.* 5 23], and ye dishonour me. **50** But I seek not mine own glory [*cp.* 7 18: *also* 5 44: *and verse 54 below*]: there is one that seeketh and judgeth. **51** Verily, verily, I say unto you, If a man keep my word [*cp. verse 52 below and* 14 23, 24; 15 20: *also verse 31 above*: *and* 14 15, 21; 15 10], he shall never see death [*cp.* 5 24; 6 50, 51, 58; 10 28; 11 25-26]. **52** The Jews said unto him, Now we know that thou hast a [8]devil [*cp. verse 48 above*]. Abraham is dead, and the prophets; and thou sayest, If a man keep my word, he shall never taste of death. **53** Art thou greater than our father [*cp.* 4 12: *also vv.* 33, 37, 39, *above*] Abraham, which is dead? and the prophets are dead: whom makest thou thyself [*cp.* 5 18; 10 33; 19 7, 12: *also* 1 22]? **54** Jesus answered, If I glorify myself [*cp. verse 50 above*: *also* 5 31; 8 13, 14, 18; *etc.*], my glory is nothing: it is my Father that glorifieth me [*cp.* 13 32; 16 14; 17 1, 5: *also* 7 39; *etc.*]; of whom ye say, that he is your God [*cp. verse 41 above*] **55** and ye have not known him [*cp.* 7 28; 8 19; 15 21; 16 3; 17 25: *also* 4 22]: but I know him [*cp.* 7 29; 10 15; 17 25: *also* 1 18; 6 46; 8 19]; and if I should say, I know him not, I shall be like unto you, a liar: but I know him, and keep his word [*cp.* 5 38; 14 24; 17 6, 14, 17, 20: *also* 5 24; 8 31; *etc.*]. **56** Your father Abraham rejoiced [9]to see my day; and he saw it, and was glad. **57** The Jews therefore said unto him, Thou art not yet fifty years old [*cp.* 2 20], and hast thou seen Abraham? **58** Jesus said unto them, Verily, verily, I say unto you, Before Abraham [10]was, I am [*cp.* 17 5, 24: *also* 1 1, 2, 18: *and* 8 24, 28; 13 19]. **59** They took up stones therefore to cast at him [*cp.* 10 31; 11 8]: but Jesus [11]hid himself, and went out of the temple [*cp.* 10 39: *also* 12 36].[12]

cp. 12 14; *etc.*	*cp.* 11 18; *etc.*	*cp.* 19 47; *etc.*
	cp. 1 38.	
cp. 15 16; 16 8-12.	*cp.* 4 13; 6 52; *etc.*	*cp.* 2 50; 9 45; 18 34.
cp. 13 19-23.	*cp.* 2 2; *etc.*	*cp.* 4 32: *also* 1 2; *etc.*
cp. 19 4.		
		cp. 18 28.
cp. 10 5: *and* 9 34; 10 25; 12 24.	*cp.* 3 22.	*cp.* 9 52-53: *and* 11 15, 18.
		cp. 2 26.
cp. 9 34; 10 25; 12 24.	*cp.* 3 22.	*cp.* 11 15, 18.
cp. 16 28. *cp.* 3 9.	*cp.* 9 1.	*cp.* 9 27. *cp.* 3 8; *etc.*
cp. 11 27.		*cp.* 10 22.
cp. 13 19-23.	*cp.* 2 2; *etc.*	*cp.* 5 1; 8 11, 21; *etc.* *cp.* 17 22; *etc.* *cp.* 3 23.
	cp. 13 6; 14 62.	*cp.* 21 8; 22 70.
		cp. 4 30.

[1] Or, *hath no place in you* [2] Or, *the Father: do ye also therefore the things which ye heard from the Father.* [3] Gr. *are.* [4] Some ancient authorities read *ye do the works of Abraham.* [5] Or, *know* [6] Some ancient authorities read *standeth.* [7] Or, *When one speaketh a lie, he speaketh of his own: for his father also is a liar.* [8] Gr. *demon.* [9] Or, *that he should see* [10] Gr. *was born.* [11] Or, *was hidden, and went &c.* [12] Many ancient authorities add *and going through the midst of them went his way and so passed by.*

John 8 35: *cp.* Gen. 21 10.   John 8 41: *cp.* Deut. 32 6; Is. 63 16; 64 8; Mal. 2 10.   John 8 44: *cp.* Wisd. 2 24. John 8 49: *cp.* Exod. 20 12; Deut. 5 16.   John 8 52; *cp.* Zech. 1 5.   John 8 58: *cp.* Exod. 3 14.

§ 41. A Blind Beggar receives his Sight

[*Cp.* Matt. 9 27-31; 12 22; 15 30-31; 20 29-34; 21 14: Mark 8 22-26; 10 46-52: Luke 7 21; 18 35-43]

John 9 1-12

1 And as he passed by, he saw a man blind from his birth. 2 And his disciples asked him, saying, Rabbi [*cp.* 1 38, 49; 3 2; 4 31; 6 25; 11 8: *also* 20 16: *and* 3 26], who did sin, this man, or his parents, that he should be born blind [*cp.* 9 34]? 3 Jesus answered, Neither did this man sin, nor his parents: but [*cp.* 11 4] that the works of God [*cp. verse* 4 *below*] should be made manifest in him [*cp.* 1 31; 2 11; 3 21; 7 4; 17 6; 21 1, 14: *also* 14 21, 22]. 4 We must work the works of him that sent me [*cp.* 3 21; 6 28-29: *also* 10 25, 32, 37; 14 10: *and* 4 34; 5 36; 17 4: *and* 5 17; 7 21], while it is day [*cp.* 11 9; 12 35]: the night cometh [*cp.* 11 10: *also* 13 30], when no man can work. 5 When I am in the world, I am the light of the world [*cp.* 8 12; 12 46: *also* 1 4, 5, 9; 3 19; 12 35-36]. 6 When he had thus spoken, he spat on the ground [*cp.* 18 6], and made clay of the spittle, ¹and anointed [*cp.* 20 17] his eyes with the clay, 7 and said unto him [*cp.* 4 50; 5 8; 11 43], Go, wash in the pool of Siloam (which is by interpretation, Sent). He went away therefore, and washed, and came seeing. 8 The neighbours therefore, and they which saw him aforetime, that he was a beggar, said, Is not this he that sat and begged? 9 Others said, It is he: others said, No, but he is like him. He said, I am *he*. 10 They said therefore unto him, How then were thine eyes opened? 11 He answered, The man that is called Jesus made clay, and anointed mine eyes, and said unto me, Go to Siloam, and wash: so I went away and washed, and I received sight. 12 And they said unto him, Where is he [*cp.* 7 11: *also* 8 10]? He saith, I know not.

cp. 26 25, 49; *also* 23 7, 8.	*cp.* 9 5; 11 21; 14 45: *also* 10 51.	*cp.* 13 1-5.
	cp. 16 12, 14.	
cp. 5 14.	*cp.* 7 33; 8 23.	
cp. 9 29; *etc.*	*cp.* 8 25; *etc.*	*cp.* 4 40; *etc.*
cp. 8 8; *etc.*	*cp.* 10 52; *etc.*	*cp.* 18 42; *etc.*
		cp. 13 4.
	cp. 10 46.	*cp.* 18 35.
cp. 11 5; 20 34.	*cp.* 10 51-52.	*cp.* 7 22; 18 41-43.

¹ Or, *and with the clay thereof anointed* his *eyes*

John 9 2: *cp.* Exod. 20 5; 34 7; Num. 14 18; Deut. 5 9.   John 9 7, 11: *cp.* II Kings 5 10, 14-15: *also* Neh. 3 15; Is. 8 6.

§ 42. The Pharisees object

[*Cp.* Matt. 12 9-14 || Mark 3 1-6 || Luke 6 6-11; Luke 13 10-17, 14 1-6; John 5 1-18, 7 21-24: *also* Matt. 12 1-8 || Mark 2 23-28 || Luke 6 1-5]

John 9 13-34

13 They bring to the Pharisees him that aforetime was blind. 14 Now it was the sabbath on the day [*cp.* 5 9] when Jesus made the clay, and opened his eyes. 15 Again therefore the Pharisees also asked him how he received his sight. And he said unto them, He put clay upon mine eyes, and I washed, and do see. 16 Some therefore of the Pharisees said, This man is not from God [*cp. verse* 33 *and* 6 46: *also* 1 14; 5 44; 7 29; 16 27, 28; 17 8], because he keepeth not the sabbath [*cp.* 5 16, 18; 7 23]. But others said, How can a man that is a sinner [*cp. vv.* 24, 25, 31] do such signs [*cp. verse* 33: *also* 3 2; 10 21: *and* 5 36; 10 25]? And there was a division among them [*cp.* 7 40-43; 10 19-21: *also* 6 52; 7 12]. 17 They say therefore unto the blind man again, What sayest thou of him, in that he opened thine eyes? And he said, He is a prophet [*cp.* 4 19, 44; 6 14; 7 40]. 18 The Jews therefore did not believe concerning him, that he had been blind, and had received his sight, until they called the parents of him that had received his sight, 19 and asked them, saying, Is this your son, who ye say was born blind? how then doth he now see? 20 His parents answered and said, We know that this is our son, and that he was born blind: 21 but how he now seeth, we know not; or who opened his eyes, we know not: ask him; he is of age

cp. 9 11, 13; 11 19; 26 45.	*cp.* 2 16, 17; 14 41.	*cp.* 5 8, 30, 32; 6 32, 33, 34; 7 34, 37, 39; 15 1, 2; *etc.*
cp. 13 57; 21 11, 46.	*cp.* 6 4, 15.	*cp.* 4 24; 7 16, 39; 13 33; 24 19.

[*cp. verse 23 below*]; he shall speak for himself. **22** These things said his parents, because they feared the Jews [*cp.* 7 13; 19 38; 20 19: *also* 12 42]: for the Jews had agreed already, that if any man should confess him *to be* Christ [*cp.* 1 41; 4 25, 26, 29, 42; 7 26, 41; 10 24, 25; 11 27: *also* 3 2; 12 42], he should be put out of the synagogue [*cp.* 12 42; 16 2]. **23** Therefore said his parents, He is of age; ask him [*cp. verse* 21 *above*]. **24** So they called a second time the man that was blind, and said unto him, Give glory to God: we know [*cp. vv.* 29 *and* 31: *also* 3 2; 4 42; 16 30; 21 24: Matt. 22 16; Mark 12 14; Luke 20 21] that this man is a sinner [*cp. vv.* 16, 25, *and* 31]. **25** He therefore answered, Whether he be a sinner, I know not: one thing I know, that, whereas I was blind, now I see. **26** They said therefore unto him, What did he to thee? how opened he thine eyes? **27** He answered them, I told you even now [*cp. verse* 15], and ye did not hear: wherefore would ye hear it again? would ye also become his disciples? **28** And they reviled him, and said, Thou art his disciple; but we are disciples of Moses [*cp.* 5 45]. **29** We know [*cp. vv.* 24 *and* 31: *also* 3 2; 4 42; 16 30; 21 24] that God hath spoken unto Moses: but as for this man, we know not whence he is [*cp.* 8 14, 19; 19 9: *also* 6 42; 7 27, 28]. **30** The man answered and said unto them, Why, herein is the marvel, that ye know not whence he is, and *yet* he opened mine eyes. **31** We know [*cp. vv.* 24 *and* 29: *also* 3 2; 4 42; 16 30; 21 24] that God heareth not sinners [*cp. vv.* 16, 24, 25, *above*]: but if any man be a worshipper of God, and do his will [*cp.* 7 17: *also* 4 34; 5 30; 6 38], him he heareth. **32** Since the world began it was never heard that any one opened the eyes of a man born blind. **33** If this man were not from God [*cp. verse* 16 and 6 46: *also* 1 14; 5 44; 7 29; 16 27, 28; 17 8], he could do nothing [*cp. verse* 16: *also* 3 2; 10 21: *and* 5 36; 10 25]. **34** They answered and said unto him, Thou wast altogether born in sins [*cp.* 9 2], and dost thou teach us? And they cast him out.

cp. 16 16: *also* 26 63, 68; 27 17, 22.	*cp.* 8 29: *also* 14 61-62; 15 32.	*cp.* 9 20: *also* 22 67; 23 2, 35, 39.	
cp. 5 16; 9 8; 15 31.	*cp.* 2 12.	*cp.* 17 18: *also* 2 20; 5 25, 26; 7 16; 13 13; 17 15; 18 43; 23 47.	
cp. 22 16.	*cp.* 12 14.	*cp.* 20 21. *cp.* 13 25, 27.	
cp. 22 16.	*cp.* 12 14.	*cp.* 20 21.	
cp. 7 21; 12 50; 21 31: *also* 6 10; 26 39, 42.	*cp.* 3 35: *also* 14 36.	*cp.* 22 42.	

John 9 24: *cp.* Josh. 7 19; Jer. 13 16: *also* I Sam. 6 5; Is. 42 12.   John 9 31: *cp.* Job 27 9; Ps. 66 18; Prov. 28 9; Is. 1 15: *also* Ps. 34 15-16; 145 18-20; Prov. 15 29.

§ 43. Jesus answers the Pharisees

John 9 35-41

35 Jesus heard that they had cast him out; and finding him, he said, Dost thou believe on [1]the Son of God? **36** He answered and said, And who is he, Lord, that I may believe on him? **37** Jesus said unto him, Thou hast both seen him, and he it is that speaketh with thee [*cp.* 4 26]. **38** And he said, Lord, I believe [*cp.* 6 69; 11 27; 16 30: *also* 16 27; 17 8; 20 31]. And he worshipped him [*cp.* 11 32; 18 6]. **39** And Jesus said, For judgement came I [*cp.* 5 22, 27: *also* 8 26: *and* 3 17; 12 47] into this world [*cp.* 12 46; 16 28; 18 37: *also* 1 9; 3 19; 6 14; 11 27: *and* 3 17; 10 36; 17 18], that they which see not may see; and that they which see may become blind. **40** Those of the Pharisees which were with him heard these things, and said unto him, Are we also blind? **41** Jesus said unto them, If ye were blind, ye would have no sin [*cp.* 15 22, 24]: but now ye say, We see: your sin remaineth.

cp. 16 16.	*cp.* 9 24: *also* 8 29.	*cp.* 9 20.	
cp. 2 11; 8 2; 9 18; 14 33; 15 25; 20 20; 28 9, 17: *also* 17 14.	*cp.* 5 6: *also* 1 40; 3 11; 5 22, 33; 7 25; 10 17.	*cp.* 24 52: *also* 5 8, 12; 8 28, 41, 47; 17 16.	
cp. 11 5.		*cp.* 4 18: *also* 7 22.	
cp. 13 13.	*cp.* 4 12.	*cp.* 8 10.	
cp. 15 14; 23 16, 17, 19, 24, 26.		*cp.* 6 39.	

[1] Many ancient authorities read *the Son of man*.

John 9 39: *cp.* Is. 29 18; 35 5; 42 16: *and* 6 9-10.

§ 44. The Parable of the Shepherd

[*Cp.* Matt. 18 12-13 ‖ Luke 15 3-7]

John 10 1-6

1 Verily, verily, I say unto you, He that entereth not by the door into the fold of the sheep, but climbeth up some other way, the same is a thief and a robber. 2 But he that entereth in [*cp. verse 1 above and* 10 9: *also* 3 5] by the door is [1]the shepherd of the sheep. 3 To him the porter openeth; and the sheep hear his voice: and he calleth his own sheep by name, and leadeth them out. 4 When he hath put forth all his own, he goeth before them, and the sheep follow him [*cp.* 10 27]: for they know his voice [*cp.* 10 14: *also* 10 16, 27]. 5 And a stranger will they not follow, but will flee from him: for they know not the voice of strangers. 6 This [2]parable [*cp.* 16 25, 29] spake Jesus unto them: but they understood not what things they were which he spake unto them [*cp.* 12 16: *also* 3 10; 4 33; 8 27, 43; 11 13; 13 7, 28, 36; 14 5-10, 22; 16 17-18].

cp. 5 20; 7 21; 18 3; 19 23, 24; 21 31; 23 13: *also* 7 13; 18 8, 9; 19 17; 25 21, 23.

cp. 9 47; 10 15, 23, 24, 25: *also* 9 43, 45.

cp. 18 17, 24, 25: *also* 11 52; 13 24; 24 26.

cp. 15 16; 16 8-12.

cp. 4 13; 6 52; 7 18; 8 17-21; 9 10, 32; 16 14.

cp. 2 50; 9 45; 18 34.

[1] Or, *a shepherd*   [2] Or, *proverb*

§ 45. Jesus the Good Shepherd

John 10 7-18

7 Jesus therefore said unto them again, Verily, verily, I say unto you, I am the door of the sheep. 8 All that came before me are thieves and robbers: but the sheep did not hear them. 9 I am the door: by me if any man enter in [*cp.* 10 1, 2: *also* 3 5], he shall be saved [*cp.* 3 16-17; 5 34; 12 47: *also* 4 42], and shall go in and go out, and shall find pasture. 10 The thief cometh not, but that he may steal, and kill, and destroy: I came that they may have life [*cp.* 1 4; 5 40; *etc.*], and may [1]have *it* abundantly. 11 I am the good shepherd [*cp. verse* 14 *below and* 21 15-17]: the good shepherd layeth down his life [*cp. vv.* 15 *and* 17 *below: also* 13 37, 38; 15 13: *and* 11 51-52] for the sheep. 12 He that is a hireling, and not a shepherd, whose own the sheep are not, beholdeth the wolf coming, and leaveth the sheep, and fleeth, and the wolf snatcheth them [*cp.* 10 28, 29], and scattereth *them* [*cp.* 16 32]: 13 *he fleeth* because he is a hireling, and careth not for the sheep. 14 I am the good shepherd [*cp. verse* 11 *above and* 21 15-17]; and I know mine own [*cp.* 10 27: *also* 16 14, 15; 17 10], and mine own know me [*cp.* 10 4: *also* 10 16, 27], 15 even as the Father knoweth me, and I know the Father [*cp.* 7 29; 8 55; 17 25: *also* 1 18; 6 46; 8 19]; and I lay down my life [*cp. verses* 11 *and* 17] for the sheep. 16 And other sheep I have, which are not of this fold [*cp.* 11 52]: them also I must [2]bring, and they shall hear my voice [*cp.* 10 27: *also* 10 4: *and* 5 25, 28; 18 37]; and [3]they shall become one flock [*cp.* 11 52; 17 11, 21, 22, 23: *also* 12 32], one shepherd. 17 Therefore doth the Father love me [*cp.* 3 35; 5 20; 15 9-10; 17 23, 24, 26], because I lay down my life [*cp. vv.* 11 *and* 15 *above*], that I may take it again. 18 No one [4]taketh it away from me, but I lay it down of myself [*cp.* 5 19, 30, 31; 7 17; *etc.*]. I have [5]power [*cp.* 5 27; 17 2] to lay it down, and I have [5]power to take it again [*cp.* 2 19, 21: *also* 5 26: *and* 5 27]. This commandment received I from my Father [*cp.* 12 49; 14 31: *also* 15 10].

cp. 5 20; *etc.*
cp. 1 21: *also* 18 11: *and* 20 28.

cp. 9 47; *etc.*
cp. 10 45.

cp. 18 17; *etc.*
cp. 2 11: *also* 9 55; 19 10.

cp. 9 36: *also* 10 6; 15 24: *and* 26 31.

cp. 6 34: *and* 14 27.

cp. 20 28: *also* 26 28.

cp. 10 45: *also* 14 24.

cp. 26 31.

cp. 14 27.

cp. 9 36: *also* 10 6; 15 24: *and* 26 31.
cp. 11 27.

cp. 6 34: *and* 14 27.

cp. 10 22.

cp. 8 11; 10 18; 21 31, 41, 43; 22 7-10; *etc.*

cp. 12 9; 13 10; 14 9; 16 15.

cp. 2 30-32; 36; 13 29; 14 21-24; *etc.*

cp. 3 17; 17 5.

cp. 1 11; 9 7; 12 6.

cp. 3 22; 20 13.

cp. 28 18.

[1] Or, *have abundance*   [2] Or, *lead*   [3] Or, *there shall be one flock*   [4] Some ancient authorities read *took it away.*   [5] Or, *right*

John 10 8, 10, 12-13: *cp.* Jer. 23 1-2; Ezek. 34 1-6; Zech. 11 16-17.   John 10 9: *cp.* Ps. 23 2; Ezek. 34 14. John 10 11: *cp.* Ps. 23 1-6; Is. 40 11; Ezek. 34 11-12, 23.   John 10 16: *cp.* Ezek. 34 11-13, 23; 37 24.

§ 46. The Jews are again divided

John 10 19-21

19 There arose a division again among the Jews [*cp.* 7 40-43; 9 16: *also* 6 52; 7 12] because of these words. **20** And many of them said, He hath a [1]devil [*cp.* 7 20; 8 48, 52], and is mad; why hear ye him? **21** Others said, These are not the sayings of one possessed with a [1]devil. Can a [1]devil open the eyes of the blind [*cp.* 3 2; 9 16, 33: *also* 5 36; 10 25]?

[1] Gr. *demon*.

cp. 9 34; 10 25; 12 24.	*cp.* 3 22: *and* 3 21.	*cp.* 11 15, 18.

§ 47. At the Feast of the Dedication

John 10 22-39	Matt. 26 63	Mark 14 61	Luke 22 66-68
22 [1]And it was the feast of the dedication at Jerusalem: it was winter; **23** and Jesus was walking in the temple in Solomon's porch. **24** The Jews therefore came round about him, and said unto him, How long dost thou hold us in suspense?			**66** And as soon as it was day, the assembly of the elders of the people was gathered together, both chief priest and scribes; and they led him away into their council, saying,
If thou art the Christ [*cp.* 1 41; 4 25, 26, 29; 7 26, 41; 9 22; 11 27], tell us plainly [*cp.* 7 4, 13, 26: *also* 11 14, 54; 16 25, 29; 18 20]. **25** Jesus answered them, I told you, and ye believe not [*cp.* 6 36; 12 37: *also* 1 11; *etc.*]:	And the high priest said unto him, I adjure thee by the living [*cp.* 16 16] God, that thou tell us whether thou be the Christ [*cp.* 16 16: *also* 26 68; 27 17, 22].	Again the high priest asked him, and saith unto him, Art thou the Christ [*cp.* 8 29: *also* 15 32]? *cp.* 8 32.	**67** If thou art the Christ [*cp.* 9 20: *also* 23 2, 35, 39] tell us. But he said unto them, If I tell you, ye will not believe: **68** and if I ask you, ye will not answer.
the works [*cp. vv.* 32, 37, *and* 14 10: *also* 4 34; 5 36; 17 4: *and* 3 21; 6 28-29; 9 3-4: *and* 10 38; 14 11: *and* 5 17; 7 21; 15 24] that I do in my Father's name [*cp.* 5 43: *also* 12 13: *and* 17 12], these bear witness of me [*cp.* 5 36: *also* 3 2; 9 16, 33; 10 21]. **26** But ye believe not, because ye are not of my sheep. **27** My sheep hear my voice [*cp.* 10 16: *also* 10 4: *and* 3 25, 28; 18 37], and I know them [*cp.* 10 14], and they follow me [*cp.* 10 4: *also* 8 12: *and* 1 43; 12 26; 21 19, 22]: **28** and I give unto them eternal life [*cp.* 17 2: *also* 3 15, 16, 36; 5 24; 6 40; *etc.*: *and* 8 51; 11 25-26]; and they shall never perish [*cp.* 3 16: *also* 17 12; 18 9: *and* 6 39], and no one shall snatch them [*cp.* 10 12] out of my hand. **29** [2]My Father, which hath given *them* unto me [*cp.* 6 37, 39; 17 2, 6, 9, 11, 12, 24; 18 9], is greater [*cp.* 14 28] than all; and no one is able to snatch [3]*them* [*cp.* 10 12] out of the Father's hand. **30** I and the Father are one [*cp.* 17 11, 22: *also* 5 19, 12 45; 14 9-11; 15 24]. **31** The Jews took up stones again to stone him [*cp.* 8 59; 11 8]. **32** Jesus answered them, Many good works have I shewed you from the Father [*cp. vv.* 25, 37, *and* 38]; for which of those works do ye stone me? **33** The Jews answered him, For a good work we	*cp.* 16 24; *etc.*	*cp.* 8 34; *etc.*	*cp.* 9 23; *etc.*
stone thee not, but for blasphemy [*cp. verse* 36]; and because that thou, being a man, makest thyself [*cp.* 5 18; 8 53; 19 7, 12] God [*cp. verse* 36: *also* 5 17, 18: *and* 19 7]. **34** Jesus answered them, Is it not written in your law [*cp.* 8 17; 18 31: *also* 15 25: *and* 7 51; 19 7], I said, Ye are gods? **35** If he called them gods, unto whom the word of God came (and the scripture cannot be broken), **36** say ye of him, whom the Father [4]sanctified [*cp.* 17 17, 19] and sent into the world [*cp.* 3 17; 17 18: *also* 3 34; 5 38; *etc.*: *and* 1 9; 3 19; *etc.*], Thou blasphemest [*cp. verse* 33]; because I said, I am *the* Son of God [*cp. verse* 33: *also* 5 17, 18: *and* 19 7]?	*cp.* 9 3; 26 65. *cp.* 26 63-64. *cp.* 5 17-19. *see above. see above.*	*cp.* 2 7; 14 64. *cp.* 14 61-62. *see above. see above.*	*cp.* 5 21. *cp.* 22 70. *cp.* 16 17. *see above. see above.*

37 If I do not the works of my Father [*cp. vv.* 25, *32, and* 38], believe me not. **38** But if I do them, though ye believe not me, believe the works [*cp.* 14 11: *also vv.* 25, 32, 37, *above*; *etc.*]: that ye may know and understand that the Father is in me, and I in the Father [*cp.* 14 10, 11; 17 21: *also* 14 20; 17 23]. **39** They sought again to take him [*cp.* 7 30, 32, 44; 11 57: *also* 5 18; 7 1, 19, 25; 8 37, 40; 11 53: *and* 5 16]: and he went forth out of their hand [*cp.* 8 59: *also* 12 36: Luke 4 30].

*cp.*21 46: *also* 12 14; 26 4; 27 1.	*cp.* 12 12: *also* 3 6; 11 18; 14 1.	*cp.*20 19: *also* 19 47; 22 2: *and* 6 11.

[1] Some ancient authorities read *At that time was the feast.*   [2] Some ancient authorities read *That which my Father hath given unto me.*   [3] Or, *aught*   [4] Or, *consecrated*

John 10 22: *cp.* I Macc. 4 59.   John 10 33: *cp.* Lev. 24 16.   John 10 34 = Ps. 82 6.

(viii) Beyond Jordan (§ 48)

§ 48. Many acknowledge that John's Witness to Jesus was true

John 10 40-42

40 And he went away again beyond Jordan into the place where John was at the first baptizing [*cp.* 1 28: 3 26: *also* 3 23]; and there he abode. **41** And many came unto him; and they said, John indeed did no sign: but all things whatsoever John spake of this man were true [*cp.* 1 7, 15, 29-34; 3 27-36; 5 33]. **42** And many believed on him there [*cp.* 2 11, 23; 4 39, 41; 7 31; 8 30; 11 45; 12 11, 42: *also* 7 48].

cp. 19 1. *cp.* 3 1, 6.	*cp.* 10 1. *cp.* 1 4-5.	*cp.* 3 3.
cp. 18 6.	*cp.* 9 42.	

C. The Passion and Resurrection (§§ 49-85)

(i) The Prologue to the Passion (§§ 49-59)

§ 49. Mary and Martha appeal to Jesus to come and help Lazarus

John 11 1-16

1 Now a certain man was sick, Lazarus of Bethany [*cp.* 12 1], of the village of Mary and her sister Martha. **2** And it was that Mary which anointed the Lord [*cp.* 4 1; 6 23; 20 2, 18, 20, 25; 21 7, 12] with ointment, and wiped his feet with her hair [*cp.* 12 3], whose brother Lazarus was sick. **3** The sisters therefore sent unto him, saying, Lord, behold, he whom thou lovest [*cp. verses* 5 *and* 36] is sick. **4** But when Jesus heard it, he said, This sickness is not unto death, but [*cp.* 9 3] for the glory of God [*cp.* 11 40], that the Son of God may be glorified thereby [*cp.* 12 23; 13 31: *also* 7 39; 12 16; 17 10: *and* 8 54; 13 32; 16 14; 17 1 *ff.*]. **5** Now Jesus loved [*cp. verses* 3 *and* 36] Martha, and her sister, and Lazarus. **6** When therefore he heard that he was sick, he abode at that time two days in the place where he was. **7** Then after this he saith to the disciples, Let us go into Judæa again. **8** The disciples say unto him, Rabbi [*cp.* 1 38, 49; 3 2; 4 31; 6 25; 9 2: *also* 20 16: *and* 3 26], the Jews were but now seeking to stone thee [*cp.* 10 31: *also* 8 59]; and goest thou thither again? **9** Jesus answered, Are there not twelve hours in the day? If a man walk in the day [*cp.* 9 4; 12 35], he stumbleth not, because he seeth the light of this world. **10** But if a man walk in the night [*cp.* 8 12; 12 35: *also* 9 4; 13 30], he stumbleth, because the light is not in him. **11** These things spake he: and after this he saith unto them, Our friend Lazarus is fallen asleep; but I go, that I may awake him out of sleep. **12** The disciples therefore said unto him, Lord, if he is fallen asleep, he will [1]recover. **13** Now Jesus had spoken

	cp. 16 19, 20.	*cp.* 10 38, 39. *cp.* 7 13, 19; 10 1, 39, 41; 11 39; 12 42; 13 15; 17 5, 6; 18 6; 19 8; 22 61; 24 34: *also* 24 3.
*cp.*26 25, 49: *also* 23 7, 8.	*cp.*9 5; 11 21; 14 45: *also* 10 51.	
cp. 9 24.	*cp.* 5 39.	*cp.* 8 52.

of his death: but they thought [*cp.* 3 10; 4 33; 8 27, 43; 10 6; 12 16; 13 7, 28, 36; 14 5-10, 22; 16 17-18] that he spake of taking rest in sleep. **14** Then Jesus therefore said unto them plainly [*cp.* 7 4, 13, 26; 10 24; 11 54; 16 25, 29; 18 20: *and* Mark 8 32], Lazarus is dead [*cp.* 1 48; 2 24, 25; 4 19, 29; 5 6, 42; 6 61, 64; 13 11, 18; 16 19, 30; 18 4; 21 17]. **15** And I am glad for your sakes that I was not there, to the intent ye may believe [*cp.* 13 19; 14 29: *also* 19 35; 20 31: *and* 11 42]; nevertheless let us go unto him. **16** Thomas [*cp.* 14 5; 20 24, 26-29; 21 2] therefore, who is called ²Didymus [*cp.* 20 24; 21 2], said unto his fellow-disciples, Let us also go, that we may die with him [*cp.* 13 37].

cp. 15 16; 16 8-12.	*cp.*4 13; 6 52; 7 18; 8 17-21; 9 10, 32; 16 14.	*cp.*2 50; 9 45; 18 34.
*cp.*9 4; 12 25; 16 8.	*cp.* 2 8; 8 17.	*cp.* 5 22; 6 8; 9 47; 11 17.
cp. 10 3.	*cp.* 3 18.	*cp.* 6 15.
cp. 26 35.	*cp.* 14 31.	*cp.* 22 33.

¹ Gr. *be saved.*   ² That is, *Twin.*

§ 50. **The Raising of Lazarus**

John 11 17-44

17 So when Jesus came, he found that he had been in the tomb four days already [*cp. verse* 39]. **18** Now Bethany was nigh unto Jerusalem, about fifteen furlongs off; **19** and many of the Jews [*cp.* 11 45] had come to Martha and Mary, to console them concerning their brother [*cp. verse* 31]. **20** Martha therefore, when she heard that Jesus was coming, went and met him: but Mary still sat in the house. **21** Martha therefore said unto Jesus, Lord, if thou hadst been here, my brother had not died [*cp. verse* 32: *also* 4 49]. **22** And even now I know that, whatsoever thou shalt ask of God, God will give thee. **23** Jesus saith unto her, Thy brother shall rise again. **24** Martha saith unto him, I know that he shall rise again in the resurrection at the last day [*cp.* 6 39, 40, 44, 54; 12 48]. **25** Jesus said unto her, I am the resurrection [*cp.* 5 21; 6 39, 40, 44, 54], and the life [*cp.* 14 6: *also* 1 4; 5 26; 6 57]: he that believeth on me, though he die, yet shall he live: **26** and whosoever liveth and believeth on me shall never die [*cp.* 3 15, 16, 36; 5 24; 6 40, 47; 20 31: *also* 6 50, 51, 54, 58; 8 51; 10 28]. Believest thou this? **27** She saith unto him, Yea, Lord: I have believed [*cp.* 6 69; 9 38; 16 30: *also* 16 27; 17 8: *and* 20 31] that thou art the Christ [*cp.* 1 41; 4 25, 26, 29; 7 26, 41; 9 22; 10 24; 20 31], the Son of God [*cp.* 1 34, 49: *also* 3 18; 5 25; 9 35; 10 36; 11 4; 19 7: *and* 1 18; 3 16-17, 35-36; *etc.*: *and* 20 31], *even* he that cometh [*cp.* 1 15, 27; 3 31; 6 14; 12 13: *also* 1 30] into the world. **28** And when she had said this, she went away, and called Mary ¹her sister secretly, saying, The ²Master [*cp.* 13 13, 14: *also* 1 38; *etc.*] is here, and calleth thee. **29** And she, when she heard it, arose quickly, and went unto him. **30** (Now Jesus was not yet come into the village, but was still in the place where Martha met him.) **31** The Jews then which were with her in the house, and were comforting her [*cp. verse* 19], when they saw Mary, that she rose up quickly and went out, followed her, supposing that she was going unto the tomb to ³weep there. **32** Mary therefore, when she came where Jesus was, and saw him, fell down [*cp.* 18 6: *also* 9 38] at his feet, saying unto him, Lord, if thou hadst been here, my brother had not died [*cp. verse* 21: *also* 4 49]. **33** When Jesus therefore saw her ⁴weeping, and the Jews *also* ⁴weeping which came with her, he ⁵groaned in the spirit, and ⁶was troubled [*cp.* 12 27; 13 21: *also* 14 1, 27], **34** and said, Where have ye laid him? They say unto him, Lord, come and see [*cp.* 1 39, 46; 4 29]. **35** Jesus wept. **36** The Jews therefore said, Behold how he loved him [*cp.* 11 3, 5]! **37** But some of them said, Could not this man, which opened the eyes of him that was blind [*cp.* 9

		cp. 10 39.
cp. 16 16: *also* 26 63, 68; 27, 17, 22.	*cp.* 8 29: *also* 14 61; 15 32.	*cp.* 9 20: *also* 22 67; 23 2, 35, 39.
cp. 4 3, 6; 8 29; 14 33; 16 16; 26 63; 27 40, 43, 54: *also* 3 17; 17 5.	*cp.* 1 1; 3 11; 5 7; 15 39: *also* 1 11; 9 7.	*cp.* 1 35; 4 3, 9, 41; 8 28; 22 70: *also* 3 22; 9 35.
cp. 3 11; 11 3; 21 9; 23 39.	*cp.* 11 9: *also* 1 7.	*cp.* 7 19, 20; 13 35; 19 38: *also* 3 16.
cp. 26 18.	*cp.* 14 14.	*cp.* 22 11.
cp. 2 11: *also* 17 14: *and* 8 2; 9 18; 14 33; 15 25; 20 20; 28 9, 17.	*cp.* 3 11; 5 22, 33; 7 25: *also* 1 40; 10 17: *and* 5 6.	*cp.* 5 8, 12; 8 28, 41, 47; 17 16: *also* 24 52.

6-7], have caused that this man also should not die? **38** Jesus therefore again [7]groaning in himself cometh to the tomb. Now it was a cave, and a stone lay [8]against it. **39** Jesus saith, Take ye away the stone. Martha, the sister of him that was dead, saith unto him, Lord, by this time he stinketh: for he hath been *dead* four days [*cp. verse* 17]. **40** Jesus saith unto her, Said I not unto thee [*cp. verses* 25 *and* 26], that, if thou believedst, thou shouldest see the glory of God [*cp.* 11 4]? **41** So they took away the stone.

	John	Matt.	Mark	Luke
And Jesus lifted up his eyes [*cp.* 17 1], and said, Father [*cp.* 12 27, 28; 17 1, 5, 11, 21, 24, 25], I thank thee that thou heardest me. **42** And I knew that thou hearest me always: but because of the multitude which standeth around [*cp.* 12 29] I said it, that they may believe [*cp.* 11 15; 13 19; 14 29; 19 35; 20 31] that thou didst		*cp.* 14 19. *cp.* 11 25, 26; 26 39, 42: *also* 14 23; 19 13; 26 36, 39, 42, 44: *and* 6 9.	*cp.* 6 41; 7 34. *cp.* 14 36: *also* 1 35; 6 46; 14 32, 35, 39.	*cp.* 9 16. *cp.* 10 21, 22; 22 42; 23 34, 46: *also* 3 21; 5 16; 6 12; 9 18; *etc.*: *and* 11 2.
		cp. 16 28; 27 47: *also* 26 73.	*cp.* 9 1; 11 5; 14 47; 15 35: *also* 14 69, 70; 15 39.	*cp.* 9 27; 19 24.

send me [*cp.* 17 8, 21: *also* 17 25: *and* 5 36, 38; 6 29: *and* 3 17, 34; *etc.*]. **43** And when he had thus spoken, he cried with a loud voice [*cp.* 4 50; 5 8], Lazarus, come forth [*cp.* 5 28]. **44** He that was dead came forth [*cp.* 5 29], bound hand and foot with [9]graveclothes [*cp.* 19 40]; and his face was bound about with a napkin [*cp.* 20 7]. Jesus saith unto them, Loose him, and let him go.

	Mark	Mark	Luke
	cp. 8 8, 13; *etc.*	*cp.* 10 52; *etc.*	*cp.* 18 42; *etc.*

[1] Or, *her sister, saying secretly*   [2] Or, *Teacher*   [3] Gr. *wail.*   [4] Gr. *wailing.*
[5] Or, *was moved with indignation in the spirit* 6 Gr. *troubled himself.*   [7] Or, *being moved with indignation in himself*   [8] Or, *upon*   [9] Or, *grave-bands*

§ 51. A Report is made to the Pharisees

John 11 45-46

John	Matt.	Mark
45 Many therefore of the Jews [*cp.* 11 19], which came to Mary and beheld [1]that which he did [*cp.* 2 23; 6 2; 7 3], believed on him [*cp.* 12 11: *also* 2 11, 23; 4 39, 41; 7 31; 8 30; 10 42; 12 42: *and* 7 48]. **46** But some of them went away to the Pharisees, and told them the things which Jesus had done.	*cp.* 18 6.	*cp.* 9 42.

[1] Many ancient authorities read *the things which he did.*

§ 52. The Plot to destroy Jesus

John 11 47-53	Matt. 26 1-5	Mark 14 1-2	Luke 22 1-2
	1 And it came to pass, when Jesus had finished all these words, he said unto his disciples, **2** Ye know that after two days		
cp. 11 55.	the passover *cp.* 26 17. cometh,	**1** Now after two days was *the feast of* the passover and the unleavened bread [*cp.* 14 12]:	**1** Now the feast of unleavened bread [*cp.* 22 7] drew nigh, which is called the Passover.
cp. 2 19; 3 14; 12 32-33.	and the Son of man is delivered up to be crucified [*cp.* 16 21; 17 12, 22-23; 20 18-19: *also* 20 28; 26 24, 25]. **3** Then	*cp.* 8 31; 9 12, 31; 10 33-34: *also* 10 45; 14 21, 41.	*cp.* 9 22, 44; 18 31-33; 24 7: *also* 13 32-33; 17 25; 22 22.
47 The chief priests therefore and the Pharisees gathered a council, and said, What	were gathered together the chief priests, and the elders of the people, unto the court [*cp.* 26 57, 58: *also*	and the chief priests and the scribes *cp.* 14 53, 54: *also* 14 66.	**2** And the chief priests and the scribes *cp.* 22 55.

do we? for this man doeth many signs. **48** If we let him thus alone, all men will believe on him [*cp.* 12 19]: and the Romans will come and take away both our place [*cp.* 4 20] and our nation. **49** But a certain one of them,	26 69: *and* John 18 15]		
	cp. 21 46: *also verse* 5 *below.*	*cp.* 11 18; 12 12: *also verse* 2 *below.*	*cp.* 19 48; 20 19: *also verse* 2 *below.*
Caiaphas [*cp.* 18 13, 14, 24, 28], being high priest that year [*cp. verse* 51 *below and* 18 13], said unto them, Ye know nothing at all, **50** nor do ye take account that it is expedient [*cp.* 16 7; 18 14] for you that one man should die for the people [*cp.* 18 14], and that the whole nation perish not. **51** Now this he said not of himself: but being high priest that year [*cp. verse* 49 *above and* 18 13], he prophesied that Jesus should die for the nation [*cp.* 10 11, 15, 17]; **52** and not for the nation only [*cp.* 10 16], but that he might also gather together into one [*cp.* 10 16; 17 11, 21, 22, 23: *also* 12 32] the children of God [*cp.* 1 12: *also* 12 36] that are scattered abroad. **53** So from that day forth they took counsel that they might put him to death [*cp.* 5 18; 7 1, 19, 25; 8 37, 40: *also* 5 16; 7 30, 32, 44; 10 39; 11 57].	of the high priest, who was called Caiaphas [*cp.* 26 57];		*cp.* 3 2.
	cp. 20 28. *cp.* 8 11; 10 18; 21 31, 41, 43; 22 7-10; 24 14; 26 13; 28 19.	*cp.* 10 45. *cp.* 12 9; 13 10; 14 9; 16 15.	*cp.* 2 30-32; 3 6; 13 29; 14 21-24; 20 16; 24 47.
	cp. 5 9: *also* 5 45: *and* 8 12; 13 38.		*cp.* 20 36: *also* 6 35; 16 8.
	4 and they took counsel together that they might take Jesus by subtilty, and kill him [*cp.* 12 14; 21 46; 27 1: *also* 22 15: *and* 12 10]. **5** But they said, Not during the feast, lest a tumult arise among the people.	sought how they might take him with subtilty, and kill him [*cp.* 3 6; 11 18; 12 12: *also* 12 13: *and* 3 2]: **2** for they said, Not during the feast, lest haply there shall be a tumult of the people.	sought how they might put him to death [*cp.* 6 11; 19 47; 20 19, 20: *also* 11 53-54: *and* 6 7]; for they feared the people.

§ 53. **Jesus withdraws**

John 11 54-57			
54 Jesus therefore walked no more openly [*cp.* 7 4, 13, 26; 10 24; 11 14; 16 25, 29; 18 20] among the Jews, but departed thence into the country near to the wilderness, into a city called Ephraim; and there he tarried with the disciples [*cp.* 3 22]. **55** Now the passover of the Jews was at hand [*cp.* 2 13; 6 4: *also* 5 1; 7 2]: and many went up to Jerusalem out of the country before the passover, to purify themselves [*cp.* 18 28]. **56** They sought therefore for Jesus [*cp.* 7 11], and spake one with another, as they stood in the temple, What think ye? That he will not come to the feast? **57** Now the chief priests and the Pharisees had given commandment, that, if any man knew where he was, he should shew it, that they might take him [*cp.* 7 30, 32, 44; 10 39: *also* 5 18; 7 1, 19, 25; 8 37, 40; 11 53: *and* 5 16].	*cp.* 17 25; 18 12; 21 28; 22 17, 42; 26 66.	*cp.* 8 32.	

John 11 55: *cp.* II Chron. 30 17: *also* Num. 9 6.

§ 54. The Anointing in Bethany

John 12 1-8	Matt. 26 6-13	Mark 14 3-9	Luke 7 36-50
1 Jesus therefore six days before the pass-over [*cp.* 13 1] came to Bethany [*cp.* 11 1],	6 Now when Jesus was in Bethany, in the house of Simon the leper,	3 And while he was in Bethany [*cp.* 11 1] in the house of Simon the leper,	*cp.* 19 29. *cp.* 7 40, 43, 44. **36** And one of the Pharisees desired him that he would eat [*cp.* 7 34] with him. And he entered into the Pharisee's house,
where Lazarus was, whom Jesus raised from the dead. **2** So they made him a supper there: and Martha served; but Lazarus was one of them that sat at meat with him. **3** Mary therefore	7 there came unto him a woman	as he sat at meat, there came a woman	*cp.* 10 40. and sat down to meat [*cp.* 11 37; 14 1]. **37** And behold, a woman which was in the city, a sinner [*cp.* 7 34]; and when she knew that he was sitting at meat in the Pharisee's house, she
took a pound of ointment of ¹spikenard, very precious,	having ¹an alabaster cruse of exceeding precious ointment, and she poured it upon his head, as he sat at meat.	having ¹an alabaster cruse of ointment of ²spikenard very costly; *and* she brake the cruse, and poured it over his head.	brought ¹an alabaster cruse of ointment,
and anointed the feet of Jesus, and wiped his feet with her hair [*cp.* 11 2]: and the house was filled with the odour of the ointment. **4** But Judas Iscariot [*cp.* 14 22: *also* 6 71; 13 2, 26], one of his disciples, which should betray him [*cp.* 6 64, 71; 13 11; 18 2, 5: *also* 13 2, 21], saith,	8 But *cp.* 10 4; 26 14. when the disciples *cp.* 10 4; 26 25, 46, 48; 27 3: *also* 26 21, 23, 24. saw it, they had indignation, saying,	4 But *cp.* 3 19; 14 10. there were some *cp.* 3 19; 14 42, 44: *also* 14 18, 21. they had indignation among themselves, *saying,*	**38** and standing behind at his feet [*cp.* 8 35; 10 39], weeping, she began to wet his feet with her tears, and wiped them with the hair of her head, and ²kissed his feet, and anointed them with the ointment. 39 Now *cp.* 6 16; 22 3. *cp.* 22 21, 22. when the Pharisee which had bidden him saw it, he spake within himself [*cp.* 11 38], saying,
	To what purpose is this waste? 9 For this *ointment* might have been sold for much, and given to the poor.	To what purpose hath this waste of the ointment been made? 5 For this ointment might have been sold for above three hundred ³pence, and given to the poor.	
5 Why was not this ointment sold for three hundred ²pence, and given to the poor [*cp.* 13 29]? **6** Now this he said, not because he cared for the poor; but because he was a thief, and having the ³bag [*cp.*	*cp.* 15 23; 19 13.	And they murmured against her [*cp.* 10 13].	*cp.* 18 15.

13 29] ⁴took away what was put therein. **7** Jesus therefore
cp. 5 6; 6 15.
said,

⁵Suffer her to keep it against the day of my burying. **8** For the poor ye have always with you;

but me ye have not always.

cp. 10 16; 11 52.

---

10 But Jesus perceiving it [*cp. 12 15; 16 8; 22 18*] said unto them, Why trouble ye the woman? for she hath wrought a good work upon me.
cp. 19 14.
11 For ye have the poor always with you;

but me ye have not always. **12** For in that she ²poured this ointment upon my body, she did it to prepare me for burial. **13** Verily I say unto you, Wheresoever ³this gospel [*cp. 4 23; 9 35; 24 14*] shall be preached in the whole world [*cp. 24 14: also 8 11; 10 18; 21 31, 41, 43; 22 7-10; 28 19*], that also which this woman hath done shall be spoken of for a memorial of her.

---

6 But Jesus
cp. 8 17.
said, Let her alone; why trouble ye her? she hath wrought a good work on me.
cp. 10 14.
7 For ye have the poor always with you, and whensover ye will ye can do them good: but me ye have not always. **8** She hath done what she could: she hath anointed my body aforehand for the burying. **9** And verily I say unto you, Wheresoever the gospel [*cp. 1 1, 14, 15; 8 35; 10 29; 13 10; 16 15*] shall be preached throughout the whole world [*cp. 13 10: also 12 9; 16 15*], that also which this woman hath done shall be spoken of for a memorial of her.

---

cp. 18 16.

cp. 2 30-32; 3 6; etc.

---

1 See marginal note on Mark 14 3.
2 See marginal note on Matt. 18 28.
3 Or, *box*
4 Or, *carried what was put therein*
5 Or, *Let her alone: it was that she might keep it*

1 Or, *a flask*
2 Gr. *cast.*
3 Or, *these good tidings*

1 Or, *a flask*
2 Gr. *pistic nard*, pistic being perhaps a local name. Others take it to mean *genuine*; others, *liquid.*
3 See marginal note on Matt. 18 28.

---

cp. 4 19, 44; 6 14; 7 40; 9 17.

cp. 13 57; 21 11, 46.
cp. 9 11; 11 19.
cp. 26 6.
cp. 18 23-34.
cp. 18 25.

cp. 6 4, 15.
cp. 2 16.
cp. 14 3.

cp. 1 38.

cp, 9 22; 16 23.

cp. 5 30; 8 33.

cp. 9 2.
cp. 5 12: also 12 34.
cp. 8 27; 21 10.
cp. 9 22.

cp. 2 5.
cp. 1 27; 2 7; 4 41.
cp. 5 34; 10 52.

This man, if he were ³a prophet [*cp. 4 24; 7 16; 13 33; 24 19*], would have perceived who and what manner of woman this is which toucheth him, that she is a sinner [*cp. 5 30; 15 2; 19 7*]. **40** And Jesus answering said unto him, Simon, I have somewhat to say unto thee. And he saith, ⁴Master, say on. **41** A certain lender had two debtors: the one owed five hundred ⁵pence, and the other fifty. **42** When they had not *wherewith* to pay, he forgave them both. Which of them therefore will love him most? **43** Simon answered and said, He, I suppose, to whom he forgave the most. And he said unto him, Thou hast rightly judged [*cp. 10 28*]. **44** And turning [*cp. 7 9; 9 55; 10 23; 14 25; 22 61; 23 28*] to the woman, he said unto Simon, Seest thou this woman? I entered into thine house, thou gavest me no water for my feet: but she hath wetted my feet with her tears, and wiped them with her hair. **45** Thou gavest me no kiss: but she, since the time I came in, hath not ceased to ⁶kiss my feet. **46** My head with oil thou didst not anoint: but she hath anointed my feet with ointment. **47** Wherefore I say unto thee, Her sins, which are many, are forgiven; for she loved much: but to whom little is forgiven, *the same* loveth little. **48** And he said unto her, Thy sins are forgiven [*cp. 5 20*]. **49** And they that sat at meat with him began to say ⁷within themselves, Who is this [*cp. 5 21: also 4 36; 8 25; 9 9*] that even forgiveth sins? **50** And he said unto the woman, Thy faith hath saved thee [*cp. 8 48; 17 19; 18 42*]; go in peace [*cp. 8 48*].

1 Or, *a flask*   2 Gr. *kissed much.*   3 Some ancient authorities read *the prophet*. See John 1 21, 25.   4 Or, *Teacher*   5 See footnote on Matt. 18 28.   6 Gr. *kiss much.*
7 Or, *among*

§ 55. The Common People come to see both Jesus and Lazarus

John 12 9-11

9 The common people therefore of the Jews learned that he was there: and they came, not for Jesus' sake only, but that they might see Lazarus also, whom he had raised from the dead [*cp.* 12 17-19]. **10** But the chief priests took counsel that they might put Lazarus also to death; **11** because that by reason of him many of the Jews went away, and believed on Jesus [*cp.* 11 45: *also* 2 11, 23; 4 39, 41; 7 31; 8 30; 10 42; 12 42: *and* 7 48].

cp. 18 6.   *cp.* 9 42.   *cp.* 16 31.

§ 56. The Triumphal Entry

John 12 12-19	Matt. 21 1-11	Mark 11 1-11	Luke 19 29-40
12 On the morrow [*cp.* 1 29, 35, 43; 6 22] [1]a great	*cp.* 27 62.	*cp.* 11 12.	
	1 And when they drew nigh unto Jerusalem, and came unto Bethphage,	**1** And when they draw nigh unto Jerusalem,	**29** And it came to pass, when he drew nigh
cp. 12 1.	unto the mount of Olives, then Jesus sent two	unto Bethphage and Bethany, at the mount of Olives, he sendeth two [*cp.* 14 13: *also* 6 7] of his disciples, **2** and saith unto them, Go your way	unto Bethphage and Bethany, at the mount that is called *the mount* of Olives, he sent two [*cp.* 22 8: *also* 10 1] of the disciples, **30** saying,
	disciples, **2** saying unto them, Go into the village that is over against you, and straightway	into the village that is over against you: and straightway as ye enter into it, ye shall find	Go your way into the village over against *you*; in the which as ye enter ye shall find
cp. 19 41.	ye shall find an ass tied, and a colt with her:	a colt tied, whereon no man ever yet sat;	a colt tied, whereon no man ever yet sat [*cp.* 23 53]:
	loose *them*, and bring *them* unto me. **3** And if any one say aught unto you,	loose him, and bring him. **3** And if any one say unto you, Why do ye this?	loose him, and bring him. **31** And if any one ask you, Why do ye loose him? thus shall ye say,
	ye shall say, The Lord hath need of them; and straightway he will send them.	say ye, The Lord hath need of him; and straightway he [1]will send him [2]back hither.	The Lord hath need of him.
	4 Now this is come to pass, that it might be fulfilled which was spoken [1]by the prophet, saying, **5** Tell ye the daughter of Zion,		
verse 15	Behold, thy King cometh unto thee, Meek, and riding upon an ass, And upon a colt the foal of an ass.		
	6 And the disciples went,	**4** And they went away, and found a colt tied at the door without in the open street; and they loose him. **5** And	**32** And they that were sent went away, and found even as he had said unto them [*cp.* 22 13]. **33** And as they were loosing the colt,
	and did	certain of them that stood there [*cp.* 9 1; 14 47; 15 35: *also* 14 69, 70; 15 39]	
cp. 11 42; 12 29.	*cp.* 16 28; 27 47: *also* 26 73.	*cp.* 9 27: *also* 19 24.	
		said unto them, What do	the owners thereof said unto them, Why

verse 14

multitude that had come to the feast, when they heard that Jesus was coming to Jerusalem,

13 took the branches of the palm trees,

and

went forth to meet him, and cried out,

verses 17 *and* 18

Hosanna:

Blessed *is* he that cometh [*cp.* 1 15, 27; 3 31; 6 14; 11 27: *also* 1 30] in the name [*cp.* 5 43; 10 25: *also* 17 12] of the Lord,   even the King of Israel [*cp.* 1 49: *also* 18 33, 39; 19 3, 19, 21: *and* 6 15; 12 15; 18 37].

cp. 14 27; 16 33.

14 And Jesus, having found a young ass, sat thereon; as it is written, **15** Fear not, daughter of Zion: behold, thy King cometh, sitting on an ass's colt. **16** These things understood not his disciples [*cp.* 4 33; 11 13; 13 7, 28, 36; 14 5-10, 22; 16 17-18: *also* 3 10; 8 27, 43; 10 6] at the first: but when Jesus was glorified [*cp.* 7 39; 12 23; 13 31: *also* 11 4; 17 10: *and* 17 1 *ff.*],

---

even as Jesus appointed them [*cp.* 26 19],

7 and   brought the ass, and the colt,   and   put on them their garments; and he sat thereon. **8** And the most part of the multitude

spread their garments in the way; and others cut branches from the trees,   and spread them in the way. **9** And

the   multitudes that went before   him, and that followed, cried,

saying, Hosanna [*cp.* 21 15] to the son of David [*cp.* 1 1; 9 27; 12 23; 15 22; 20 30, 31; 21 15]: Blessed *is* he that cometh [*cp.* 3 11; 11 3]

in the name   of the Lord [= 23 39]; *cp.* 27 42: *also* 2 2; 27 11, 29, 37: *and* 21 5.

cp. 5 9; 10 13.
Hosanna in the highest

verse 7

verses 4 *and* 5

cp. 15 16; 16 8-12.

---

ye, loosing the colt? **6** And they said unto them even as Jesus had said: and they let them go. **7** And they bring   the colt unto Jesus, and   cast on him their garments;   and he sat upon him. **8** And

many

spread their garments upon the way; and others ³branches, which they had cut from the fields.

9 And

they that went before,   and they that followed, cried,

Hosanna; *cp.* 10 47, 48.

Blessed *is* he that cometh [*cp.* 1 7]

in the name   of the Lord: *cp.* 15 32: *also* 15 2, 9, 12, 18, 26.

10 Blessed *is* the kingdom that cometh, *the kingdom* of our father David: *cp.* 9 50.
Hosanna in the highest.

verse 7

cp. 4 13; 6 52; 7 18; 8 17-21; 9 10, 32: *also* 16 14.

---

loose ye the colt? **34** And they said, The Lord hath need of him.

35 And they brought him   to Jesus: and they threw their garments upon the colt, and set Jesus thereon. **36** And

as he went, they spread their garments in the way.

37 And as he was now drawing nigh, *even* at the descent of the mount of Olives, the whole multitude of the disciples *cp.* 18 39. began to rejoice and praise God [*cp.* 2 13, 20; 18 43] with a loud voice for all the ¹mighty works which they had seen; **38** saying,

cp. 18 38, 39: *also* 1 32.

Blessed *is* the King [*see below*] that cometh [*cp.* 7 19, 20: *also* 3 16] in the name   of the Lord [= 13 35]: *cp.* 23 3, 37, 38: *also* 23 2: *and* 1 33.

peace [*cp.* 2 14: *also* 1 79; 2 29; 19 42] in heaven, and glory in the highest [*cp.* 2 14].

verse 35

cp. 9 45; 18 34: *also* 2 50.

then [*cp.* 13 7] remembered they that these things were written of him, and that they had done these things unto him [*cp.* 2 22: *also* 14 26; 16 4]. **17** The multitude therefore that was with him when he called Lazarus out of the tomb, and raised him from the dead, bare witness [*cp.* 12 9-11]. **18** For this cause also the multitude went and met him, for that they heard that he had done this sign [*cp.* 12 9-11]. **19** The Pharisees therefore said	*cp.* 26 75.	*cp.* 14 72.	*cp.* 24 6, 8: *also* 22 61. *cp.* 16 31. *verse* 37 **39** And some of the Pharisees from the multitude said unto him, ²Master, rebuke [*cp.* 18 39] thy disciples. **40** And he answered and said, I tell you that, if these shall hold their peace [*cp.* 18 39], the stones will cry out [*cp.* 18 39].
	cp. 21 15-16.		
among themselves, ²Behold how ye prevail nothing: lo, the world is gone after him [*cp.* 11 48: *also* 3 26].	*cp.* 21 46; 26 5. **10** And when he was come into Jerusalem, all the city was stirred, saying, Who is this [*cp.* 8 27]? **11** And the multitudes said, This is the prophet [*cp.* 13 57; 21 46], Jesus, from Nazareth [*cp.* 2 23; 26 71] of Galilee.	*cp.* 11 18; 12 12; 14 2. **11** And he entered into Jerusalem . . . *cp.* 4 41: *also* 1 27. *cp.* 6 4, 15. *cp.* 1 24; 10 47; 14 67; 16 6.	*cp.* 19 48; 20 19; 22 2.
cp. 5 12: *also* 12 34. *cp.* 4 19,44; 6 14; 7 40; 9 17. *cp.* 1 45; 18 5, 7; 19 19.			*cp.* 5 21; 7 49; 8 25; 9 9: *also* 4 36. *cp.* 4 24; 7 16, 39; 13 33; 24 19. *cp.* 4 34; 18 37; 24 19.
¹ Some ancient authorities read *the common people.* ² Or, *Ye behold*	¹ Or, *through*	¹ Gr. *sendeth.* ² Or, *again* ³ Gr. *layers of leaves.*	¹ Gr. *powers.* ² Or, *Teacher*

Matt. 21 5: *cp.* Is. 62 11.   John 12 13: *cp.* I Macc. 13 51.   John 12 13 ‖ Matt. 21 9 ‖ Mark 11 9 ‖ Luke 19 38: *cp.* Ps. 118 25-26.   John 12 15 ‖ Matt. 21 5 = Zech. 9 9.

§ 57. Certain Greeks wish to see Jesus

John 12 20-36a

20 Now there were certain Greeks [*cp.* 7 35] among those that went up to worship at the feast: **21** these therefore came to Philip [*cp.* 1 43-48; 6 5-7; 14 8-9], which was of Bethsaida [*cp.* 1 44] of Galilee, and asked him, saying, Sir, we would see Jesus. **22** Philip cometh and telleth Andrew [*cp.* 1 40, 44; 6 8]: Andrew cometh, and Philip, and they tell Jesus. **23** And Jesus answereth them, saying, The hour is come [*cp.* 13 1; 17 1: *also* 12 27: *and* 2 4; 7 6, 8, 30; 8 20], that the Son of man should be glorified [*cp.* 7 39; 12 16; 13 31: *also* 11 4; 17 10: *and* 17 1 *ff.*]. **24** Verily, verily, I say unto you, Except a grain of wheat fall into the earth and die, it abideth by itself alone; but if it die, it beareth much fruit.		*cp.* 7 26. *cp.* 10 3. *cp.* 3 18. *cp.* 11 21. *cp.* 6 45; 8 22. *cp.* 4 18; 10 *cp.* 1 16, 29; 3 2. 18; 13 3. *cp.* 26 45: *also* *cp.* 14 41: *also* 26 18. 14 35.	*cp.* 6 14. *cp.* 10 13. *cp.* 9 9; 19 3. *cp.* 6 14. *cp.* 22 14: *also* 22 53.
cp. verse 25.	Matt. 10 **37** He that loveth father or mother more than me is not worthy of me; and he that loveth son or daughter *cp.* 19 27-29.	*cp.* 10 28-30.	Luke 14 **26** If any man cometh unto me, and hateth not his own father, and mother, and wife [*cp.* 18 29], and children, and brethren, and sisters [*cp.* 18 28-30],

Column 1 (John)

more
than me is not worthy of me.
cp. 8 18-22.
38 And he that doth not take his cross and follow after me, is not worthy of me.

25 He that loveth his ¹life loseth it; and he that hateth [cp. Luke 14 26 above] his ¹life in this world shall keep it unto life eternal. **26** If any man serve me, let him

follow me [cp. 1 43; 21 19, 22]; and where I am [cp. 7 34, 36; 14 3; 17 24], there shall also my servant be [cp. 14 3; 17 24]: if any man serve me, him will

cp. 15 21.

the Father honour.

27 Now is my soul troubled [cp. 11 33; 13 21: also 14 1, 27];

and what shall I say?

cp. 11 41; 12 27-28; 17 1-26.

Father [cp. 11 41; 12 28; 17 1, 5, 11, 21, 24, 25], save me from this ²hour [cp. 12 23; 13 1; 17 1: also 2 4; 7 6, 8, 30; 8 20]. But for this cause [cp. 18 37] came I unto this hour. **28** Father [see above],

cp. 18 11.

cp. 4 34; 5 30; 6 38; 7 17; 9 31.

glorify thy name. There came therefore a voice out of heaven, saying, I have both glorified it, and will glorify it again. **29** The

Column 2 (Matt)

39 He that ¹findeth his ²life shall lose it; and he that ³loseth his ²life for my sake [see below] shall find it. Matt. 16 **24** If any man would come after me, let him deny himself, and take up his cross, and follow me [cp. 4 19; 8 22; 9 9: 19 21].

25 For whosoever would save his ²life shall lose it: and whosoever shall lose his ²life for my sake [cp. 5 11; 10 18, 39: also 10 22; 19 29; 24 9]

shall find it. 26 **38** Then saith he unto them, My soul is exceeding sorrowful, even unto death: abide ye here, and watch [cp. 24 42; 25 13; 26 41] with me.

39 And he went forward a little, and fell on his face, and prayed [cp. 14 23; 19 13; 26 36, 42, 44: also 11 25],

cp. 11 25, 26; 26 39, 42: also 6 9.

cp. 26 45: also 26 18.

saying, O my Father [see above], if it be possible, cp. 19 26. let this cup [cp. 20 22, 23] pass away from me: nevertheless, not as I will, but as thou wilt [cp. 26 42 and 6 10: also 7 21; 12 50; 21 31].

cp. 3 17; 17 5.

Column 3 (Mark)

Mark 8 **34** If any man would come after me, let him deny himself, and take up his cross, and follow me [cp. 1 17; 2 14; 10 21].

35 For whosoever would save his ¹life shall lose it; and whosoever shall lose his ¹life for my sake [cp. 10 29; 13 9: also 13 13] and the gospel's [cp. 10 29] shall save it. 14 **34** And he saith unto them, My soul is exceeding sorrowful even unto death: abide ye here, and watch [cp. 13 33, 35, 37; 14 38].

35 And he went forward a little, and fell on the ground, and prayed [cp. 1 35; 6 46; 14 32, 39] that, if it were possible, cp. 14 36.

the hour [cp. 14 41] might pass away from him.

36 And he said, Abba, Father [see above], all things are possible unto thee [cp. 10 27]; remove this cup [cp. 10 38, 39] from me: howbeit not what I will, but what thou wilt [cp. 3 35].

cp. 1 11; 9 7.

Column 4 (Luke)

yea, and his own life also, he cannot be my disciple [cp. 9 57-62]. **27** Whosoever doth not bear his own cross, and come after me, cannot be my disciple.
Luke 17 **33** Whosoever shall seek to gain his ¹life shall lose it: but whosoever shall lose

his ¹life

shall ²preserve it.
Luke 9 **23** If any man would come after me, let him deny himself, and take up his cross daily, and follow me [cp. 5 27; 9 59; 18 22].

24 For whosoever would save his ¹life shall lose it; but whosoever shall lose his ¹life for my sake [cp. 6 22; 18 29; 21 12, 17], the same shall save it.

cp. 12 50.

cp. 12 37; 21 36.

22 **41** And he was parted from them about a stone's cast; and he kneeled down and prayed [cp. 3 21; 5 16; 6 12; 9 18, 28, 29; 11 1; 22 44: also 10 21], cp. 10 21, 22; 22 42; 23 34, 46: also 11 2.

cp. 22 14, 53.

42 saying, Father [see above], if thou be willing, cp. 1 37; 18 27. remove this cup from me: nevertheless not my will, but thine,

be done.

cp. 3 22; 9 35.

John	Matthew	Mark	Luke
multitude therefore, that stood by [cp. 11 42], and heard it, said that it had thundered: others said,	cp. 16 28; 27 47: also 26 73.	cp. 9 1; 11 5; 14 47; 15 35: also 14 69, 70; 15 39.	cp. 9 27; 19 24.
An angel [cp. 1 51]	cp. 4 11; 26 53.	cp. 1 13.	**43** ³And there appeared unto him an angel from heaven, strengthening him.
hath spoken to him. **30** Jesus answered and said, This voice hath not come for my sake, but for your sakes. **31** Now is ³the judgement of this world [cp. 3 18, 19: 5 24; 16 11: and 5 29; 12 48]: now shall the prince of this world [cp. 16 11: also 14 30] be cast out.			cp. 10 18.
32 And I, if I be lifted up [cp. 3 14; 8 28] ⁴from the earth, will draw [cp. 6 44] all men [cp. 10 16; 11 52; 17 11, 21, 22, 23] unto myself [cp. 14 3: also 14 21].	cp. 8 11; 10 18; 21 31, 41, 43; 22 7-10; 24 14; 26 13; 28 19.	cp. 12 9; 13 10; 14 9; 16 15.	cp. 2 30-32; 3 6; 13 29; 14 21-24; 20 16; 24 47.
33 But this he said, signifying by what manner of death he should die [cp. 18 32: also 21 19: and 2 19-22; 3 14; 8 28]. **34** The multitude therefore answered him, We have heard out of the law that the Christ abideth for ever: and how sayest thou [cp. 8 33: also 14 9: and 3 4, 9; 6 42, 52, 60: and 4 9; 7 15], The Son of man must be lifted up?	cp. 16 21-23; 17 9, 12, 22-23; 20 17-19, 28; 26 2, 24, 32.	cp. 8 31-33; 9 9, 12, 30-32; 10 32-34, 45; 14 21, 28.	cp. 9 22, 43-45; 13 32-33; 17 25; 18 31-34; 22 22; 24 7.
	¹ Or, *found* ² Or, *soul* ³ Or, *lost*	¹ Or, *soul*	¹ Or, *soul* ² Gr. *save it alive.* ³ Many ancient authorities omit ver. 43, 44.

who is this Son of man[cp. 5 12]? **35** Jesus therefore said unto them, Yet a little while [cp. 7 33; 13 33; 14 19; 16 16-19] is the light ⁵among you. Walk while ye have the light [cp. 9 4; 11 9], that darkness overtake you not [cp. 1 5: also 3 19-20]: and he that walketh in the darkness [cp. 8 12: also 1 5; 12 46: and 11 10] knoweth not whither he goeth [cp. 8 14; etc.]. **36** While ye have the light [cp. 1 4, 5, 9; 8 12; 9 5; 12 46: also 3 19], believe on the light, that ye may become sons of light [cp. 1 12; 11 52].

Matthew	Mark	Luke
cp. 8 27; 21 10.	cp. 4 41: also 1 27.	cp. 5 21; 7 49; 8 25; 9 9: also 4 36.
	cp. 5 9, 45; 8 12; 13 38.	cp. 16 8: also 6 35; 20 36.

¹ Or, *soul* ² Or, *hour?* ³ Or, *a judgement* ⁴ Or, *out of* ⁵ Or, *in*

John 12 34: cp. Pss. 89 4 and 110 4; Is. 9 7; Ezek. 37 25.

§ 58. Jesus again withdraws

John 12 36b-43

These things spake Jesus [cp. 17 1], and he departed and ¹hid himself from them [cp. 8 59; 10 39]. **37** But though he had done so many signs before them, yet they believed not on him [cp. 6 36; 10 25: also 1 11; 3 11, 32; 5 43]: **38** that the word of Isaiah the prophet might be fulfilled, which he spake,
 Lord, who hath believed our report?
 And to whom hath the arm of the Lord been revealed?
39 For this cause they could not believe [cp. 5 44], for that Isaiah said again,
40 He hath blinded their eyes, and he hardened their heart;
 Lest they should see with their eyes, and perceive with their heart,
 And should turn,

Matthew	Mark	Luke
		cp. 4 30.
	cp. 13 15. cp. 19 8.	cp. 3 5; 10 5: also 6 52; 8 17; 16 14.

And I should heal them.

41 These things said Isaiah, because he saw his glory [*cp.* 1 14; 2 11; 17 5, 22, 24]; and he spake of him [*cp.* 1 45: *also* Luke 24 27, 44]. **42** Nevertheless even of the rulers [*cp.* 3 1; 7 26, 48] many believed on him [*cp.* 7 48: *also* 2 11, 23; 4 39, 41; 7 31; 8 30; 10 42; 11 45]; but because of the Pharisees [*cp.* 7 13; 9 22; 19 38; 20 19] they did not confess ²*it* [*cp.* 9 22: *also* 3 2], lest they should be put out of the synagogue [*cp.* 9 22; 16 2]: **43** for they loved the glory of men more than the glory of God [*cp.* 5 44].

cp. 19 28; 25 31.	*cp.* 10 37.	*cp.* 9 26, 32; 24 26.
cp. 9 18.	*cp.* 5 22.	*cp.* 14 1; 18 18; 23 13, 35; 24 20: *also* 8 41; 13 14.

¹ Or, *was hidden from them*   ² Or, *him*

John 12 38 = Is. 53 1.   John 12 40 = Is. 6 10.   John 12 41: *cp.* Is. 6 1, 5.

§ 59. **Jesus the Father's Agent**

John 12 44-50	Matt. 18 5; 10 40	Mark 9 37	Luke 9 48; 10 16
44 And Jesus cried and said, He that believeth on me, believeth not on me, but on him that sent me [*cp.* 14 1]. **45** And he that beholdeth me [*cp.* 14 19; 16 10, 16, 17, 19: *also* 6 40, 62] beholdeth him that sent me [*cp.* 14 9-11; 15 24: *also* 10 30; 17 11. 22: *and* 5 19].			
cp. 14 13, 14, 26; 15 16; 16 23, 24, 26.	**18 5** And whoso shall receive one such little child in my name [*cp.* 18 20; 24 5: *also* 7 22] receiveth me.	**9 37** Whosoever shall receive one of such little children in my name [*cp.* 9 38, 39; 13 6; 16 17], receiveth me: and whosoever receiveth me, receiveth not me, but him that sent me.	**9 48** Whosoever shall receive this little child in my name [*cp.* 9 49; 10 17; 21 8; 24 47] receiveth me: and whosoever shall receive me receiveth him that sent me.
13 20 He that receiveth whomsoever I send receiveth me; and he that receiveth me receiveth him that sent me. **46** I am come a light into the world [*cp.* 8 12; 9 5: *also* 1 4, 5, 9; 3 19; 12 35-36: *and* 9 39; 16 28; 18 37: *and* 6 14; 11 27], that whosoever believeth on me may not abide in the darkness [*cp.* 8 12; 9 5: *also* 1 5: *and* 11 10]. **47** And if any man hear my sayings, and keep them not, I judge him not [*cp.* 8 15: *also* 3 17]: for I came not to judge the world, but to save the world [*cp.* 3 17: *also* 4 42; 5 34; 10 9].	**10 40** He that receiveth you receiveth me, and he that receiveth me receiveth him that sent me.		
	cp. 7 26.		*cp.* 6 49.
	cp. 1 21; 18 11: *also* 20 28.	*cp.* 10 45.	*cp.* 9 55; 19 10: *also* 2 11. **10 16** He that heareth you heareth me; and he that rejecteth you rejecteth me; and he that rejecteth me rejecteth him that sent me.
48 He that rejecteth me [*cp.* 15 23: *also* 5 23], and receiveth not my sayings, hath one that judgeth him: the word that I spake [*cp.* 4 41; 5 24; 8 31, 37, 43, 51, 52; 14 23, 24; 15 3, 20: *also* 5 38; *etc.*],	*cp.* 13 19-23.	*cp.* 2 2; 4 33: *also* 4 14-20; 16 20.	*cp.* 4 32, 36: *also* 1 2; 8 12-15: *and* 5 1; 8 11, 21; 11 28.

the same shall judge him [*cp.* 5 28-29] in the last day [*cp.* 6 39, 40, 44, 54; 11 24]. **49** For I spake not from myself [*cp.* 14 10: *also* 7 17: *and* 5 19, 30; 8 28: *and* 7 28; 8 42: *and* 16 13]; but the Father which sent me, he hath given me a commandment [*cp.* 10 18; 14 31: *also* 15 10], what I should say, and what I should speak. **50** And I know that his commandment is life eternal: the things therefore which I speak, even as the Father hath said unto me, so I speak [*cp.* 3 34; 7 16; 8 26, 28, 38, 40; 14 24: *also* 15 15; 17 8, 14].

(ii) At Supper before the Passover (§§ 60-70)

§ 60. **Jesus washes the Disciples' Feet**

John 13 1-11

1 Now before the feast of the passover [*cp.* 12 1], Jesus knowing that his hour was come [*cp.* 12 23; 17 1: *also* 12 27: *and* 2 4; 7 6, 8, 30; 8 20] that he should depart out of this world unto the Father [*cp.* 14 12, 28; 16 10, 17, 28: *also* 7 33; 16 5: *and* 17 11, 13: *and* 20 17: *and verse* 3 *below*], having loved his own [*cp.* 1 11: *also* 8 44; 15 19; 16 32; 19 27: *and* 13 34; 15 9, 12] which were in the world, he loved them [1]unto the end. **2** And during supper, the devil [*cp.* 13 27: *also* 6 70] having already put into the heart of Judas Iscariot [*cp.* 6 71; 12 4; 13 26; 14 22], Simon's son [*cp.* 6 71; 13 26], to betray him [*see verse* 11 *below*], **3** Jesus, knowing that the Father had given all things into his hands [*cp.* 3 35; 5 27; 17 2], and that he came forth from God [*cp.* 8 42; 16 27, 28, 30; 17 8], and goeth unto God [*see verse* 1 *above*], **4** riseth from supper, and layeth aside his garments; and he took a towel, and girded himself. **5** Then he poureth water into the bason, and began to wash the disciples' feet, and to wipe them with the towel wherewith he was girded. **6** So he cometh to Simon Peter. He saith unto him, Lord, dost thou wash my feet? **7** Jesus answered and said unto him, What I do thou knowest not now [*cp.* 13 12; 15 15: *also* 4 33; 11 13; 12 16; 13 28, 36; 14 5-10, 22; 16 17-18: *and* 3 10; 8 27, 43; 10 6]; but thou shalt understand hereafter [*cp.* 13 36]. **8** Peter saith unto him, Thou shalt never wash my feet. Jesus answered him, If I [*cp.* 3 3, 5; 6 53; 8 24] wash thee not, thou hast no part with me. **9** Simon Peter saith unto him, Lord, not my feet only, but also my hands and my head. **10** Jesus saith to him, He that is bathed needeth not [2]save to wash his feet, but is clean every whit: and ye are clean [*cp.* 15 3], but not all [*cp. verse* 11 *below and* 13 18]. **11** For he knew [*cp.* 1 48; 2 24, 25; 5 6, 42; 6 61, 64; 13 18; 16 19, 30; 18 4; 21 17: *also* 4 19, 29; 11 14] him that should betray him [*cp.* 6 64; 13 21: *also* 6 71; 12 4; 18 2, 5: *and* 13 2]; therefore said he, Ye are not all clean [*cp. verse* 10 *above and* 13 18].

[1] Or, *to the uttermost*   [2] Some ancient authorities omit *save*, and *his feet*.

cp. 26 45: *also* 26 18.	*cp.* 14 41: *also* 14 35.	*cp.* 22 14: *also* 22 53.
		cp. 18 28.
		cp. 22 3.
cp. 10 4; 26 14.	*cp.* 3 19; 14 10.	*cp.* 6 16; 22 3.
cp. 9 6, 8; 11 27; 28 18.	*cp.* 2 10.	*cp.* 5 24; 10 22.
		cp. 12 37; 17 8.
		cp. 22 26-27: *also* 12 37: 17 8.
cp. 15 16; 16 8-12.	*cp.* 4 13; 6 52; 7 18; 8 17-21; 9 10, 32: *also* 16 14.	*cp.* 9 45; 18 34: *also* 2 50.
cp. 9 4; 12 25; 16 8.	*cp.* 2 8; 8 17.	*cp.* 5 22; 6 8; 9 47; 11 17.
cp. 26 21: *also* 10 4; 26 25, 46, 48; 27 3: *and* 26 23, 24.	*cp.* 14 18: *also* 3 19; 14 42, 44: *and* 14 21.	*cp.* 22 21: *and* 22 22.

§ 61. The Foot-washing explained

[*Cp.* Luke 22 24-27]

John 13 12-20

12 So when he had washed their feet, and taken his garments, and ¹sat down again, he said unto them, Know ye what I have done to you [*cp.* 13 7: *also* 15 15]? **13** Ye call me, ²Master [*cp.* 1 38; 8 4; 11 28; 20 16: *also* 1 49; *etc.*], and, Lord: and ye say well; for so I am. **14** If I then, the Lord and the ²Master, have washed your feet, ye also ought to wash one another's feet. **15** For I have given you an example, that ye also should do as I have done to you. **16** Verily, verily, I say unto you,

A ³servant is not greater than his lord; neither ⁴one that is sent greater than he that sent him.

cp. 7 20; 8 48, 52; 10 20.

| | | *cp.*8 19; *etc.*: *and* 7 21. | *cp.*4 38; *etc.* | *cp.*7 40; *etc.*: *and* 6 46. |
| | | *cp.*11 29. | | |

John 15 20

20 Remember the word that I said unto you,

A ¹servant is not greater than his lord.

If they persecuted me, they will also persecute you; if they kept my word, they will keep yours also.

¹ Gr. *bondservant.*

Matt. 10 24-25

24 A disciple is not above his ¹master, nor a ²servant above his lord.

25 It is enough for the disciple that he be as his ¹master, and the ²servant as his lord. If they have called the master of the house ³Beelzebub [*cp.* 9 34; 12 24], how much more *shall they call* them of his household!

¹ Or, *teacher*
² Gr. *bondservant.*
³ Gr. *Beelzebul.*

Luke 6 40

40 The disciple is not above his ¹master:

but every one when he is perfected shall be as his ¹master.

cp. 3 22.   *cp.* 11 15, 18.

¹ Or, *teacher*

17 If ye know these things, blessed are ye if ye do them. **18** I speak not of you all [*cp.* 13 10, 11]: I know [*cp.* 1 48; 2 24, 25; 5 6, 42; 6 61, 64; 13 11; 16 19, 30; 18 4; 21 17: *also* 4 19, 29; 11 14] whom I ⁵have chosen [*cp.* 6 70; 15 16, 19]: but that the scripture may be fulfilled,

cp. 2 19, 22; 3 14; 12 32, 33: *also* 5 39; 15 25; 17 12.

cp. 13 21.

He that eateth ⁶my bread lifted up his heel against me [*cp.* 5 39; 15 25; 17 12].

cp. 24 46.

cp. 9 4; 12 25; 16 8.

cp. 3 14.

Matt. 26 24 The Son of man goeth, even as it is written of him [*cp.* 16 21-23; 17 12, 22-23; 20 17-19, 28; 26 2, 45: *also* 26 12, 18: *and* 21 42; 26 31, 54, 56]: but woe [*cp.* 18 7: *also* 23 13 *ff.*] unto that man through whom the Son of man is betrayed! . . . **21** And as they were eating, he said, Verily I say unto you, that one of you shall betray me.

cp. 21 42; 26 24, 31, 54, 56.

cp. 2 8; 8 17.

Mark 14 21 For the Son of man goeth, even as it is written of him [*cp.* 8 31-33; 9 12, 30-32; 10 32-34, 45; 14 41: *also* 14 8: *and* 12 10; 14 27, 49]: but woe unto that man through whom the Son of man is betrayed! . . . **18** And as they ¹sat and were eating, Jesus said, Verily I say unto you, One of you shall betray me, *even he* that eateth with me.

cp. 9 12; 12 10; 14 21, 27, 49.

cp. 12 37, 43: *also* 11 28.

cp. 5 22; 6 8; 9 47; 11 17.

cp. 6 13.

Luke 22 22 For the Son of man indeed goeth, as it hath been determined [*cp.* 9 22, 43-45; 13 32-33; 17 25; 18 31-34; 24 7, 44: *also* 20 17; 22 37; 24 25-27, 46]: but woe [*cp.* 17 1: *also* 11 42 *ff.*] unto that man through whom he is betrayed! . . .

21 But behold, the hand of him that betrayeth me is with me on the table.

cp. 18 31; 20 17; 22 37; 24 25-27, 44-46.

John	Matt.	Mark	Luke
19 From henceforth [*cp.* 14 7] I tell you before it come to pass [*cp.* 14 29: *also* 16 4], that, when it is come to pass, ye may believe [*cp.* 14 29: *also* 11 15: *and* 19 35; 20 31: *and* 11 42] that [7]I am *he* [*cp.* 8 24, 28: *also* 8 58]. **20** Verily, verily, I say unto you,	*cp.* 23 39; 26 29, 64. *cp.* 24 25.	*cp.* 13 23.	
		cp. 13 6; 14 62.	*cp.* 21 8; 22 70.
He that receiveth whomsoever I send receiveth me; and he that receiveth me receiveth him that sent me [*cp.* 12 44-48: *also* 5 23: *and* 15 23].	Matt. 10 **40** He that receiveth you receiveth me, and he that receiveth me receiveth him that sent me.		Luke 10 **16** He that heareth you heareth me; and he that rejecteth you rejecteth me; and he that rejecteth me rejecteth him that sent me.
	Matt. 18 **5** And whoso shall receive one such little child in my name receiveth me.	Mark 9 **37** Whosoever shall receive one of such little children in my name, receiveth me: and whosoever receiveth me, receiveth not me, but him that sent me.	Luke 9 **48** Whosoever shall receive this little child in my name receiveth me: and whosoever shall receive me receiveth him that sent me.

[1] Gr. *reclined*.   [2] Or, *Teacher*
[3] Gr. *bondservant*.
[4] Gr. *an apostle*.   [5] Or, *chose*
[6] Many ancient authorities read *his bread with me*.   [7] Or, *I am*

[1] Gr. *reclined*.

John 13 18 = Ps. 41 9.

§ 62. **The Prophecy of the Betrayal**

John 13 21-30	Matt. 26 20-25	Mark 14 17-21	Luke 22 14, 21-23
21 When Jesus had thus said, he was troubled [*cp.* 11 33; 12 27: *also* 14 1, 27] in the spirit, and testified, *cp.* 12 23, 27: 13 1; 17 1: *also* 2 4; 7 6, 8, 30; 8 20.	**20** Now when even [*cp.* 26 45: *also* 26 18] was come, he was sitting at meat *cp.* 10 2. with the twelve [1]disciples;	**17** And when it was evening [*cp.* 14 35, 41] he cometh with the twelve. **18** And as they [1]sat *cp.* 6 30.	**14** And when the hour [*cp.* 22 53] was come, he sat down, and the apostles [*cp.* 6 13; 9 10; 17 5; 24 10] with him. . . .
and said, Verily, verily, I say unto you, that one of you shall betray me [*cp.* 6 64; 13 11]. *cp.* 13 18. **22** The disciples looked *cp.* 16 6, 20, 22. one on another, doubting of whom he spake. **23** There was at the table reclining in Jesus' bosom one of his disciples, whom Jesus loved [*cp.* 19 26; 20 2; 21 7, 20: *also* 11 36]. **24** Simon Peter therefore beckoneth to him, and saith unto him, Tell *us* who it is of whom he speaketh.	**21** and as they were eating [*cp.* 26 26], he said, Verily I say unto you, that one of you shall betray me. **22** And they were exceeding sorrowful [*cp.* 17 23; 18 31: *also* 26 37], and began	and were eating [*cp.* 14 22], Jesus said, Verily I say unto you, One of you shall betray me, *even* he that eateth with me. **19** They began to be sorrowful, and	**21** But behold, the hand of him that betrayeth me is with me on the table. *cp.* 22 45.

25 He leaning back [*cp.* 21 20], as he was [*cp.* 4 6], on Jesus' breast saith unto him, Lord, who is it? **26** Jesus therefore answereth, He it is, for whom I shall dip the sop, and give it him. *cp.* 13 18.	to say unto him every one, Is it I, Lord? **23** And he answered and said, He that dipped his hand with me in the dish, the same shall betray me.	*cp.* 4 36. to say unto him one by one, Is it I? **20** And he said unto them, *It is* one of the twelve, he that dippeth with me in the dish.	*verse 23*
cp. 2 19, 22; 3 14; 12 32, 33: *also* 5 39; 15 25; 17 12.	**24** The Son of man goeth, even as it is written of him [*cp.* 16 21-23; 17 12, 22-23; 20 17-19, 28; 26 2, 45: *also* 26 12, 18: *and* 21 42; 26 31, 54, 56]: but woe [*cp.* 18 7: *also* 23 13 *ff.*] unto that man through whom the Son of man is betrayed! good were it [2]for that man if he had not been born.	**21** For the Son of man goeth, even as it is written of him [*cp.* 8 31-33; 9 12, 30-32; 10 32-34, 45; 14 41: *also* 14 8: *and* 12 10; 14 27, 49]: but woe unto that man through whom the Son of man is betrayed! good were it [2]for that man if he had not been born.	**22** For the Son of man indeed goeth, as it hath been determined [*cp.* 9 22, 43-45; 13 32-33; 17 25; 18 31-34; 24 7, 44: *also* 20 17; 22 37; 24 25-27, 46]: but woe [*cp.* 17 1: *also* 11 42 *ff.*] unto that man through whom he is betrayed!
verse 22	*verse 22*	*verse 19*	**23** And they began to question among themselves, which of them it was that should do this thing.
So when he had dipped the sop, he taketh and giveth it to Judas, *the son* of Simon Iscariot [*cp.* 6 71: *also* 13 2: *and* 12 4; 14 22].	**25** And Judas, *cp.* 10 4; 26 14. which betrayed him, answered and said, Is it I, Rabbi [*cp.* 26 49: *also* 23 7, 8]? He saith unto him, Thou has said [*cp.* 26 64: *also* 27 11].		
cp. 1 38, 49; *etc.*: *also* 20 16.		*cp.* 3 19; 14 10.	*cp.* 6 16; 22 3.
cp. 18 37.		*cp.* 9 5; 11 21; 14 45: *also* 10 51. *cp.* 15 2.	*cp.* 23 3: *also* 22 70.
27 And after the sop, then entered Satan [*cp.* 13 2: *also* 6 70] into him. Jesus therefore saith unto him, That thou			*cp.* 22 3.
	[1] Many authorities, some ancient, omit *disciples.* [2] Gr. *for him if that man.*	[1] Gr. *reclined.* [2] Gr. *for him if that man.*	

doest, do quickly. 28 Now no man at the table knew for what intent he spake this unto him [*cp.* 4 33; 11 13; 12 16; 13 7, 36; 14 5-10, 22; 16 17-18: *also* 3 10; 8 27, 43; 10 6]. **29** For some thought, because Judas had the [1]bag [*cp.* 12 6], that Jesus said unto him, Buy what things we have need of for the feast; or, that he should give something to the poor [*cp.* 12 5]. **30** He then having received the sop went out straightway: and it was night [*cp.* 9 4; 11 10: *also* 12 35].

cp. 26 50. *cp.* 15 16; 16 8-12.	*cp.* 4 13; 6 52; 7 18; 8 17-21; 9 10, 32: *also* 16 14.	*cp.* 9 45; 18 34: *also* 2 50.

[1] Or, *box*

Mark 14 18 ‖ Luke 22 21: *cp.* Ps. 41 9.

§ 63. A New Commandment of Love

John 13 31-35

31 When therefore he was gone out, Jesus saith, Now [1]is the Son of man glorified [*cp.* 7 39; 12 16, 23: *also* 11 4; 17 10: *and* 17 1*ff.*], and God [1]is glorified in him [*cp.* 14 13: *also* 15 8]; **32** and God shall glorify him in himself, and straightway shall he glorify him [*cp.* 8 54; 16 14; 17 1, 5: *also* 7 39; *etc.*]. **33** Little children, yet a little while [*cp.* 7 33; 12 35; 14 19; 16 16-19] I am with you. Ye shall seek me [*cp.* 7 34, 36; 8 21]: and as I said unto the Jews, Whither I go [*cp.* 8 14, 21, 22; 13 36; 14 4: *also* 7 35; 13 36; 14 5;

16 5: *and* 3 8; 12 35], ye cannot come [*cp.* 7 34, 36; 8 21, 22: *also* 13 36]; so now I say unto you. **34** A new commandment I give unto you [*cp.* 15 12: *also* 14 15, 21; 15 10], that ye love one an-other [*cp. verse* 35 *below and* 15 12, 17]; [2]even as I have loved you [*cp.* 15 12: *also* 13 1; 15 9], that ye also love one another. **35** By this shall all men know that ye are my disciples [*cp.* 8 31; 15 8], if ye have love one to another [*cp. verse* 34 *above and* 15 12, 17].

| | | | cp. 14 26, 27, 33. |

[1] Or, *was* [2] Or, *even as I loved you, that ye also may love one another*

§ 64. The Prophecy of Peter's Denial

[*For* John 13 36-14 4 *cp.* Matt. 19 27-29 ‖ Mark 10 28-30 ‖ Luke 18 28-30 *and* 22 28-30]

John 13 36-38	Matt. 26 33-35	Mark 14 29-31	Luke 22 31-34
36 Simon Peter [*cp.* 21 21: *also* 6 68]	**33** But Peter [*cp.* 14 28; 15 15; 16 22; 17 4; 18 21; 19 27: *also* 16 16; 17 24] answered and said unto him,	**29** But Peter [*cp.* 8 32; 9 5; 10 28; 11 21: *also* 8 29]	*cp.* 8 45; 9 33; 12 41; 18 28: *also* 5 8; 9 20.
saith unto him, Lord, whither goest thou [*cp.* 16 5: *also* 4 33; 11 13; 12 16; 13 7, 28; 14 5-10, 22; 16 17-18: *and* 3 10; 8 27, 43; 10 6]?	*cp.* 15 16; 16 8-12.	said unto him, *cp.* 4 13; 6 52; 7 18; 8 17-21; 9 10, 32: *also* 16 14.	*cp.* 9 45; 18 34: *also* 2 50.
	If all shall be [1]offended in thee, I will never be offended.	Although all shall be [1]offended, yet will not I.	
Jesus answered, Whither I go [*cp.* 8 14, 21, 22; 13 33; 14 4: *also* 7 35; 14 5; 16 5: *and* 3 8; 12 35], thou canst not follow me now [*cp.* 7 34, 36; 8 21, 22; 13 33]; but thou shalt follow afterwards [*cp.* 13 7: *also* 21 18-19]. *cp.* 1 42; 21 15, 16, 17.	*cp.* 16 17; 17 25.	*cp.* 14 37.	**31** Simon, Simon, be hold, Satan [*cp.* 22 3] [1]asked to have you, that he might sift you as wheat: **32** but I made supplication for thee, that thy faith [*cp.* 8 25; 12 28; 17 5, 6: *also* 24 11, 12, 38, 41: *and* 24 25] fail not: and do thou, when once thou hast turned again, stablish thy brethren.
cp. 3 12; 6 64; 14 10; 20 25, 27.	*cp.* 8 26; 14 31; 16 8; 17 20; 21 21; 28 17.	*cp.* 4 40; 11 22; 16 11, 13, 14.	**33** And he said unto him, Lord, with thee I am ready to go both to prison and to death.
cp. 21 15-17. **37** Peter saith unto him, Lord, why cannot I follow thee even now? I will lay down my life [*cp.* 10 11, 15, 17; 15 13] for thee [*cp.* 11 16].	*cp.* 16 18-19. *verse* 35	*verse* 31	
38 Jesus answereth, Wilt thou lay down thy life for me? Verily, verily, I say unto thee,	**34** Jesus said unto him, Verily I say unto thee, that	**30** And Jesus saith unto him, Verily I say unto thee, that thou to-day, *even* this night, before	**34** And he said, I tell thee, Peter,
The cock shall not crow,	this night, before the cock crow,	the cock crow twice [*cp.* 14 68, 72],	the cock shall not crow this day, until thou
till thou hast denied	thou shalt deny	shalt deny	shalt thrice deny that thou

cp. 18 17, 25, 27. me thrice [*cp.* 18 27]. *verse* 37	*cp.* 26 70, 72, 74. me thrice [*cp.* 26 75]. **35** Peter saith into him, Even if I must die with thee, *yet* will I not deny thee. Likewise also said all the disciples.	*cp.* 14 68, 70, 71. me thrice [*cp.* 14 72]. **31** But he spake exceed- ing vehemently, If I must die with thee, I will not deny thee. And in like manner also said they all.	knowest [*cp.* 22 57, 58, 60] me [*cp.* 22 61]. *verse* 33
	[1] Gr. *caused to stumble.*	[1] Gr. *caused to stumble.*	[1] Or, *obtained you by asking*

§ 65. **Jesus the Way, the Truth, and the Life: The Promise of the Spirit**

[*For* John 13 36-14 4 *cp.* Matt. 19 27-29 ‖ Mark 10 28-30 ‖ Luke 18 28-30 *and* 22 28-30]

John 14 1-24

1 Let not your heart be troubled [*cp.* 14 27: *also* 11 33; 12 27; 13 21]: [1]ye believe in God, believe also in me [*cp.* 12 44]. **2** In my Father's house [*cp.* 2 16] are many [2]mansions; if it were not so, I would have told you; for I go to prepare a place for you. **3** And if I go and prepare a place for you, I come again [*cp.* 14 28: *also verse* 18 *below: and* 21 22, 23], and will receive you unto myself [*cp.* 12 32]; that where I am [*cp.* 7 34, 36; 12 26; 17 24], *there* ye may be also [*cp.* 17 24: *also* 12 26]. **4** [3]And whither I go [*cp.* 8 14, 21, 22; 13 33, 36: *also* 7 35; 13 36; 14 5; 16 5: *and* 3 8; 12 35], ye know the way. **5** Thomas [*cp.* 11 16; 20 24, 26-29; 21 2] saith unto him, Lord, we know not whither thou goest; how know we the way [*cp. vv.* 8 *and* 22 *below*; 4 33; 11 13; 12 16; 13 7, 36; 16 17-18: *also* 3 10; 8 27, 43; 10 6]? **6** Jesus saith unto him, I am the way, and the truth [*cp.* 1 14, 17; 5 33; 8 32; 18 37], and the life [*cp.* 11 25: *also* 1 4; 5 26; 6 57: *and* 3 15; *etc.*]: no one cometh unto the Father, but [4]by me. **7** If ye had known me, ye would have known my Father also [*cp.* 8 19]: from hence-forth [*cp.* 13 19] ye know him, and have seen him. **8** Philip [*cp.* 1 43-48; 6 5-7; 12 21-22] saith unto him, Lord, shew us the Father, and it sufficeth [*cp.* 6 7] us. **9** Jesus saith unto him, Have I been so long time with you, and dost thou not know me [*cp.* 1 10, 26, 31, 33; 8 19; 16 3: *also* 20 14; 21 4: *and* 8 55; 14 17; 17 25], Philip? he that hath seen me hath seen the Father [*cp.* 12 45; 15 24: *also* 10 30; 17 11, 22: *and* 5 19]; how sayest thou [*cp.* 8 33; 12 34], Shew us the Father? **10** Believest thou not [*cp.* 3 12; 6 64; 20 27] that I am in the Father, and the Father in me [*cp. verse* 11; 10 38; 17 21: *also* 14 20; 17 23]? the words that I say unto you [*cp.* 3 34; 8 26, 47; 12 47-50; 17 8, 14: *also* 6 63, 68] I speak not from myself [*cp.* 12 49: *also* 7 17: *and* 5 19, 30; 8 28: *and* 7 28; 8 42: *and* 16 13: *see also verse* 24 *below*]: but the Father abiding in me doeth his works [*cp.* 10 25, 32, 37: *also* 4 34; 5 36; 17 4: *and* 3 21; 6 28-29; 9 3-4: *and* 10 38; 14 11: *and* 5 17; 7 21; 15 24]. **11** Believe me that I am in the Father, and the Father in me: or else believe me for the very works' sake. **12** Verily, verily, I say unto you, He that believeth on me, the works that I do shall he do also; and greater *works* than these [*cp.* 1 50; 5 20] shall he do; because I go unto the Father [*cp.* 14 28; 16 10, 17, 28: *also* 7 33; 16 5: *and* 17 11, 13: *and* 20 17: *and* 13 1, 3].

cp. 10 3.	*cp.* 3 18.	*cp.* 6 15.
cp. 15 16; 16 8-12.	*cp.* 4 13; 6 52; 7 18; 8 17-21; 9 10, 32: *also* 16 14.	*cp.* 9 45; 18 34: *also* 2 50.
cp. 23 39; 26 29, 64.		
cp. 10 3.	*cp.* 31 8.	*cp.* 6 14.
cp. 17 17.	*cp.* 9 19.	*cp.* 9 41.
cp. 8 26; 14 31; 16 8; 17 20; 21 21; 28 17.	*cp.* 4 40; 11 22; 16 14.	*cp.* 8 25; 12 28; 17 5-6; 22 32; 24 25, 38.

| **13** And whatsoever ye shall ask   in my name [*cp. verse* 14 *below*; 16 23, 24, 26: *also* 14 26],

that will I do, that the Father may be | John 15 16; 16 23-24
15 16 . . . that whatsoever ye shall ask of the Father in my name,

he may give it you. | Matt. 21 22; 7 7
21 22 And all things, whatsoever ye shall ask   in
cp. 18 5, 20; 24 5: *also* 7 22.

prayer, believing,

ye shall receive. | Mark 11 24
11 24 All things whatsoever ye

cp. 9 37, 38, 39; 13 6; 16 17.

pray   and ask for, believe that ye have received them, and ye shall have them. | Luke 11 9
11 24 All things whatsoever ye

cp. 9 48, 49; 10 17; 21 8; 24 47. |

glorified in the Son [cp. 13 31: also 15 8].

14 If ye shall ask [5]me anything

in my name, that will I do.

15 7 Ask whatsoever ye will, and it shall be done unto you.

16 23 If ye shall ask anything of the Father, he will give it you in my name. **24** Hitherto have ye asked nothing in my name: ask,

and ye shall receive.

cp. 18 19.

7 7 Ask,

and it shall be given you; seek, and ye shall find; knock, and it shall be opened unto you.

11 9 Ask,

and it shall be given you; seek, and ye shall find; knock, and it shall be opened unto you.

cp. 28 20.

cp. 24 49.

15 If ye love me, ye will keep my commandments [cp. verse 21 and 15 10: also 13 34; 15 12: and 8 51, 52; 14 23, 24; 15 20]. **16** And I will [6]pray the Father [cp. 16 26: also 17 9, 15, 20], and he shall give you another [7]Comforter [cp. 14 26; 15 26; 16 7], that he may be with you for ever, **17** even the Spirit of truth [cp. 15 26; 16 13]: whom the world cannot receive; for it beholdeth him not, neither knoweth him: ye know him; for he abideth with you, and shall be in you. **18** I will not leave you [8]desolate: I come unto you [cp. verse 3 above and 14 28: also 21 22, 23]. **19** Yet a little while [cp. 7 33; 12 35; 13 33; 16 16-19], and the world beholdeth me no more; but ye behold me [cp. 12 45; 16 10, 16, 17, 19: also 6 40, 62]: because I live, [9]ye shall live also. **20** In that day [cp. 16 23, 26] ye shall know that I am in my Father [cp. verse 10 above], and ye in me, and I in you [cp. 17 21, 23, 26: also 6 56; 15 4, 5, 7]. **21** He that hath my commandments, and keepeth them [cp. verse 15 above], he it is that loveth me [cp. verse 15 and 15 10: also 13 34; 15 12]: and he that loveth me shall be loved of my Father [cp. verse 23 below; 16 27; 17 23: also 21 15-17], and I will love him, and will manifest myself [cp. 7 4, 21 1, 14: also 1 31; 2 11; 3 21; 9 3; 17 6] unto him. **22** Judas (not Iscariot) saith unto him, Lord, what is come to pass that thou wilt manifest thyself unto us, and not unto the world [cp. 7 4: also verse 5 above]? **23** Jesus answered and said unto him, If a man love me, he will keep my word [cp. 8 51, 52; 15 20: also verse 24 below: and 14 15, 21; 15 10]: and my Father will love him [cp. verse 21 above], and we will come unto him, and make our abode with him. **24** He that loveth me not keepeth not my words [cp. verse 23 above: also 4 41; 5 24; 8 31, 37, 43, 51, 52; 12 48; 15 3, 20]: and the word [cp. 5 38; 8 55; 17 6, 14, 17, 20] which ye hear is not mine, but the Father's who sent me [cp. 7 16: also 3 34; 8 26, 28, 38, 40; 12 49, 50; 14 10; 15 15].

cp. 7 22; 24 36: also 26 29.

cp. 13 32: also 14 25.

cp. 10 12; 17 31; 21 34.

cp. 16 12, 14.

cp. 6 16: also Acts 1 13.

cp. 28 20.

[1] Or, believe in God   [2] Or, abiding-places   [3] Many ancient authorities read And whither I go ye know, and the way ye know.
[4] Or, through   [5] Many ancient authorities omit me.   [6] Gr. make request of.   [7] Or, Advocate Or, Helper Gr. Paraclete.   [8] Or, orphans   [9] Or, and ye shall live

§ 66. The Gift of Peace

John 14 25-31

25 These things have I spoken unto you [cp. 15 11; 16 1, 4, 6, 25, 33], while yet abiding with you [cp. 16 4]. **26** But the [1]Comforter [cp. 14 16; 15 26; 16 7], even the Holy Spirit, whom the Father will send [cp. 15 26: also 14 16: and 16 7] in my name [cp. 14 13, 14; 15 16; 16

cp. 24 44.

cp. 18 5, 20; 24 5: also 7 22.

cp. 9 37, 38, 39; 13 6; 16 17.

cp. 24 49.

cp. 9 48, 49; 10 17; 21 8; 24 47.

23, 24, 26], he shall teach you all things [*cp.* 15 26; 16 13], and bring to your remembrance [*cp.* 16 4: *also* 2 22; 12 16] all that I said unto you. **27** Peace I leave with you; my peace I give unto you [*cp.* 16 33: *also* 20 19, 21, 26]: not as the world giveth, give I unto you. Let not your

cp. 10 19, 20.

cp. 26 75.

cp. 13 11.

cp. 14 72.

cp. 12 11, 12.

cp. 22 61: *also* 24 6, 8.

cp. 5 9; 10 13.

cp. 9 50.

cp. 1 79; 2 14, 29; 10 6; 19 38: *also* 24 36.

heart be troubled [*cp.* 14 1: *also* 11 33; 12 27; 13 21], neither let it be fearful. **28** Ye heard how I said to you, I go away [*cp.* 8 21: *also* 7 33; *etc.*], and I come unto you [*cp.* 14 3, 18: *also* 21 22, 23]. If ye loved me, ye would have rejoiced, because I go unto the Father [*cp.* 14 12; 16 10, 17, 28: *also* 7 33; 16 5: *and* 17 11, 13: *and* 20 17: *and* 13 1, 3]: for the Father is greater [*cp.* 10 29] than I. **29** And now I have told you before it come to pass [*cp.* 13 19: *also* 16 4], that, when it is come to pass, ye may believe [*cp.* 13 19: *also* 11 15: *and* 19 35; 20 31: *and* 11 42]. **30** I will no more speak much with you [*cp.* 8 26; 16 12], for the prince of the world [*cp.* 12 31; 16 11] cometh: and he hath nothing in me; **31** but that the world may know [*cp.* 17 23: *also* 17 21] that I love the Father, and as the Father gave me commandment [*cp.* 10 18; 12 49: *also* 15 10], even so I do.

cp. 24 25.

cp. 13 23.

Matt. 26 **44** And he left them again, and went away, and prayed a third time, saying again the same words. **45** Then cometh he to the disciples, and saith unto them, Sleep on now, and take your rest:

Mark 14 **41** And he cometh the third time, and saith unto them, Sleep on now, and take your rest: it is enough;

cp. 12 23, 27; 13 1; 17 1: *also* 2 4; 7 6, 8, 30; 8 20.

behold, the hour [*cp.* 26 18] is at hand, and the Son of man is betrayed into the hands of sinners.

the hour [*cp.* 14 35] is come; behold, the Son of man is betrayed into the hands of sinners.

cp. 22 14, 53.

Arise, let us go hence.

46 Arise, let us be going: behold, he is at hand that betrayeth me.

42 Arise, let us be going: behold, he that betrayeth me is at hand.

[1] Or, *Advocate* Or, *Helper* Gr. *Paraclete.*

§ 67. Jesus the True Vine

John 15 1-27

1 I am the true [*cp.* 1 9; 6 32: *also* 6 55; 17 3] vine, and my Father is the husbandman. **2** Every branch in me that beareth not fruit, he taketh it away [*cp. verse* 6 *below*]: and every *branch* that beareth fruit, he cleanseth it, that it may bear more fruit. **3** Already ye are clean [*cp.* 13 10] because of the word which I have spoken unto you [*cp.* 4 41; 5 24; 8 31, 37, 43, 51, 52; 12 48; 14 23, 24; 15 20: *also* 5 38; *etc.*]. **4** Abide in me, and I in you [*cp. verses* 5, 7, *and* 6 56: *also* 8 31: *and* 14 20; 17 21, 23, 26]. As the branch cannot bear fruit [*cp. verses* 5, 8, *and* 16] of itself, except it abide in the vine; so neither can ye, except ye abide in me. **5** I am the vine, ye are the branches: He that abideth in me, and I in him [*cp. verses* 4 *and* 7], the same beareth much fruit [*cp. verses* 4, 8, *and* 16]: for apart from me ye can do nothing. **6** If a man abide not in me, he is cast forth as a branch, and is withered; and they gather them, and cast them into the fire, and they are burned. **7** If ye abide in me, and my words abide in you [*cp. verses* 4 *and* 5 *above*], ask [*cp. verse* 16 *below*]

cp. 3 10; 7 19.

cp. 3 9; 13 7, 9.

cp. 13 23.

cp. 4 20.

cp. 8 15.

cp. 13 23.

cp. 4 20.

cp. 8 15.

cp. 3 10; 7 19: *also* 3 12; 5 22, 29; *etc.*

cp. 9 43, 45, 47.

cp. 3 9: *also* 3 17; 12 5.

whatsoever ye will, and it shall be done unto you. **8** Herein [1]is my Father glorified [*cp.* 13 31; 14 13], [2]that ye bear much fruit [*cp. verses* 4, 5, *and* 16], and *so* shall ye be my disciples [*cp.* 8 31; 13 35]. **9** Even as the Father hath loved me [*cp.* 3 35; 5 20; 10 17; 17 23, 24, 26], I also have loved you [*cp.* 13 1, 34; 15 12]: abide ye in my love. **10** If ye keep my commandments [*cp.* 14 15, 21: *also* 13 34; 15 12: *and* 8 51, 52; 14 23, 24; 15 20], ye shall abide in my love; even as I have kept my Father's commandments [*cp.* 10 18; 12 49; 14 31], and abide in his love. **11** These things have I spoken unto you [*cp.* 14 25; 16 1, 4, 6, 25, 33], that my joy may be in you, and *that* your joy may be fulfilled [*cp.* 3 29; 16 24; 17 13]. **12** This is my commandment [*cp. verse* 17 *below and* 13 34: *also* 14 15, 21; 15 10], that ye love one another [*cp. verse* 17 *below and* 13 34, 35], even as I have loved you [*cp.* 13 34: *also* 13 1; 15 9]. **13** Greater love hath no man than this, that a man lay down his life [*cp.* 10 11, 15, 17; 13 37, 38] for his friends. **14** Ye are my friends, if ye do the things which I command you. **15** No longer do I call you [3]servants; for the [4]servant knoweth not [*cp.* 13 7, 12] what his lord doeth: but I have called you friends; for all things that I heard from my Father I have made known unto you [*cp.* 14 24; 17 8, 14: *also* 3 34; 7 16; 8 26, 28, 38, 40; 12 49, 50]. **16** Ye did not choose me, but I chose you, and appointed you, that ye should go and bear fruit, and *that* your fruit should abide: that

cp. 13 23.	*cp.* 4 20.	*cp.* 8 15. *cp.* 14 26; *etc.*	
cp. 3 17; 17 5.	*cp.* 1 11; 9 7; 12 6.	*cp.* 3 22; 20 **13**.	
cp. 28 20.			
cp. 25 21, 23.			
cp. 12 50.	*cp.* 3 35.	*cp.* 12 4: *also* 8 21.	

John 14 13-14; 15 7	Matt. 21 22; 7 7	Mark 11 24	Luke 11 9
cp. 15 19: *also* 6 70; 13 18.		*cp.* 3 14.	*cp.* 6 13.
cp. 15 4, 5, 8.	*cp.* 13 23.	*cp.* 4 20.	*cp.* 8 15.

whatsoever ye shall ask of the Father in my name [*cp.* 14 13, 14; 16 23, 24, 26: *also* 14 26],

John 14	Matt.	Mark	Luke
14 13 And whatsoever ye shall ask in my name,	**21 22** And all things, whatsoever ye shall ask	**11 24** All things whatsoever ye	
	cp. 18 5, 20; 24 5: *also* 7 22.	*cp.* 9 37, 38, 39; 13 6; 16 17.	*cp.* 9 48, 49; 10 17; 21 8; 24 47.
	in prayer, believing,	pray and ask for, believe that ye have received them, and	

he may give it you. — that will I do, that the Father may be glorified in the Son. *(Matt.)* ye shall receive. *(Mark)* ye shall have them.

16 23 If ye shall ask anything of the Father, he will give it you in my name. — **14** If ye shall ask [1]me anything in my name, that will I do. *(Matt. cp. 18 19.)*

24 Hitherto have ye asked nothing in my name: ask, and ye shall receive.

John 14	Matt.	Luke
15 7 Ask whatsoever ye will, and it shall be done unto you.	**7 7** Ask, and it shall be given you; seek, and ye shall find; knock, and it shall be opened unto you.	**11 9** Ask, and it shall be given you; seek, and ye shall find; knock, and it shall be opened unto you.

[1] Many ancient authorities omit *me*.

17 These things I command you [*cp. verse* 12 *above and* 13 34: *also* 14 15, 21; 15 10], that ye may love one another [*cp. verse* 12 *above and* 13 34, 35]. **18** If the world hateth you [*cp.* 17 14: *also* 7 7], [5]ye know that it hath hated me [*cp.* 7 7; 15 24] before *it hated* you. **19** If ye were of the world, the world would love its own [*cp* 1 11; 8 44; 16 32; 19 27]: but because ye are not of the world [*cp.* 8 23; 17 14, 16; 18 36], but I chose you [*cp. verse* 16 *above: also* 6 70; 13 18] out of the world, therefore the world hateth you. **20** Remember the word that I said unto you,

cp. 10 22; 24 9.	*cp.* 13 13.	*cp.* 1 71; 6 22, 27; 21 17. *cp.* 18 28.	
	cp. 3 14.	*cp.* 6 13.	

John 13 16	Matt. 10 24-25	Luke 6 40
16 Verily, verily, I say unto you,	**24** A disciple is not above	**40** The disciple is not above

A ⁴servant is not greater than his lord.

A ¹servant is not greater than his lord; neither ²one that is sent greater than he that sent him.

his ¹master, nor a ²servant above his lord.

25 It is enough for the disciple that he be as his ¹master, and the ²servant as his lord. If they have

his ¹master:

but everyone when he is perfected shall be as his ¹master.

If they persecuted me [*cp.* 5 16, 18],

called the master of the house ³Beelzebub [*cp.* 9 34; 12 24], how much more *shall they call* them of his household!

they will also persecute you; if they have kept my word [*cp.* 8 51, 52; 14 23, 24: *also* 14 15, 21; 15 10: *and* 4 41; 5 24; 8 31; *etc.*], they will keep yours also. **21** But all these things will they do [*cp.* 16 3] unto you for my name's sake, because they know not [*cp.* 7 28; 8 19, 55; 16 3; 17 25: *also* 4 22] him that sent me. **22** If I had not come and spoken unto them, they had not had sin [*cp. verse* 24 *below and* 9 41]: but now they have no excuse for their sin.

cp. 7 20; 8 48, 52; 10 20.	*cp.* 5 11; 10 23: *also* 23 34.	*cp.* 3 22.	*cp.* 11 15, 18.
			cp. 21 12: *also* 11 50.
cp. 10 22; 19 29; 24 9: *also* 5 11; 10 18, 39; 16 25.	*cp.* 13 13: *also* 8 35; 10 29; 13 9.		*cp.* 21 12, 17: *also* 6 22; 9 24: *and* 18 29.

¹ Gr. *bondservant.*
² Gr. *an apostle.*

¹ Or, *teacher*
² Gr. *bondservant.*
³ Gr. *Beelzebul.*

¹ Or, *teacher*

23 He that hateth me hateth my Father also [*cp.* 5 23; 12 44-45; 13 20]. **24** If I had not done among them the works [*cp.* 10 25, 32, 37, 38; 14 10, 11: *also* 3 21; 4 34; 5 36; *etc.*] which none other did, they had not had sin [*cp. verse* 24 *above and* 9 41]: but now have they both seen and hated [*cp. verse* 18 *above*] both me and my Father [*cp.* 12 45; 14 9-11: *also* 10 30; 17 11, 22: *and* 5 19]. **25** But *this cometh to pass*, that the word may be fulfilled that is written in their law [*cp.* 7 51; 8 17; 10 34; 18 31: *also* 19 7], They hated me without a cause. **26** But when the ⁶Comforter [*cp.* 14 16, 26; 16 7] is come, whom I will send unto you from the Father [*cp.* 14 26: *also* 14 16: *and* 16 7], *even the Spirit of truth* [*cp.* 14 17; 16 13], which ⁷proceedeth from the Father, he shall bear witness of me: **27** ⁸and ye also bear witness [*cp.* 19 35; 21 24], because ye have been with me from the beginning [*cp.* 6 64; 16 4: *also* 8 44].

cp. 10 40.	*cp.* 9 37.	*cp.* 9 48; 10 16.
		cp. 24 49.
		cp. 24 48. *cp.* 1 2.

¹ Or, *was*   ² Many ancient authorities read *that ye bear much fruit, and be my disciples.*
³ Gr. *bondservants.*   ⁴ Gr. *bondservant.*   ⁵ Or, *know ye*   ⁶ Or, *Advocate* Or, *Helper* Gr. *Paraclete.*   ⁷ Or, *goeth forth from*   ⁸ Or, *and bear ye also witness*

John 15 1: *cp.* Jer. 2 21.   John 15 6: *cp.* Ezek. 15 4; 19 12.   John 15 25 = Pss. 35 19 *and* 69 4.

§ 68. The Spirit will guide the Disciples into all the Truth: Their Sorrow will be turned into Joy

John 16 1-24

1 These things have I spoken unto you [*cp.* 14 25; 15 11; 16 4, 6, 25, 33], that ye should not be made to stumble [*cp.* 6 61]. **2** They shall put you out of the synagogues [*cp.* 9 22, 12 42]: yea, the hour cometh [*cp.* 4 21, 23; 5 25, 28; 16 25, 32], that whosoever killeth you shall think that he offereth service unto God. **3** And these things will they do [*cp.* 15 21], because they have not known the Father [*cp.* 7 28; 8 19, 55; 15 21; 17 25: *also* 4 22], nor me [*cp.* 1 10, 26, 31, 33; 8 19; 14 9: *also* 20 14; 21 4: *and* 8 55; 14 17; 17 25]. **4** But these things have I spoken unto you [*cp. verse* 1 *above*], that when their hour is come, ye may remember them [*cp.* 14 26: *also* 2 22; 12 16], how that I told you [*cp.* 13 19; 14 29]. And these things I said not unto you from the beginning [*cp.* 6 64; 15 27: *also* 8 44], because I was with you [14 25]. **5** But now I go unto him that sent me [*cp.* 7 33: *also* 14 12, 28; 16 10, 17, 28: *and* 17 11, 13: *and* 20 17: *and* 13 1, 3]; and none of you asketh me, Whither goest thou [*cp.* 13 36: *also* 8 14; *etc.*]? **6** But because I have spoken these things unto you [*cp. verse* 1 *above*], sorrow hath filled your heart [*cp. verses* 20 *and* 22]. **7** Nevertheless I tell you the truth; It is expedient [*cp.* 11 50, 18 14] for you that I go away: for if I go not away, the [1]Comforter [*cp.* 14 16, 26; 15 26] will not come unto you; but if I go, I will send him unto you [*cp.* 15 26: *also* 14 16, 26]. **8** And he, when he is come, will convict the world in respect of sin [*cp.* 8 46], and of righteousness, and of judgement: **9** of sin, because they believe not on me [*cp.* 8 24]: **10** of righteousness, because I go to the Father [*cp.* 14 12, 28; 16 17, 28: *also* 7 33; 16 5: *and* 17 11, 13: *and* 20 17: *and* 13 1, 3], and ye behold me no more [*cp. verses* 16, 17, 19, *and* 14 19: *also* 12 45: *and* 6 40, 62: *and* 14 17]; **11** of judgement, because the prince of this world [*cp.* 12 31: *also* 14 30] hath been judged [*cp.* 3 18, 19; 5 24; 12 31: *and* 5 29; 12 48]. **12** I have yet many things to say unto you [*cp.* 16 25: *also* 6 60], but ye cannot bear them now [*cp.* 16 25: *also* 6 60]. **13** Howbeit when he, the Spirit of truth [*cp.* 14 17; 15 26], is come, he shall guide you into all the truth: for he shall not speak from himself [*cp.* 5 19, 30; 8 28: *also* 7 17; 12 49; 14 10: *and* 8 42]; but what things soever he shall hear, *these* shall he speak: and he shall declare unto you [*cp. verses* 14 *and* 15 *and* 4 25] the things that are to come [*cp.* 14 26]. **14** He shall glorify me [*cp.* 8 54; 13 32; 17 1, 5: *also* 7 39; *etc.*]: for he shall take of mine [*cp.* 10 14; 16 15; 17 10], and shall declare *it* unto you. **15** All things whatsoever the Father hath are mine: therefore said I, that he taketh of mine, and shall declare *it* unto you. **16** A little while [*cp.* 7 33; 12 35; 13 33; 14 19], and ye behold me no more [*cp. verse* 10 *above*]; and again a little while, and ye shall see me [*cp. verse* 22 *below*]. **17** *Some* of his disciples therefore said one to another [*cp.* 4 33; 11 13; 12 16; 13 7, 28, 36; 14 5-10, 22: *also* 3 10; 8 27, 43; 10 6], What is this that he saith unto us, A little while, and ye behold me not; and again a little while, and ye shall see me: and, Because I go to the Father [*cp. verse* 10 *above*]? **18** They said therefore, What is this that he saith, A little while? We know not what he saith. **19** Jesus perceived [*cp.* 1 48; 2 24, 25; 5 6, 42; 6 61, 64; 13 11, 18; 16 30; 18 4; 21 17: *also* 4 19, 29; 11 14] that they were desirous to ask him, and he said unto them, Do ye inquire among yourselves concerning this, that I said, A little while, and ye behold me not, and again a little while, and ye shall see me? **20** Verily, verily, I say unto you, that ye shall weep and lament, but the world shall rejoice: ye shall be sorrowful [*cp. verses* 6 *and* 22], but your sorrow shall be turned into joy. **21** A woman when she is in travail hath sorrow, because her hour is come: but when she is delivered of the child, she remembereth no more the anguish, for the joy that a man is born into the world. **22** And ye therefore now have sorrow [*cp. verses* 6 *and* 20 *above*]: but I will see	*cp.* 11 6; 13 21, 57; 15 12; *etc.* *cp.* 10 17-21; 24 9. *cp.* 26 75: *also* 24 25. *cp.* 17 23: *also* 26 22, 37. *cp.* 15 16; 16 8-12. *cp.* 9 40; 12 25; 16 8. *cp.* 9 15. *cp.* 5 4. *see above.*	*cp.* 4 17; 6 3; 14 27, 29. *cp.* 13 9-12. *cp.* 14 72: *also* 13 23. *cp.* 14 19. *cp.* 4 13; 6 52; 7 18; 8 17-21; 9 10, 32: *also* 16 14. *cp.* 2 8; 8 17. *cp.* 2 20; 16 10. *see above.*	*cp.* 7 23. *cp.* 21 12-16: *also* 12 11. *cp.* 22 61: *also* 24 6, 8. *cp.* 24 44. *cp.* 22 45. *cp.* 24 49. *cp.* 10 18. *cp.* 9 45; 18 34: *also* 2 50. *cp.* 5 22; 6 8; 9 47; 11 17. *cp.* 5 35. *cp.* 6 21. *see above.*

	John 14 13-14; 15 7	Matt. 21 22; 7 7	Mark 11 24	Luke 11 9
you again [*cp. verse 16 above*], and your heart shall rejoice, and your joy [*cp. 20 20*] no one taketh away from you. **23** And in that day [*cp. 14 20; 16 26*] ye shall ²ask me nothing. Verily, verily, I say unto you, 15 **16** . . . that whatsoever ye shall ask of the Father in my name,		*cp. 28 8.* *cp. 7 22; 24 36: also 26 29.*	*cp. 13 32: also 14 25.*	*cp. 24 41, 52.* *cp. 10 12; 17 31; 21 34.*
	14 **13** And whatsoever ye shall ask in my name,	21 **22** And all things, whatsoever ye shall ask in prayer, believing ye shall receive.	11 **24** All things whatsoever ye pray and ask for, believe that ye have received them, and ye shall have them.	
he may give it you.	that will I do, that the Father may be glorified in the Son. **14** If ye shall ask ¹me anything			
If ye shall ask anything of the Father, he will give it you in my name [*cp. 14 13, 14; 15 16; 16 24, 26: also 14 26*].	in my name,	*cp. 18 19.* *cp. 18 5, 20; 24 5: also 7 22.*	*cp. 9 37, 38, 39; 13 6; 16 17.*	*cp. 9 48, 49; 10 17; 21 8; 24 47.*
24 Hitherto have ye asked nothing in my name:	that will I do.			
ask, and ye shall receive,	15 **7** Ask whatsoever ye will, and it shall be done unto you.	7 **7** Ask, and it shall be given you; seek, and ye shall find; knock, and it shall be opened unto you.		11 **9** Ask, and it shall be given you; seek, and ye shall find; knock, and it shall be opened unto you.
that your joy may be fulfilled [*cp. 3 29; 15 11; 17 13*].		*cp. 25 21, 23.*		
¹ Or, *Advocate* Or, *Helper* Gr. *Paraclete.* ² Or, *ask me no question*	¹ Many ancient authorities omit *me.*			

John 16 20: *cp.* Jer. 31 13.   John 16 21: *cp.* Is. 26 17.   John 16 22: *cp.* Is. 66 14.

§ 69. The Prophecy of the Flight of the Disciples

John 16 25-33

25 These things have I spoken unto you [*cp. 14 25; 15 11; 16 1, 4, 6, 33*] in ¹proverbs [*cp. verse 29 below and 10 6*]: the hour cometh [*cp. 4 21, 23; 5 25, 28; 16 2, 32*], when I shall no more speak unto you in ¹proverbs, but shall tell you plainly [*cp. 10 24; 11 14, 54; 16 29; 18 20: also 7 4, 13, 26*] of the Father. **26** In that day [*cp. 14 20; 16 23*] ye shall ask in my name [*cp. 14 13, 14; 15 16; 16 23, 24: also 14 26*]: and I say not unto you, that I will ²pray the Father [*cp. 14 16: also 17 9, 15, 20*] for you; **27** for the Father himself loveth you [*cp. 14 21, 23; 17 23*], because ye have loved me [*cp. 14 21, 23; 17 23: also 21 15-17*], and have believed [*cp. verse 30 below*] that I came forth from the Father [*cp. 8 42; 13 3; 16 28, 30: also 1 14; 5 44; 7 29; 9 16; 33, 17 8*]. **28** I came out from the Father, and am come into the world [*cp. 9 39; 12 46; 18 37: also 1 9; 3 19; 6 14; 11 27: and 3 17; 10 36; 17 18*]: again, I leave the world, and go unto the Father [*cp. 14 12, 28; 16 10, 17: also 7 33; 16 5: and 17 11, 13: and 20 17: and 13 1, 3*]. **29** His disciples say, Lo, now speakest thou plainly [*cp. verse 25 above*],	*cp. 13 34.* *cp. 7 22; etc.: and 8 5; etc.*	*cp. 8 32: also 4 33-34.* *cp. 13 32; etc.: and 9 37; etc.* *cp. 1 38.* *cp. 8 32.*	*cp. 10 12; etc.: and 9 48; etc.*

and speakest no ³proverb [cp. verse 25 above]. **30** Now know we [cp. 3 2; 4 42; 9 24, 29, 31; 21 24: also 17 7] that thou knowest all things [cp. 21 17: also 2 24, 25: and 1 48; 4 19, 29; 5 6, 42; 6 61, 64; 11 14; 13 11, 18; 16 19; 18 4], and needest not that any man should ask thee: by this we believe [cp. 6 69; 9 38; 11 27: also 16 27; 17 8; and 20 31] that thou camest forth from God [cp. verse 27 above]. **31** Jesus answered them, Do ye now believe?

cp. 6 61: also 16 1.

32 Behold, the hour cometh [cp. verse 25 above], yea, is come [cp. 4 23; 5 25], that ye

cp. 10 11-16.

shall be scattered, every man to his own [cp. 19 27: also 1 11; 8 44; 13 1; 15 19], and shall leave me alone: and *yet* I am not alone [cp. 8 16, 29], because the Father is with me. **33** These things have I spoken unto you [cp. verse 25 above], that in me ye may have peace [cp. 14 27: also 20 19, 21, 26]. In the world ye have tribulation: but be of good cheer; I have overcome the world.

¹ Or, *parables*
² Gr. *make request of.*
³ Or, *parable*

---

cp. 4 34.

cp. 22 16; *also* 9 4; 12 25; 16 8.   *cp.* 12 14: *also* 2 8; 8 17.   *cp.* 20 21: *also* 5 22; 6 8; 9 47; 11 17.

Matt. 26 31

Then saith Jesus unto them,
All ye shall be ¹offended [cp. 11 6; 13 57; 15 12: also 13 21; 24 10] in me this night:

for it is written, I will smite the shepherd, and the sheep [cp. 9 36; 10 6; 15 24] of the flock shall be scattered abroad.

cp. 26 56.

cp. 5 9; 10 13.

cp. 9 2, 22; 14 27.

¹ Gr. *caused to stumble.*

Mark 14 27

And Jesus saith unto them,
All ye shall be ¹offended [cp. 6 3: also 4 17]:

for it is written, I will smite the shepherd, and the sheep [cp. 6 34] shall be scattered abroad.

cp. 14 50.

cp. 9 50.

cp. 6 50; 10 49.

¹ Gr. *caused to stumble.*

cp. 7 23.

cp. 18 28.

cp. 1 79; 2 14, 29; 10 6; 19 38: also 24 36.

Matt. 26 31 || Mark 14 27 = Zech. 13 7.

§ 70. The High Priestly Prayer

John 17 1-26

1 These things spake Jesus [cp. 12 36]; and lifting up his eyes to heaven [cp. 11 41], he said, Father [cp. verses 5, 11, 21, 24, 25, and 11 41; 12 27, 28], the hour is come [cp. 12 23; 13 1: also 12 27: and 2 4; 7 6, 8, 30; 8 20]; glorify thy Son [cp. verse 5 and 8 54; 13 32; 16 14], that the Son may glorify thee [cp. verse 4 below]: **2** even as thou gavest him authority [cp. 3 35; 5 27; 13 3: also 10 18] over all flesh, that whatsoever thou hast given him [cp. verses 6, 9, 11, 12, 24, and 6 37, 39; 10 29; 18 9], to them he should give eternal life [cp. 10 28: also 3 15, 16; etc.]. **3** And this is life eternal, that they should know thee the only [cp. 5 44] true [cp. 1 9; 6 32; 15 1: also 6 55] God, and him whom thou didst send, *even* Jesus Christ. **4** I glorified thee [cp. verse 1 above] on the earth, having accomplished the work [cp. 4 34; 5 36: also 19 28, 30: and 10 25, 32, 37; 14 10:

cp. 14 19.
cp. 11 25, 26; 26 39, 42: also 14 23; etc.: and 6 9.

cp. 26 45: also 26 18.

cp. 6 41; 7 34.
cp. 14 36: also 1 35; etc.

cp. 14 41: also 14 35.

cp. 9 16.
cp. 10 21, 22; 22 42; 23 34, 46: also 3 21; etc.: and 11 2.

cp. 22 14: also 22 53.

cp. 9 6, 8; 11 27; 28 18.   *cp.* 2 10.   *cp.* 5 24; 10 22.

cp. 12 50; 13

and 3 21; 6 28-29; 9 3-4: and 5 17; 7 21] which thou hast given me to do. **5** And now, O Father [*cp. verse* 1 *above*], glorify thou me [*cp. verse* 1 *above*] with thine own self with the glory [*cp. verses* 22 *and* 24 *and* 1 14; 2 11; 12 41] which I had with thee before the world was [*cp. verse* 24 *and* 1 1, 2, 18; 8 58]. **6** I manifested [*cp.* 1 31; 2 11; 3 21; 7 4; 9 3; 21 1, 14: *also* 14 21, 22] thy name [*cp. verse* 26: *and* 1 18; 3 11, 32; 8 26, 40; 15 15] unto the men whom thou gavest me [*cp. verse* 2 *above*] out of the world: thine they were, and thou gavest them to me; and they have kept thy word [*cp.* 8 55: *also* 5 38; 14 24; 17 14, 17: *and* 5 24; 8 31; *etc.*]. **7** Now they know [*cp.* 16 30] that all things whatsoever thou hast given me are from thee: **8** for the words which thou gavest me [*cp.* 3 34; 8 26; 12 49, 50; 14 10] I have given unto them [*cp. verse* 14 *and* 14 24; 15 15: *also* 3 34; 7 16; 8 26, 28, 38, 40; 12 49, 50]; and they received *them*, and knew of a truth that I came forth from thee [*cp.* 8 42; 13 3; 16 27, 28, 30: *also* 1 14; 5 44; 7 29; 9 16, 33], and they believed [*cp.* 16 27, 30: *also* 6 69; 9 38; 11 27; 20 31] that thou didst send me [*cp. verses* 21, 25, *and* 11 42: *also* 5 36, 38; 6 29: *and* 3 17, 34; *etc.*]. **9** I ¹pray [*cp. verses* 15 *and* 20; 14 16; 16 26] for them: I ¹pray not for the world, but for those whom thou hast given me [*cp. verse* 2 *above*]; for they are thine: **10** and all things that are mine are thine, and thine are mine [*cp.* 10 14; 16 14, 15]: and I am glorified [*cp.* 7 39; 12 16, 23; 13 31: *also* 11 4] in them. **11** And I am no more in the world, and these are in the world, and I come to thee [*cp. verse* 13: *also* 7 33; 13 1, 3; 14 12, 28; 16 5, 10, 17, 28: *and* 20 17]. Holy Father [*cp. verse* 1 *above*], keep them in thy name [*cp. verse* 12 *and* 5 43; 10 25: *also* 12 13] which thou hast given me [*cp. verse* 2 *above*], that they may be one [*cp. verses* 21, 22, 23 *and* 10 16; 11 52: *also* 12 32], even as we *are* [*cp. verse* 22 *and* 10 30: *also* 5 19; 12 45; 14 9-11; 15 24]. **12** While I was with them, I kept them in thy name which thou hast given me [*cp. verse* 2 *above*]: and I guarded them, and not one of them perished [*cp.* 18 9: *also* 3 16; 10 28: *and* 6 39], but the son of perdition; that the scripture might be fulfilled. **13** But now I come to thee [*cp. verse* 11 *above*]; and these things I speak in the world, that they may have my joy fulfilled [*cp.* 3 29; 15 11; 16 24] in themselves. **14** I have given them thy word [*cp. verse* 8 *above*]; and the world hated them [*cp.* 15 18, 19: *also* 7 7], because they are not of the world [*cp. verse* 16 *and* 15 19], even as I am not of the world [*cp. verse* 16 *and* 8 23: *also* 18 36: *and* 15 19]. **15** I ¹pray [*cp. verses* 9 *and* 20] not that thou shouldest take them ²from the world, but that thou shouldest keep them ²from ³the evil *one*. **16** They are not of the world, even as I am not of the world [*cp. verse* 14 *above*]. **17** ⁴Sanctify them [*cp. verse* 19 *and* 10 36] in the truth: thy word is truth [*cp.* 3 33; 7 28; 8 26]. **18** As thou didst send me into the world [*cp.* 3 17; 10 36: *also* 3 34; 5 38; *etc.*: *and* 1 9; 3 19; *etc.*], even so sent I them into the world [*cp.* 20 21]. **19** And for their sakes I ⁴sanctify myself [*cp. verse* 17 *and* 10 36], that they themselves also may be sanctified in truth. **20** Neither for these only do I ¹pray [*cp. verses* 9 *and* 15], but for them also that believe on me through their word [*cp.* 4 39]; **21** that they may all be one[*cp. verses* 11, 22, 23]; even as thou, Father [*cp. verse* 1 *above*], *art* in me, and I in thee [*cp. verse* 23 *and* 10 38; 14 10, 11, 20], that they also may be in us [*cp. verses* 23, 26, *and* 14 20: *also* 6 56; 15 4-7: *and* 8 31]: that the world may believe [*cp.* 14 31; 17 23] that thou didst send me [*cp. verses* 8 *and* 25]. **22** And the glory [*cp. verses* 5 *and* 24] which thou hast given me I have given unto them; that they may be one [*cp. verses* 11, 21, 23], even as we *are* one [*cp. verse* 11]; **23** I in them, and thou in me [*cp. verses* 21 *and* 26], that they may be perfected into one [*cp. verse* 11, 21, 22]; that the world may know [*cp.* 14 31: *also* 17 21] that thou didst send me, and lovedst them [*cp.* 14 21, 23; 16 27], even as thou lovedst me [*cp. verses* 24 *and* 26 *below*: *also* 3 35; 5 20; 10 17; 15 9]. **24** Father [*cp. verse* 1 *above*], ⁵that which thou hast given me, I will that, where I am [*cp.* 7 34, 36; 12 26; 14 3], they also may be [*cp.* 14 3: *also* 12 26] with me; that they may behold my glory [*cp. verses* 5 *and* 22], which thou hast given me [*cp. verse* 2 *above*]: for thou lovedst me [*cp. verses* 23 *and* 26] before the foundation of the world [*cp. verse* 5 *and* 1 1, 2, 18; 8 58]. **25** O righteous Father [*cp. verse* 1 *above*], the world knew

Marginal references:

(col. 1)	(col. 2)	(col. 3)
cp. 19 28; 25 31.	cp. 10 37.	32; 18 31; 22 37. cp. 9 26, 32; 24 26.
cp. 11 27.	cp. 16 12, 14.	cp. 10 22.
	cp. 1 38.	
cp. 25 21, 23.		
cp. 10 22; 24 9.	cp. 13 13.	cp. 1 71; 6 22, 27; 21 17.
cp. 5 37, 39; 6 13; 13 19, 38.		
cp. 28 19-20.	cp. 16 15.	cp. 24 47-49.
cp. 3 17; 17 5.	cp. 1 11; 9 7; 12 6.	cp. 3 22; 20 13.
cp. 13 35; 25 34.		cp. 11 50.

thee not [*cp.* 7 28; 8 19, 55; 15 21; 16 3: *also* 4 22], but I knew thee [*cp.* 7 29; 8 55; 10 15: *also* 1 18; 6 46; 8 19]; and these knew that thou didst send me [*cp. verses* 8 *and* 21]; **26** and I made known unto them thy name [*cp. verse* 6 *above*], and will make it known; that the love wherewith thou lovedst me [*cp. verses* 23 *and* 24] may be in them, and I in them [*cp. verses* 21 *and* 23].	*cp.* 11 27.	*cp.* 10 22.

¹ Gr. *make request.*   ² Gr. *out of.*   ³ Or, *evil*   ⁴ Or, *Consecrate*   ⁵ Many ancient authorities read *those whom.*

John 17 8, 26: *cp.* Ps. 22 22.   John 17 12: *cp.* Is. 34 16 *and* Ps. 109 8.   John 17 17: *cp.* II Sam. 7 28 *and* Ps 119 160.

(iii) In the Garden (§ 71)

§ 71. The Arrest

John 18 1-11	Matt. 26 30, 36, 47-54	Mark 14 26, 32, 43-47	Luke 22 39-40, 47-51
1 When Jesus had spoken these words, he went forth *cp. verse* 2.	**30** And when they had sung a hymn, they went out [*cp.* 21 17] unto the mount of Olives.	**26** And when they had sung a hymn, they went out [*cp.* 11 11, 19] unto the mount of Olives.	**39** And he came out, and went, [*cp.* 21 37] as his custom was [*cp.* 21 37: *also* 4 16: *and* 1 9; 2 42], unto the mount of Olives; and the disciples also followed him.
with his disciples over the ¹brook ²Kidron, where was a garden [*cp.* 18 26: *also* 19 41], into the which he entered, himself and his disciples. **2** Now Judas also, which betrayed him [*cp. verse* 5 *and* 6 64, 71; 13 11: *also* 13 2, 21], knew the place: for Jesus ofttimes resorted thither with his disciples.	**36** Then cometh Jesus with them unto *cp.* 10 4; 26 25, 46, 48; 27 3: *also* 26 21, 23, 24. ¹a place called Gethsemane, . . .	**32** And they come unto *cp.* 3 19; 14 42, 44: *also* 14 18, 21. ¹a place which was named Gethsemane: . . .	**40** And when he was at *cp.* 21 21, 22. the place . . .
3 Judas then, having received the ³band *of soldiers,* and officers from the chief priests and the Pharisees, cometh thither with lanterns and torches and weapons. **4** Jesus therefore, knowing [*cp.* 1 48; 2 24, 25; 5 6, 42; 6 61, 64; 13 11, 18; 16 19, 30; 21 17: *also* 4 19, 29; 11 14] all the things that were coming upon him, went forth, and saith unto them, Whom seek ye [*cp. verse* 7 *and* 20 15: *also* 1 38: *and* 4 27]? **5** They answered him, Jesus of Nazareth [*cp. verse* 7 *and* 1 45; 19 19]. Jesus saith unto them, I	**47** And while he yet spake, lo, Judas, one of the twelve, came, and with him a great multitude with swords and staves, from the chief priests and elders of the people. *cp.* 9 4; 12 25; 16 8. *cp.* 2 23; 26 71: *also* 21 11.	**43** And straightway, while he yet spake, cometh Judas, one of the twelve, and with him a multitude with swords and staves, from the chief priests and the scribes and the elders. *cp.* 2 8; 8 17. *cp.* 1 24; 10 47; 14 67; 16 6.	**47** While he yet spake, behold, a multitude, and he that was called Judas, one of the twelve, went before them; *cp.* 22 52. *cp.* 5 22; 6 8; 9 47; 11 17. *cp.* 4 34; 18 37; 24 19.

am *he*. And Judas also, which betrayed him [*cp. verse 2 above*], was standing with them.	**48** Now he that betrayed him	**44** Now he that betrayed him	
	gave them a sign, saying, Whomsoever I shall kiss, that is he: take him.	had given them a token, saying, Whomsoever I shall kiss, that is he; take him, and lead him away safely. **45** And when he was come, straightway he came to him, and saith,	and he drew near unto Jesus
cp. 19 3.	**49** And straightway he came to Jesus, and said, Hail [*cp.* 27 29; 28 9], Rabbi; and ²kissed him. **50** And Jesus said unto him,	[*cp.* 15 18] Rabbi; and ²kissed him.	*cp.* 1 28. to kiss him. **48** But Jesus said unto him, Judas, betrayest thou the Son of man with a kiss?
cp. 13 27. **6** When therefore he said unto them, I am *he*, they went backward, and fell [*cp.* 11 32: *also* 9 38] to the ground [*cp.* 9 6]. **7** Again therefore he asked them, Whom seek ye [*cp. verse 4 above*]? And they said, Jesus of Nazareth [*cp. verse* 5]. **8** Jesus answered, I told you that I am *he*: if therefore ye seek me, let these go their way: **9** that the word might be fulfilled which he spake, Of those whom thou hast given me [*cp.* 6 37, 39; 10 29; 17 2, 6, 9, 11, 12, 24] I lost not one [*cp.* 17 12: *also* 6 39; 10 28: *and* 3 16].	Friend [*cp.* 20 13; 22 12], *do* that for which thou art come.

cp. 2 11: *also* 17 14: *and* 8 2; 9 18; 14 33; 15 25; 20 20; 28 9, 17.

cp. 2 23; *etc.* | *cp.* 3 11; 5 22, 33; 7 25: *also* 1 40; 10 17: *and* 5 6.

cp. 1 24; *etc.* | *cp.* 5 8, 12; 8 28, 41, 47; 17 16: *also* 24 52.

cp. 4 34; *etc.* |
| | | | **49** And when they that were about him saw what would follow, they said, Lord, shall we smite with the sword? |
| **10** Simon Peter therefore *cp.* 11 42; 12 29. having a sword drew it, and struck the high priest's ⁴servant, and cut off his right ear. Now the ⁴servant's name was Malchus. **11** Jesus therefore said unto Peter, Put up the sword into the sheath: the cup which the Father hath given me, shall I not drink it? | Then they came and laid hands on Jesus, and took him. **51** And behold, one of them that were with [*cp.* 16 28; 27 47: *also* 26 73] Jesus stretched out his hand, and drew his sword, and smote the ³servant of the high priest, and struck off his [*cp.* 5 29, 30, 39; 27 29] ear. **52** Then saith Jesus unto him, Put up again thy sword into its place: *cp.* 26 39: *also* 20 22, 23. for all they that take the sword shall perish with the sword. **53** Or thinkest thou that I cannot beseech my Father, and he shall even now send me more | **46** And they laid hands on him, and took him. **47** But a certain one of them that stood by [*cp.* 9 1; 11 5; 15 35: *also* 14 69, 70; 15 39] drew his sword, and smote the ³servant of the high priest, and struck off his ear.

cp. 14 36: *also* 10 38, 39. | **50** And a certain one of them *cp.* 9 27: *also* 19 24. *cp.* 22 26, 38. smote the ¹servant of the high priest, and struck off his right [*cp.* 6 6] ear. **51** But Jesus answered and said, Suffer ye thus far. *cp.* 22 42. |

cp. 1 51; 12 29.	than twelve legions of angels [*cp.* 4 11]? **54** How then should the scriptures be fulfilled, that thus it must be?	*cp.* 1 13.	*cp.* 22 43.
			And he touched his ear, and healed him.

[1] Or, *ravine* Gr. *winter-torrent.* [2] Or, *of the Cedars* [3] Or, *cohort* [4] Gr. *bondservant.*	[1] Gr. *an enclosed piece of ground.* [2] Gr. *kissed him much.* [3] Gr. *bondservant.*	[1] Gr. *an enclosed piece of ground.* [2] Gr. *kissed him much.* [3] Gr. *bondservant.*	[1] Gr. *bondservant.*

(iv) The Trial (§§ 72-79)

§ 72. **Jesus led to Annas**

John 18 12-14	Matt. 26 57	Mark 14 53	Luke 22 54
12 So the [1]band and the [2]chief captain, and the officers of the Jews, seized Jesus and bound him [*cp.* 18 24], **13** and led him to Annas [*cp.* 18 24] first;	**57** And they that had taken Jesus [*cp.* 27 2] led him away	**53** And they [*cp.* 15 1] led Jesus away	**54** And they seized him, and led him away, [*cp.* 3 2]
cp. 18 24.	to *the house of* Caiaphas [*cp.* 26 3] the high priest.	to the high priest.	and brought him into the high priest's house.
for he was father in law to Caiaphas [*cp.* 11 49; 18 24, 28], which was high priest that year [*cp.* 11 49, 51]. **14** Now Caiaphas was he which gave counsel to the Jews that it was expedient [*cp.* 11 50; 16 7] that one man should die for the people [*cp.* 11 50].			*cp.* 3 2.
[1] Or, *cohort* [2] Or, *military tribune* Gr. *chiliarch.*			

§ 73. **Peter's Denial** (i)

John 18 15-18	Matt. 26 58, 69-71	Mark 14 54, 66-68	Luke 22 54, 56-57, 55
15 And Simon Peter followed Jesus, and *so did* another disciple [*verse* 16 *and* 20 2, 3, 4, 8]. Now that disciple was known unto the high priest, and entered in with Jesus into the court of the high priest; **16** but Peter was standing at the door without. So the other disciple, which was known unto the high priest, went out and spake unto her that kept the door, and brought in	**58** But Peter followed him afar off,	**54** And Peter had followed him afar off,	**54** But Peter followed afar off.
	unto the court [*cp.* 26 3, 69] of the high priest,		
		even within, into the court [*cp. verse* 66; *also* 15 16] of the high priest, . . .	
Peter.	**69** Now Peter was sitting without in the court [*cp.* 26 3, 58]:	**66** And as Peter was beneath in the court [*cp. verse* 54], there	
cp. verse 15.			*cp. verse* 55.

17 The maid therefore that kept the door	and	cometh one of the maids of the high priest;	**56** And a certain maid
cp. 18 18, 25.		**67** and seeing Peter cp. verse 54. warming himself [cp. verse 54], she looked upon him, and saith,	seeing him as he sat in the light of the fire, and looking stedfastly upon him, said,
saith unto Peter, Art thou also one of cp. 18 5, 7; 19 19: also 1 45.	came unto him, saying, Thou also wast with cp. 26 71.	Thou also wast with the Nazarene [cp. 1 24; 10 47; 16 6], even Jesus. cp. 14 70.	This man also was with him. [cp. 4 34; 18 37; 24 19] cp. 22 59.
this man's disciples? He saith, I am not.	Jesus the Galilaean. **70** But he denied before them all, saying, I know not what thou sayest. **71** And when he was gone out into the porch ...	**68** But he denied, saying, [1]I neither know, nor understand what thou sayest: and he went out into the [2]porch; [3]and the cock crew.	**57** But he denied, saying, Woman, I know him not.
18 Now the [1]servants and the officers were standing there, having made [2]a fire of coals [cp. 21 9]; for it was cold; and they were warming themselves: and Peter also was with them, standing and warming himself [cp. 18 25].	**58** ... and sat with the officers, to see the end.	**54** ... and he was sitting with the officers, and warming himself [cp. verse 67] in the light of the fire.	**55** And when they had kindled a fire in the midst of the court, and had sat down together, Peter sat in the midst of them. cp. verse 56.
[1] Gr. bondservants. [2] Gr. a fire of charcoal.		[1] Or, I neither know, nor understand: thou, what sayest thou? [2] Gr. forecourt. [3] Many ancient authorities omit and the cock crew.	

§ 74. Jesus before Annas

John 18 19-24	Matt. 26 62-63, 55, 67-68, 57	Mark 14 60-61, 48-49, 65, 53	Luke 22 52-53, 63-65, 54
19 The high priest therefore asked Jesus of his disciples, and of his teaching. cp. 19 10.	**62** And the high priest stood up, and said unto him, Answerest thou nothing? what is it which these witness against thee? **63** But Jesus held his peace. cp. 27 12, 14: also 15 23.	**60** And the high priest stood up in the midst, and asked Jesus, saying, Answerest thou nothing? what is it which these witness against thee? **61** But he held his peace, and answered nothing [cp. 15 5]. ... **48** And Jesus answered and	
cp. 19 9.			cp. 23 9.
20 Jesus answered him,	**55** In that hour said Jesus to the multitudes,	said unto them,	**52** And Jesus said unto the chief priests, and captains of the temple, and elders, which were come against him,
I have spoken openly [cp. 7 4, 13, 26; 10 24; 11 14, 54; 16 25, 29] to the world [cp. 8 26]; I ever taught in [1]synagogues [cp. 6 59], and in the	Are ye come out as against a robber with swords and staves to seize me? I sat daily cp. 4 23; 9 35; 13 54. in the	Are ye come out, as against a robber, with swords and staves to seize me? cp. 8 32. **49** I was daily with you [cp. 1 21, 39; 6 2] in the	Are ye come out, as against a robber, with swords and staves? **53** When I was daily with you [cp. 4 15, 16, 44; 6 6; 13 10] in the

Column 1 (John)

temple [cp. 7 14, 28; 8 2, 20], where all the Jews come together; and in secret [cp. 7 4, 10] spake I nothing.

21 Why askest thou me? ask them that have heard *me*, what I spake unto them: behold, these know the things which I said. **22** And when he had said this,

cp. 19 3.

cp. 1 41; 4 25, 26, 29; 7 26, 41; 9 22; 10 24; 11 27.

one of the officers standing by struck Jesus ²with his hand [cp. 19 3], saying, Answerest thou the high priest so? **23** Jesus answered him, If I have spoken evil, bear witness of the evil: but if well, why smitest thou me?

18 **12** So the ³band and the ⁴chief captain, and the officers of the Jews, seized Jesus and bound him, **13** and led him to Annas first; for he was father in law to Caiaphas, which was high priest that year. . . . **24** Annas therefore sent him bound unto Caiaphas [cp. 18 13, 14, 28: *and* 11 49] the high priest.

¹ Gr. *synagogue.*
² Or, *with a rod*
³ Or, *cohort*
⁴ Or, *military tribune* Gr. *chiliarch.*

Column 2 (Matt.)

temple [cp. 21 23]

teaching, and ye took me not.

cp. 27 29, 31, 41: *also* 20 19.

67 Then did they spit [cp. 27 30] in his face and buffet him: and some smote him ¹with the palms of their hands, **68** saying, Prophesy unto us, thou Christ [cp. 27 17, 22: *also* 26 63: *and* 16 16]: who is he that struck thee?

57 And they that had taken Jesus led him away to *the house of* Caiaphas [cp. 26 3] the high priest.

¹ Or, *with rods*

Column 3 (Mark)

temple [cp. 11 27; 12 35]

teaching, and ye took me not.

65 And some cp. 15 20, 31: *also* 10 34.

began to spit [cp. 15 19: *also* 10 34] on him, and to cover his face, and to buffet him,

and to say unto him, Prophesy: cp. 15 32: *also* 14 61: *and* 8 29.

and the officers received him with ¹blows of their hands.

53 And they led Jesus away to the high priest.

¹ Or, *strokes of rods*

Column 4 (Luke)

temple [cp. 19 47; 20 1; 21 37],

ye stretched not forth your hands against me.

63 And the men that held ¹Jesus mocked [cp. 23 11, 35, 36: *also* 18 32] him, and beat him. cp. 18 32.

64 And they blindfolded him,

and asked him, saying, Prophesy: cp. 23 35, 39: *also* 22 67; 23 2: *and* 9 20. who is he that struck thee?

65 And many other [cp. 3 18] things spake they against him, reviling him. . . . **54** And they seized him, and led him *away,*

cp. 3 2. and brought him into cp. 3 2. the high priest's house.

¹ Gr. *him.*

John 18 20: cp. Is. 45 19; 48 16.

§ 75. Peter's Denial (ii)

John 18 25-27	Matt. 26 71-74	Mark 14 69-72	Luke 22 58-60
25 Now Simon Peter was standing and warming himself [cp. 18 18].		cp. 14 54, 67.	
	71 . . . another	**69** And the	**58** And after a little while another

John	Matt.	Mark	Luke
They said therefore unto him, Art thou also *one* of his disciples? *cp.* 18 5, 7; 19 19: *also* 1 45.	*maid* saw him, and saith unto them that were there, This man also was with Jesus the Nazarene [*cp.* 2 23: *also* 21 11]. **72** And again he denied with an oath, I know not the man. **73** And after a little while	maid saw him, and began again to say to them that stood by [*cp. verse* 70], This is *one* of them. *cp.* 14 67. **70** But he again denied it.	saw him, and said, Thou also art *one* of them. *cp.* 4 34; 18 37; 24 19. But Peter said, Man, I am
He denied and said, I am not.			not. **59** And after the space of about one hour
cp. 11 42; 12 29. **26** One of the ¹servants of the high priest, being a kinsman of him whose ear Peter cut off, saith,	they that stood by [*cp.* 16 28; 27 47]	And after a little while again they that stood by [*cp.* 9 1; 11 5; 14 47, 69; 15 35, 39]	*cp.* 9 27; 19 24.
	came and said to Peter, Of a truth thou also art *one* of them; [*cp.* 26 69] for thy speech bewrayeth thee.	said to Peter, Of a truth thou art *one* of them; for thou art a Galilæan.	another confidently affirmed, saying, Of a truth this man also was with him: for he is a Galilæan.
Did not I see thee in the garden [*cp.* 18 1: *also* 19 41] with him? **27** Peter therefore	**74** Then began he to curse and to swear, I know not the man. And straightway	**71** But he began to curse, and to swear, I know not this man of whom ye speak. **72** And straightway the second time [*cp.* 14 68]	**60** But Peter said, Man, I know not what thou sayest. And immediately, while he yet spake,
denied again: and straightway the cock crew [*cp.* 13 38].	the cock crew [*cp.* 26 34].	the cock crew [*cp.* 14 30].	the cock crew [*cp.* 22 34].

¹ Gr. *bondservants.*

§ 76. Jesus led to Pilate

John 18 28-32	Matt. 27 1-2	Mark 15 1	Luke 23 1-2
28 They	**1** Now when morning was come, all the chief priests and the elders of the people took counsel [*cp.* 12 14; 22 15; 27 7; 28 12] against Jesus to put him to death: **2** and	**1** And straightway in the morning the chief priests with the elders and scribes, and the whole council, held a consultation [*cp.* 3 6],	**1** And *cp.* 22 66.
cp. 18 12, 24. lead Jesus therefore from Caiaphas [*cp.* 18 13, 14, 24: *and* 11 49]	they bound him, and led him away, *cp.* 26 3, 57.	and bound Jesus, and carried him away,	the whole company of them rose up,
into the ¹palace [*cp.* 18 33; 19 9]: and it was early; and they themselves entered not into the ¹palace, that they might not be defiled [*cp.* 11 55], but might eat the passover. **29** Pilate therefore went out [*cp.* 18 38;	and delivered him up to Pilate the governor [*cp.* 27 11, 14, 15, 21, 27; 28 14]. *cp.* 27 27.	and delivered him up to Pilate. *cp.* 15 16.	*cp.* 3 2. and brought him before Pilate. *cp.* 20 20.

John	Matt.	Mark	Luke
19 4] unto them, and saith, What accusation bring ye against this man? **30** They answered and said unto him, If this man *cp.* 7 12: *also* 7 47.	*cp.* 27 12.	*cp.* 15 3.	**2** And they began to accuse him, saying, We found this man perverting [*cp.* 23 14] our nation, and forbidding to give tribute [*cp.* 20 20-26] to Cæsar, and saying that he himself is [1]Christ [*cp.* 22 67: *also* 23 35, 39: *and* 9 20] a king [*cp.* 23 3].
cp. 19 12.	*cp.* 22 15-22.	*cp.* 12 13-17.	
cp. 4 25, 26: *also* 1 41; 4 29; 7 26, 41; 9 22; 11 27. were not an evil-doer, we	*cp.* 26 63-64: *also* 26 68; 27 17, 22: *and* 16 16.	*cp.* 14 61-62: *also* 15 32: *and* 8 29.	

should not have delivered him up unto thee. **31** Pilate therefore said unto them, Take him yourselves [*cp.* 19 6], and judge him according to your law [*cp.* 8 17; 10 34: *also* 7 51; 15 25: *and* 19 7]. The Jews said unto him, It is not lawful for us to put any man to death: **32** that the word of Jesus might be fulfilled, which he spake, signifying by what manner of death he should die [*cp.* 12 33: *also* 21 19: *and* 2 19-22; 3 14; 8 28].

[1] Gr. *Prætorium.*

[1] Or, *an anointed king*

John 18 28: *cp.* Num. 9 6.

§ 77. Jesus before Pilate

John 18 33-38a	Matt. 27 11	Mark 15 2	Luke 23 3
33 Pilate therefore entered again into the [1]palace [*cp.* 18 28; 19 9], and called Jesus,	*cp.* 27 27.	*cp.* 15 16.	
			cp. 20 20.
and said unto him, Art thou the King of the Jews [*cp.* 18 39; 19 3, 19, 21: *also* 1 49; 12 13: *and* 6 15; 12 15; 18 37; 19 12, 14, 15]?	**11** Now Jesus stood before the governor [*cp.* 27 2, 14, 15, 21, 27; 28 14]: and the governor asked him, saying, Art thou the King of the Jews [*cp.* 2 2; 27 29, 37: *also* 27 42: *and* 21 5]?	**2** And Pilate asked him, Art thou the King of the Jews [*cp.* 15 9, 12, 18, 26: *also* 15 32]?	**3** And Pilate asked him, saying, Art thou the King of the Jews [*cp.* 23 37, 38: *and* 19 38; 23 2]?

34 Jesus answered, Sayest thou this of thyself, or did others tell it thee concerning me? **35** Pilate answered, Am I a Jew? Thine own nation and the chief priests delivered thee unto me: what hast thou done? **36** Jesus answered, My kingdom is not of this world [*cp.* 8 23; 17 14, 16: *also* 15 19]: if my kingdom were of this world, then would my [2]servants fight, that I should not be delivered to the Jews: but now is my kingdom not from hence. **37** Pilate therefore said unto him, Art thou a king then? Jesus answered,

		cp. 16 28; 20 21.	*cp.* 22 29, 30; 23 42.
[3]Thou sayest that I am a	And Jesus said unto him, Thou sayest [*cp.* 26 25, 64].	And he answering saith unto him, Thou sayest.	And he answered him and said, Thou sayest [*cp.* 22 70].

king. To this end [*cp.* 12 27] have I been born, and to this end am I come into the world [*cp.* 9 39; 12 46; 16 28: *also* 1 9; 3 19; 6 14; 11 27: *and* 3 17; 10 36; 17 18], that I should bear witness unto the truth [*cp.* 5 33: *also* 1 14, 17; 8 32; 14 6]. Every one that is of the truth heareth my voice [*cp.* 10 16, 27: *also* 5 25, 28]. **38** Pilate saith unto him, What is truth?

[1] Gr. *Prætorium.*
[2] Or, *officers*: as in ver. 3, 12, 18, 22.
[3] Or, *Thou sayest it, because I am a king.*

§ 78. **Who should be released?**

John 18 38b-40	Matt. 27 15-21	Mark 15 6-11	Luke 23 4, 13-14, 16, 18-19
38b And when he had said this, he went out again [cp. 18 29; 19 4] unto the Jews, and saith unto them, I find no crime [cp. 19 4, 6] in him.	cp. 27 24. **15** Now at [1]the feast the governor [cp. 27 2, 11, 14, 21, 27; 28 14] was wont to release unto the multitude one prisoner, whom they would. **16** And they had then a notable prisoner, called Barabbas.	**6** Now at [1]the feast he used to release unto them one prisoner, whom they asked of him. **7** And there was one called Barabbas, *lying* bound with them that had made insurrection, men who in the insurrection had committed murder. **8** And the multitude went up and began to ask him *to do* as he was wont to do unto them. **9** And Pilate answered them, saying,	**4** And Pilate said unto the chief priests and the multitudes, I find no fault [cp. 23 14, 22] in this man. cp. 20 20. *verse* 19 **13** And Pilate called together the chief priests and the rulers and the people, **14** and said unto them, Ye . . . . . **16** I will therefore chastise him, and release him [cp. 23 22].[1]
39 But ye have a custom, that I should release unto you, one at the passover: cp. 19 1. will ye therefore that I release unto you the King of the Jews [cp. 18 33; 19 3, 19, 21: *also* 1 49; 12 13: *and* 6 15; 12 15; 18 37; 19 12, 14, 15]? cp. 4 25, 26: *also* 1 41; 4 29; 7 26, 41; 9 22; 11 27.	cp. 27 26. Whom will ye that I release unto you? cp. 2 2; 27 11, 29, 37: *also* 27 42: *and* 21 5. Barabbas, or Jesus which is called Christ [cp. 1 16; 27 22: *also* 26 63, 64, 68: *and* 16 16]? **18** For he knew that for envy they had delivered him up. **19** And while he was sitting on the judgement-seat, his wife sent unto him, saying, Have thou nothing to do with that righteous man [cp. 27 24]: for I have suffered many things this day in a dream because of him. **20** Now the chief priests and the elders persuaded the multitudes that they should ask for Barabbas, and destroy Jesus. **21** But the governor [cp. *verse* 15] answered and said unto them, Whether of the twain will ye that I release unto you? And they said,	cp. 15 15. Will ye that I release unto you the King of the Jews [cp. 15 2, 12, 18, 26: *also* 15 32]? cp. 14 61, 62; 15 32: *and* 8 29. **10** For he perceived that for envy the chief priests had delivered him up. **11** But the chief priests stirred up the multitude, that he should rather release Barabbas unto them.	cp. 23 3, 37, 38: *and* 19 38; 23 2. cp. 22 67; 23 2, 35, 39: *and* 9 20. cp. 23 47. cp. 23 5.
40 They cried out therefore again, saying, [cp. 19	**said,**		**18** But they cried out all together, saying, Away

15] Not this man, but Barabbas. Now Barabbas was a robber.	Barabbas.	*verse 7*	with this man, and release unto us Barabbas: **19** one who for a certain insurrection made in the city, and for murder, was cast into prison.
	[1] Or, *a feast*	[1] Or, *a feast*	[1] Many ancient authorities insert ver. 17 *Now he must needs release unto them at the feast one prisoner.* Others add the same words after ver. 19.

§ 79. Jesus is scourged, mocked, and delivered to be crucified

John 19 1-16a	Matt. 27 27-30, 22-23, 13-14, 23-26	Mark 15 16-19, 12-14, 4-5, 14-15	Luke 23 13-14, 20-22, 6, 23-25
1 Then Pilate therefore took Jesus, and scourged him. **2** And the soldiers	*cp.* 27 26. **27** Then the soldiers of the governor [*cp.* 27 2, 11, 14, 15, 21; 28 14] took Jesus into	*cp.* 15 15. **16** And the soldiers led him away within the court [*cp.* 14 54, 66], which is the [1]Prætorium; and they call together the	*cp.* 23 16, 22. *cp.* 20 20. *cp.* 22 55.
cp. 18 15. *cp.* 18 28, 33; 19 9.	the [1]palace, and gathered unto him the whole [2]band. **28** And they [3]stripped him, and put on him a scarlet robe. **29** And	whole [2]band. **17** And they clothe him with purple, and	
plaited a crown of thorns, and put it on his head, and arrayed him in a purple garment; *cp.* 18 10. **3** and they came unto him,	they plaited a crown of thorns and put it upon his head, and a reed in his right [*cp.* 5 29, 30, 39] hand; and they kneeled down before him, and mocked [*cp.* 27 31, 41: *also* 20 19] him,	plaiting a crown of thorns, they put it on him; **18** and they began to salute him,	*cp.* 23 11. *cp.* 23 11. *cp.* 6 6; 22 50. *cp.* 22 63; 23 11, 35, 36: *also* 18 32.
and said, Hail, King of the Jews [*cp.* 18 33, 39; 19 19, 21: *also* 1 49; 12 13: *and* 6 15; 12 15; 18 37; 19 12, 14, 15]! and they struck him [1]with their hands [*cp.* 18 22].	saying, Hail, King of the Jews [*cp.* 2 2; 27 11, 37: *also* 27 42: *and* 21 5]! **30** And they	Hail, King of the Jews [*cp.* 15 2, 9, 12, 26: *also* 15 32]! **19** And they smote his head with a reed, [*cp.* 14 65]	*cp.* 23 3, 37, 38: *and* 19 38; 23 2.
	cp. 26 67. spat [*cp.* 26 67] upon him, and took the reed and smote him on the head.	and did spit [*cp.* 14 65: *also* 10 34] upon him, and bowing their knees worshipped him.	*cp.* 18 32.
4 And Pilate went out again [*cp.* 18 29, 38], and saith unto them, Behold, I bring him out to you, that ye may know that I find no crime [*cp.* 18 38; 19 6] in him.	*cp.* 27 24.		**13** And Pilate called together the chief priests and the rulers and the people, **14** and said unto them, Ye brought unto me this man, as one that perverteth [*cp.* 23 2] the people: and behold, I, having examined him before you, found no fault [*cp.* 23 4, 22] in this man touching those things whereof ye accuse him.
5 Jesus therefore came out, wearing the crown of thorns and the purple			

garment. And *Pilate* saith unto them, Behold, the man [*cp. verse* 14]!

22 Pilate saith unto them, What then shall I do unto Jesus which is called

Christ [*cp.* 27 17]?

12 And Pilate again answered and said unto them, What then shall I do unto him whom ye call the King of the Jews [*cp.* 15 9]?

20 And Pilate spake unto them again,

cp. verse 12.
6 When therefore the chief priests and the officers saw him, they cried out, saying, Crucify *him*, crucify *him*. Pilate saith unto them,

They all say, Let him be crucified.
23 And he said,

Why, what evil hath he done? . . .

13 And they cried out again, Crucify him.
14 And Pilate said unto them, Why, what evil hath he done? . . .

desiring to release Jesus; **21** but they shouted, saying, Crucify, crucify him. **22** And he said unto them the third time, Why, what evil hath this man done [*cp.* 23 41]?

Take him yourselves [*cp.* 18 31], and crucify him: for I find no crime [*cp.* 18 38; 19 4] in him.
cp. verse 1.
7 The Jews answered him, We have a law [*cp.* 7 51: *also* 8 17; 10 34; 15 25; 18 31], and by that law he ought to die, because he made himself the Son of God [*cp.* 5 17, 18; 10 33, 36: *also* 8 53; 19 12]. **8** When Pilate therefore heard this saying, he was the more afraid; **9** and he entered into the ²palace again, and saith unto Jesus, Whence art thou [*cp.* 7 27, 28; 8 14; 9 29, 30]?

cp. 27 24.

cp. 27 26.

cp. 26 63-64.

cp. 15 15.

cp. 14 61-62.

I have found no cause [*cp.* 23 4, 14] of death in him: I will therefore chastise him and release him [*cp.* 23 16].

cp. 22 70.

6 But when Pilate heard it,
he asked

cp. 13 25, 27.
whether the man were a Galilæan.

13 Then saith Pilate unto him,

4 And Pilate again asked him, saying,

But Jesus gave him no answer.

Hearest thou not how many things they witness against thee? **14** And he gave him no answer [*cp.* 26 63; 27 12: *also* 15 23], not even to one word: insomuch that the governor [*cp.* 27 2, 11, 15; *etc.*] marvelled greatly.

Answerest thou nothing? behold how many things they accuse thee of. **5** But Jesus no more answered [*cp.* 14 61] anything; insomuch that Pilate marvelled.

cp. 23 9.

10 Pilate therefore saith unto him, Speakest thou not unto me? knowest thou not that I have ³power to release thee, and have ³power to crucify thee? **11** Jesus answered him, Thou wouldest have no ³power against me, except it were given thee [*cp.* 3 27; 6 65] from above: therefore he that delivered me unto thee hath greater sin. **12** Upon this Pilate sought to release him: but the Jews cried out, saying, If thou release this man, thou art not Cæsar's friend: every one that maketh himself [*cp. verse* 7 *above*] a king ⁴speaketh against Cæsar. **13** When Pilate therefore heard these words, he brought Jesus out, and sat down on the judgement-seat at a place called The Pavement, but in Hebrew, Gabbatha. **14** Now it was the Preparation [*cp.* 19 31, 42] of the passover: it was about the sixth hour [*cp.* 4 6: *also* 1 39: *and* 4 52]. And he saith unto the Jews, Behold, your King [*cp. verse* 5]! **15** They therefore cried out,

cp. 26 62.

cp. 14 60.

cp. 23 20.

cp. 23 2.

cp. 27 19.

cp. 27 62.
cp. 27 45.

cp. 15 42.
cp. 15 33.

cp. 23 54.
cp. 23 44.

23 . . . But they cried out exceedingly,

14 . . . But they cried out exceedingly,

23 But they were instant with

John	Matt.	Mark	Luke
Away with *him*, away with *him*, crucify him. Pilate saith unto them, Shall I crucify your King? The chief priests answered, We have no king but Cæsar.	saying, Let him be crucified.	Crucify him.	loud voices, asking that *cp. 23 18.* he might be crucified.
	24 So when Pilate saw that he prevailed nothing, but rather that a tumult [*cp. 26 5*] was arising, he took water, and washed his hands before the multitude, saying, I am innocent [*cp. 27 4*] ⁴of the blood of this righteous man [*cp. 27 19*]: see ye *to it* [*cp. 27 4*]. **25** And all the people answered and said, His blood *be* on us, and on our children.	**15** And Pilate,	And their voices prevailed. **24** And Pilate
			cp. 23 47.
		wishing to content the multitude,	gave sentence that what they asked for should be done. **25** And he released
	26 Then released he unto them Barabbas:	released unto them Barabbas,	him that for insurrection and murder had been cast into prison, whom they asked for; but Jesus
16 Then therefore he delivered him *cp. verse 1.* unto them to be crucified.	but Jesus he scourged and delivered to be crucified.	and delivered Jesus, when he had scourged him, to be crucified.	he delivered up *cp. 23 16, 22.* to their will.

¹ Or, *with rods*
² Gr. *Prætorium.*
³ Or, *authority*
⁴ Or, *opposeth Caesar*

¹ Gr. *Prætorium.* See Mark 15 16.
² Or, *cohort*
³ Some ancient authorities read *clothed.*
⁴ Some ancient authorities read *of this blood: see ye &c.*

¹ Or, *palace*
² Or, *cohort*

John 19 7: *cp.* Lev. 24 16.

(v) On Golgotha (§§ 80-83)

§ 80. The Crucifixion

John 19 16b-22	Matt. 27 32-35, 38, 37	Mark 15 21-24, 27, 26	Luke 23 26, 32-33a, 36, 33b, 38
16b They took therefore: he went out, Jesus **17** and bearing the cross for himself,	*cp. 27 31.* **32** And as they came out, they found a man of Cyrene, Simon by name: him they ¹compelled to go *with them,* that he might bear his cross.	*cp. 15 20.* **21** And they ¹compel one passing by, Simon of Cyrene, coming from the country, the father of Alexander and Rufus, to go *with them,* that he might bear his cross.	**26** And when they led him away, they laid hold upon one Simon of Cyrene, coming from the country, and laid on him the cross, to bear it after Jesus. **32** And there were also two others, male-

John	Matt.	Mark	Luke
unto the place called The place of a skull, which is called in Hebrew Golgotha: *cp.* 19 29-30. **18** where they crucified him, and with him two others, on either side one, and Jesus in the midst. **19** And Pilate wrote a title also, and put it on the cross. And there was written, JESUS OF NAZARETH [*cp.* 1 45; 18 5, 7], THE KING OF THE JEWS [*cp.* 18 33, 39; 19 3, 21: *also* 1 49; 12 13: *and* 6 15; 12 15; 18 37; 19 12, 14, 15]. **20** This title therefore read many of the Jews: [1]for the place where Jesus was crucified was nigh to	**33** And when they were come unto a place called Golgotha, that is to say, The place of a skull, **34** they gave him wine to drink mingled with gall [*cp.* 27 48]: and when he had tasted it, he would not drink. **35** And when they had crucified him, . . . **38** Then are there crucified with him two robbers, one on the right hand, and one on the left. **37** And they set up over his head his accusation written, THIS IS JESUS *cp.* 2 23; 26 71: *also* 21 11. THE KING OF THE JEWS [*cp.* 2 2; 27 11, 29: *also* 27 42: *and* 21 5]. [1] Gr. *impressed.*	**22** And they bring him unto the place Golgotha, which is, being interpreted, The place of a skull. **23** And they offered him wine mingled with myrrh [*cp.* 15 36]: but he received it not. **24** And they crucify him, . . . **27** And with him they crucify two robbers; one on his right hand, and one on his left. **26** And the superscription of his accusation was written over, *cp.* 1 24; 10 47; 14 67; 16 6. THE KING OF THE JEWS [*cp.* 15 2, 9, 12, 18: *also* 15 32]. [1] Gr. *impress.*	factors, led with him to be put to death. **33** And when they came unto the place which is called [1]The skull, . . . **36** And the soldiers also mocked him, coming to him, offering him vinegar. **33b** there they crucified him, and the malefactors, one on the right hand and the other on the left. **38** And there was also a superscription over him, THIS IS *cp.* 4 34; 18 37; 24 19. THE KING OF THE JEWS [*cp.* 23 3, 37: *and* 19 38; 23 2]. [1] According to the Latin, *Calvary,* which has the same meaning.

20 (cont.) the city: and it was written in Hebrew, *and* in Latin, *and* in Greek. **21** The chief priests of the Jews therefore said to Pilate, Write not, The King of the Jews; but, that he said, I am King of the Jews. **22** Pilate answered, What I have written I have written.

[1] Or, *for the place of the city where Jesus was crucified was nigh at hand*

§ 81. The Garments of Jesus parted among the Soldiers: His Mother committed to the Disciple whom He loved

John 19 23-27	Matt. 27 35, 55-56	Mark 15 24, 40-41	Luke 23 34, 49
23 The soldiers therefore, when they had crucified Jesus, took his garments, and made four parts, to every soldier a part; and also the [1]coat: now the [1]coat was without seam, woven from the top throughout. **24** They said therefore one to another, Let us not rend it, but cast lots for it, whose it shall be: that the scripture might be fulfilled, which saith, They parted my gar-	**35** And when they had crucified him, they parted his garments among them, *cp.* 5 40. casting lots.	**24** And they crucify him, and part his garments among them, casting lots upon them, what each should take.	**34** And parting his garments among them, *cp.* 6 29. they cast lots.

John	Matt.	Mark	Luke
ments among them, And upon my vesture did they cast lots. These things therefore the soldiers did. **25** But there were	**55** And many women were there		**49** And all his acquaintance, and the women [cp. 8 2; 23 55; 24 1, 10, 22, 24] that followed with him from Galilee [cp. 23 55[stood afar off,
standing	beholding from afar, which had followed Jesus from Galilee, ministering unto him:	**40** And there were also women beholding from afar: *verse 41*	
by the cross of Jesus			cp. 8 3. seeing these things.
his mother, and his mother's sister, Mary the *wife* of Clopas, and Mary Magdalene [cp. 20 1, 18].	**56** among whom was Mary Magdalene [cp. 27 61; 28 1], and Mary the mother of James and Joses [cp. 27 61; 28 1], and the mother [cp. 20 20] of the sons of Zebedee [cp. 20 20].	among whom *were* both Mary Magdalene [cp. 15 47; 16 1, 9], and Mary the mother of James the [1]less and of Joses [cp. 15 47; 16 1], and Salome [cp. 16 1];	cp. 8 2; 24 10. cp. 24 10.
	verse 55	**41** who, when he was in Galilee, followed him, and ministered unto him; and many other women which came up with him unto Jerusalem. [1] Gr. *little*.	*verse 49* cp. 8 3.
26 When Jesus therefore saw his mother, and the disciple standing by, whom he loved [cp. 13 23; 20 2; 21 7, 20: also 11 36], he saith unto his mother, Woman [cp. 2 4: also 4 21; 20 13, 15], behold, thy son! **27** Then saith he to the disciple, Behold, thy mother! And from that hour the disciple took her unto his own [cp. 16 32: also 1 11; 8 44; 13 1; 15 19] home. [1] Or, *tunic*	cp. 15 28.		cp. 13 12. cp. 18 28.

John 19 24 = Ps. 22 18.

§ 82. The Death of Jesus

John 19 28-30	Matt. 27 45-51	Mark 15 33-38	Luke 23 44-46
cp. 19 14.	**45** Now from the sixth hour there was darkness over all the [1]land until the ninth hour.	**33** And when the sixth hour was come, there was darkness over the whole [1]land until the ninth hour.	**44** And it was now about the sixth hour, and a darkness came over the whole [1]land until the ninth hour, **45** [2]the sun's light failing: and the veil of the [3]temple was rent in the midst. **46** [4]And when Jesus
28 After this Jesus, knowing that all things are now finished [cp. verse 30 and 4 34; 5 36: 17 4], that the scripture might be accomplished, saith,	*verse 51* **46** And about the ninth hour Jesus	*verse 38* **34** And at the ninth hour Jesus	cp. 12 50; 18 31; 22 37: also 13 32.
	cried with a loud voice, saying, Eli, Eli, lama sabachthani? that is, My God, my	cried with a loud voice, Eloi, Eloi, lama sabachthani? which is, being interpreted, My God, my	had cried with a loud voice,

I thirst.	God, ²why hast thou forsaken me? **47** And some of them that stood there when they heard it, said, This man calleth Elijah.	God, ²why hast thou forsaken me? **35** And some of them that stood by, when they heard it, said, Behold, he calleth Elijah.	
29 There was set there a vessel full of vinegar: so they put a sponge full of the vinegar upon hyssop, and brought it to his mouth.	**48** And straightway one of them ran, and took a sponge, and filled it with vinegar [*cp.* 27 34], and put it on a reed, and gave him to drink. **49** And the rest said, Let be; let us see whether Elijah cometh to save him.³	**36** And one ran, and filling a sponge full of vinegar [*cp.* 15 23], put it on a reed, and gave him to drink, saying, Let be; let us see whether Elijah cometh to take him down.	*cp. 23 36.*
30 When Jesus therefore had received the vinegar, he said,	**50** And Jesus cried again with a loud voice,	**37** And Jesus uttered a loud voice,	he said, Father into thy hands I commend my spirit [*cp.* 12 50; 18 31; 22 37: *also* 13 32]:
It is finished [*cp. verse* 28 *and* 4 34; 5 36; 17 4]: and he bowed his head, and gave up his spirit.	and yielded up his spirit. **51** And behold, the veil of the ⁴temple was rent in twain from the top to the bottom; and the earth did quake; . . .	and gave up the ghost. **38** And the veil of the ³temple was rent in twain from the top to the bottom.	and having said this, he gave up the ghost. *verse 45*
	¹ Or, *earth* ² Or, *why didst thou forsake me?* ³ Many ancient authorities add *And another took a spear and pierced his side, and there came out water and blood.* See John 19 34. ⁴ Or, *sanctuary*	¹ Or, *earth* ² Or, *why didst thou forsake me?* ³ Or, *sanctuary*	¹ Or, *earth* ² Gr. *the sun failing.* ³ Or, *sanctuary* ⁴ Or, *And Jesus, crying with a loud voice, said*

John 19 28-29 ‖ Matt. 27 48 ‖ Mark 15 36 (‖ Luke 23 36): Ps. 69 21.

§ 83. One of the Soldiers pierces the Side of Jesus with a Spear

John 19 31-37	Matt. 27 57	Mark 15 42	
31 The Jews therefore, because it was the Preparation [*cp.* 19 14, 42], that the bodies	**57** And when even was come, . . . *cp.* 27 62.	**42** And when even was now come, because it was the Preparation, that is, the day before the sabbath, . . .	*cp. 23 54.*

should not remain on the cross upon the sabbath (for the day of that sabbath was a high *day*), asked of Pilate that their legs might be broken, and *that* they might be taken away. **32** The soldiers therefore came, and brake the legs of the first, and of the other which was crucified with him: **33** but when they came to Jesus, and saw that he was dead already, they brake not his legs: **34** howbeit one of the soldiers with a spear pierced his side [*cp.* 20 20, 25, 27], and straightway there came out blood and water [*cp.* 7 38]. **35** And he that hath seen hath borne witness [*cp.* 21 24: *also* 15 27], and his witness is true [*cp.* 21 24: *also* 5 31, 32; 8 13, 14]: and he knoweth that he saith true, that ye also may believe [*cp.* 20 31: *also* 11 15; 13 29; 14 29: *and* 11 42]. **36** For these things came to pass, that the scripture might be fulfilled, A bone of him shall not be ¹broken. **37** And again another scripture saith, They shall look on him whom they pierced.

cp. 15 44.

cp. 24 48.

¹ Or, *crushed*

John 19 31: *cp.* Deut. 21 23 *and* Exod. 12 16.   John 19 36: Exod. 12 46; Num. 9 12; Ps. 34 20.
John 19 37 = Zech. 12 10.

(vi) The Burial (§ 84)

§ 84. The Body of Jesus laid in the Tomb

John 19 38-42	Matt. 27 57-60	Mark 15 42-46	Luke 23 50-54
38 And after these things *verse 42* Joseph of Arimathæa,	**57** And when even was come, *cp. 27 62.* there came a rich man from Arimathæa, named Joseph,	**42** And when even was now come, because it was the Preparation, that is, the day before the sabbath, **43** there came Joseph of Arimathæa, a councillor of honourable estate,	*verse 54* **50** And behold, a man named Joseph, who was a councillor, a good man and a righteous **51** (he had not consented to their counsel and deed), *a man* of Arimathæa, a city of the Jews, who was looking for [*cp.* 2 25, 38] the kingdom of God:
being a disciple of Jesus, but secretly for fear of the Jews [*cp.* 7 13; 20 19: *also* 9 22: *and* 12 42],	who also himself was Jesus' disciple:	who also himself was looking for the kingdom of God;	
asked of Pilate that he might take away the body of Jesus: *cp.* 19 33.	**58** this man went to Pilate, and asked for the body of Jesus.	and he boldly went in unto Pilate, and asked for the body of Jesus. **44** And Pilate marvelled if he were already dead: and calling unto him the centurion, he asked him whether he ¹had been any while dead. **45** And when he learned it of the centurion, he	**52** this man went to Pilate, and asked for the body of Jesus.
and Pilate gave *him* leave. He came therefore, and took away his body. **39** And there came also Nicodemus, he who at the first came to him by night [*cp.* 3 1-2; 7 50], bringing a ¹mixture of myrrh and aloes, about a hundred pound *weight.* **40** So they took the body of Jesus, and bound it [*cp.* 11 44] in	Then Pilate commanded it to be given up. **59** And Joseph took the body,	granted the corpse to Joseph. **46** And he bought a linen cloth, and taking him down, *cp.* 16 1.	**53** And he took it down,
linen cloths [*cp.* 20 5, 6, 7: *and* Luke 24 12] with the spices, as the custom is to the Jews to bury. **41** Now in the place where he was crucified there was a garden [*cp.* 20 1, 5: *also* 18 1, 26]; and in the garden a new tomb	and wrapped it in a clean linen cloth,	wound him in the linen cloth,	*cp.* 23 56. and wrapped it in a linen cloth,
wherein was never man yet laid. *cp.* 20 1.	**60** and laid it in his own new tomb, which he had hewn out in the rock: and he rolled a great stone [*cp.* 27 66; 28 2] to the	and laid him in a tomb which had been hewn out of a rock; *cp.* 11 2. and he rolled a [*cp.* 16 4] stone [*cp.* 16 3, 4] against the	and laid him in a tomb that was hewn in stone, where never man had yet lain [*cp.* 19 30]. *cp.* 24 2.

	door of the tomb, and departed.	door of the tomb.	
42 There then because of the Jews' Preparation [*cp.* 19 14, 31] (for the tomb was nigh at hand) they laid Jesus.	*cp. 27 62.*	*verse 42*	**54** And it was the day of the Preparation,
			and the sabbath ¹drew on.
¹ Some ancient authorities read *roll*.		¹ Many ancient authorities read *were already dead*.	¹ Gr. *began to dawn.*

John 19 39: *cp.* Ps. 45 8; Song 4 14.

(vii) The Resurrection (§ 85)

§ 85. **The Empty Tomb**

John 20 1-10	Matt. 28 1-8	Mark 16 1-8	Luke 24 1-12
	1 Now late on the sabbath day,	**1** And when the sabbath was past, Mary Magdalene [*cp.* 15 40, 47; 16 9], and Mary the *mother* of James [*cp.* 15 40, 47], and Salome [*cp.* 15 40], bought spices, that they might come and anoint him.	*verse 10*
cp. 19 25.			*cp.* 23 56.
cp. 19 39, 40.			
1 Now on the first *day* of the week [*cp.* 20 19] cometh Mary Magdalene [*cp.* 19 25; 20 18] *cp.* 19 25. early, while it was yet dark, unto the tomb,	as it began to dawn toward the first *day* of the week, came Mary Magdalene [*cp.* 27 56, 61] and the other Mary [*cp.* 27 56, 61] to see the sepulchre.	**2** And very early on the first day of the week, they come to the tomb when the sun was risen. *cp. verse* 1.	**1** But on the first day of the week, at early dawn, they came unto the tomb, bringing the spices [*cp.* 23 56] which they had prepared.
cp. 19 39, 40.		**3** And they were saying among themselves, Who shall roll us away the stone [*cp.* 15 46; 16 4] from the door of the tomb?	
cp. 20 12.	**2** And behold, there was a great earthquake; for an angel of the Lord descended from heaven, and came and rolled away the stone [*cp.* 27 60, 66], and sat upon it. **3** His appearance was as lightning,		
cp. 20 12.	and his raiment white as snow [*cp.* 17 2]: **4** and for fear [*cp. verse* 8] of him the watchers did quake, and became as dead men.	*cp. verse* 5.	*cp. verse* 4.
and seeth the stone taken away from the tomb.	*cp.* 27 60, 66; 28 2. *cp.* 27 60.	[*cp.* 9 26]. **4** and looking up, they see that the stone [*cp.* 15 46; 16 3] is rolled back: for it was exceeding great. **5** And entering into the tomb, *cp.* 16 19.	**2** And they found the stone rolled away from the tomb. **3** And they entered in, and found not the body [*cp.* 24 23] ¹of the Lord Jesus. **4** And it came to pass, while they were per-
cp. vv. 6-8.			

cp. 20 12.

cp. 20 12.
cp. 7 15, 21, 46.

cp. verse 3.
cp. 8 27; 9 33; 12 23; 15 31; 21 20; 27 14: *also* 7 28; *etc.*

cp. 9 8; 17 6; 27 54; 28 4, 8.

cp. 20 13.

cp 18 5, 7; 19 19; *also* 1 45.

they saw a young man sitting on the right side, arrayed in a white [cp. 9 3] robe; and they were amazed [cp. 1 27; 2 12; 5 20, 42; 6 51; 7 37; 10 32; 15 5; 16 8: *also* 1 22; *etc.*]. cp. 4 41; 5 15, 33; 9 6, 32; 10 32; 16 8.

plexed thereabout, behold, two men [cp. 24 23] stood by them in dazzling [cp. 9 29] apparel: **5** and as they were   [cp. 5 9, 26; 8 25, 56; 9 43; 11 14; 24 12, 41: *also* 2 47, 48; *etc.*] affrighted [cp. 1 12, 65; 2 9; 5 26; 7 16; 8 25, 35, 37, 47; 9 34, 45; 24 37], and bowed down their faces to the earth,

5 And the angel answered and said unto the women,   Fear not ye: for I know that ye seek Jesus,   [cp. 2 23; 26 71: *also* 21 11] which hath been crucified. **6** He is not here; for he is risen, even as he said. Come, see the place ¹where the Lord lay. **7** And go quickly, and tell his disciples, He is risen from the dead [cp. 27 64]; and lo, he goeth before you into Galilee [cp. 26 32]; there shall ye see him [cp. 28 10]: lo, I have told you. *cp. verse 6.*

6 And he saith unto them, Be not amazed: ye seek Jesus, the Nazarene [cp. 1 24; 10 47; 14 67], which hath been crucified: he is risen; he is not here: *cp. verse 7.* behold, the place where they laid him! **7** But go, tell his disciples and Peter, He goeth before you into Galilee [cp. 14 28]: there shall ye see him as he said unto you.

they   said unto them,

cp. 4 34; 18 37; 24 19.

Why seek ye ²the living among the dead?   **6** ³He is not here, but is risen: remember [cp. *verse* 8] how he spake unto you when he was yet

cp. 24 34.   in Galilee,

cp. 26 45.
cp. 20 19: *also* 23 34.
cp. 16 21; *etc.*

cp. 2 19-22; 3 14; 12 32-33.

cp. 14 41.

cp. 8 31; *etc.*

7 saying that the Son of man must be delivered up into the hands of sinful men, and be crucified, and the third day rise again [cp. 9 22, 43-44; 18 31-33: *also* 13 32, 33; 17 25; 22 22: *and* 24 26, 44, 46]. **8** And they remembered [cp. 22 61] his words, **9** and returned ⁴from the tomb,

cp. 2 22; 12 16.

cp. 26 75.
8 And they departed quickly from the tomb

cp. 14 72.
8 And they went out, and fled from the tomb; for trembling and astonishment [cp. *verse* 5] had come upon them: and they said nothing to any one; for they were afraid [cp. 4 41; 5 15, 33; 9 6, 32; 10 32].

cp. 20 20: *also* 16 22.

with fear [cp. *verse* 4: *also* 9 8; 17 6; 27 54] and great joy, and ran to bring his disciples word.
¹ Many ancient authorities read *where he lay.*

cp. 1 12, 65; 2 9; 5 26; 7 16; *etc.*
cp. 24 41, 52.

2 She runneth therefore, and cometh to Simon Peter, and to the other disciple [cp. *verses* 3, 4, 8, *and* 18 15, 16], whom Jesus loved [cp. 13 23; 19 26; 21 7, 20: *also* 11 36], cp. 20 18.

cp. 19 25.
cp. 19 25.

verse 1

verse 1

cp. 16 10.

and told all these things [cp. 24 10, 23] to the eleven, and to all the rest. **10** Now they were Mary Magdalene [cp. 8 2], and Joanna [cp. 8 3], and Mary the *mother* of James: and the other women [cp. 8 2, 3; 23 49, 55; 24 22, 24] with them told these things unto the apostles.

and saith unto them,   They have taken away the Lord [cp. 4 1; 6 23; 11 2; 20 18, 20, 25; 21 7, 12] out of the tomb, and we know not where they have laid him [cp. 20 13].

cp. 27 55.

cp. 15 40-41.

cp. 16 19, 20.

cp. 7 13, 19; 10 1, 39, 41; 11 39; 12 42; 13 15; 17 5, 6; 18 6; 19 8; 22 61; 24 3, 34.

cp. 20 25.

cp. 28 17.

cp. 16 11, 13, 14.

11 And these words appeared in their sight as idle talk; and they disbelieved [cp. 24 38, 41: *also* 24 25] them. **12** ⁵But Peter arose,

3 Peter therefore went forth, and the other disciple, and they went toward the tomb. **4** And they ran both together: and the other disciple outran Peter,

and   ran

and came first to the tomb; **5** and stooping and looking in, he seeth the linen cloths [*cp. verses* 6, 7, *and* 19 40] lying; yet entered he not in. **6** Simon Peter therefore also cometh, following him, and entered into the tomb; and he beholdeth the linen cloths lying, **7** and the napkin [*cp.* 11 44], that was upon his head, not lying with the linen cloths, but rolled up in a place by itself. **8** Then entered in therefore the other disciple also, which came first to the tomb, and he saw, and believed. **9** For as yet they knew not the scripture, that he must rise again from the dead [*cp.* 2 22: *also* 2 19-22]. **10** So the disciples went away again unto their own home.

cp. 27 59.	*cp.* 15 46.	
	cp. verse 5.	
	cp. verse 5.	
cp. 22 29: *and* 16 21; *etc.*	*cp.* 12 24: *and* 8 31; *etc.*	

unto the tomb; and stooping and looking in, he seeth the linen cloths [*cp.* 23 53]

　　　　　cp. verse 3.

by themselves;
　　　　　cp. verse 3.

　　cp. 24 46: *also* 9 22; *etc.*

and he 　　　　[6]departed to his 　　　home, wondering at that which was come to pass [*cp. verse* 5].

[1] Some ancient authorities omit *of the Lord Jesus*.
[2] Gr. *him that liveth*.
[3] Some ancient authorities omit *He is not here, but is risen*.
[4] Some ancient authorities omit *from the tomb*.
[5] Some ancient authorities omit ver. 12.
[6] Or, *departed, wondering with himself*

D. The Appearances after the Resurrection and the Commissioning of the Disciples (§§ 86-92)

(i) The Appearances in Jerusalem (§§ 86-90)

§ 86. **The Appearance to Mary Magdalene**

John 20 11-18

11 But Mary was standing without at the tomb weeping: so, as she wept, she stooped and looked into the tomb; **12** and she beholdeth two angels in white sitting, one at the head, and one at the feet, where the body of Jesus had lain. **13** And they say unto her, Woman, why weepest thou [*cp. verse* 15 *below*]? She saith unto them, Because they have taken away my Lord, and I know not where they have laid him [*cp.* 20 2]. **14** When she had thus said, she turned herself back, and beholdeth Jesus standing, and knew not that it was Jesus [*cp.* 21 4]. **15** Jesus saith unto her, Woman, why weepest thou [*cp. verse* 13 *above*]? whom seekest thou [*cp.* 18 4, 7: *also* 1 38; 4 27]?

cp. 28 2, 3, 5: *also* 17 2.	*cp.* 16 5: *also* 9 3. *cp.* 5 39.	*cp.* 24 4: *also* 9 29. *cp.* 7 13; 8 52; 23 28.

Matt. 28 9-10

9 And behold, Jesus met them,
saying,

　cp. 19 3.
　　cp. verse 17.
　cp. 9 38: *also* 11 32; 18 6.

	cp. 16 9.	*cp.* 24 16.

All hail [*cp.* 26 49; 27 29]. And they came and took hold of his feet, and worshipped him [*cp.* 2 11; 8 2; 9 18; 14 33; 15 25; 20 20; 28 17: *also* 17 14].

	cp. 5 39.	*cp.* 7 13; 8 52; 23 28.
	cp. 15 18.	*cp.* 1 28.
	cp. 5 6: *also* 1 40; 3 11; *etc.*	*cp.* 24 52: *also* 5 8, 12; 8 28; *etc.*

She, supposing him to be the gardener [*cp.* 19 41], saith unto him, Sir, if thou hast borne him hence, tell me where thou has laid him, and I will take him away. **16** Jesus saith unto her, Mary. She turneth herself, and saith unto him in Hebrew, Rabboni [*cp.* 1 38, 49; 3 2; 4 31; 6 25; 9 2; 11 8: *also* 3 26]; which is to say, [1]Master. **17** Jesus saith to [*cp.* 6 20] her [2]Touch me not; for I am not yet ascended unto the Father: but go unto my brethren,

cp. 26 25, 49: *also* 23 7, 8.

10 Then saith Jesus unto them, Fear not [*cp.* 14 27; 17 7]:
　cp. verse 9.
　go tell my brethren

	cp. 10 51: *and* 9 5; 11 21; 14 45. *cp.* 6 50.	

and say to them, I ascend [*cp*. 6 62: *also* 3 13] unto my Father and your Father [*cp*. 13 1; 14 12, 28; 16 10, 17, 28], and my God and your God [*cp*. 13 3: *also* 7 33; 16 5: *and* 17 11, 13].

18 Mary Magdalene cometh and telleth the disciples, I have seen the Lord [*cp*. 20 25: *also* 4 1; 6 23; 11 2; 20 2, 20; 21 7, 12]; and *how that* he had said these things unto her.

that they depart into Galilee, and there shall they see me [*cp*. 28 7 and 16-20].
cp. 28 8.

cp. 16 10.
cp. 16 19, 20.

cp. 24 9, *etc. cp*. 7 13, 19; 10 1; *etc.*

¹ Or, *Teacher*
² Or, *Take not hold on me*

§ 87. The First Appearance to the Disciples and their Commissioning

John 20 19-23	Mark 16 14-16	Luke 24 36-49
19 When therefore it was evening, on that day, the first *day* of the week [*cp*. 20 1], and when the doors were shut [*cp*. 20 26] where the disciples were, for fear of the Jews [*cp*. 7 13; 19 38: *also* 9 22: *and* 12 42], Jesus		
came and stood in the midst [*cp*. 20 26], and saith unto them, Peace *be* unto you [*cp*. 20 21, 26: *also* 14 27].	**14** And afterward he was manifested unto the eleven themselves as they sat at meat;	**36** And as they spake these things, he himself stood in the midst of them, ¹and saith unto them, Peace *be* unto you.

cp. 9 8; 17 6; 27 54; 28 4, 8.
cp. 14 26.

cp. 4 41; 5 15, 33; 9 6, 32; 10 32; 16 8.

cp. 6 49.

37 But they were terrified and affrighted [*cp*. 1 12, 65; 2 9; 5 26; 7 16; 8 25, 35, 37, 47; 9 34, 45; 24 5], and supposed that they beheld a spirit. **38** And he said unto them,

cp. 20 25, 27.
cp. 12 40.

cp. 28 17: also 13 58.
cp. 19 8.

and he upbraided them with their unbelief [*cp*. 16 11, 13: *also* 6 6] and hardness of heart [*cp*. 6 52; 8 17: *also* 3 5; 10 5], because they believed not them which had seen him after he was risen.

cp. 20 25, 27.
cp. 20 27.

cp. 28 17.

Why are ye troubled? and wherefore do reasonings arise in your heart [*cp*. 24 11, 41: *also* 25]? **39** See my hands and my feet, that it is I myself: handle me, and see; for a spirit hath not flesh and bones, as ye behold me having. **40** ²And when he had said this, he shewed them his hands and his feet.

20 And when he had said this, he shewed unto them his hands and his side [*cp*. 20 25, 27: *and* 19 34]. The disciples therefore were
cp. 20 25, 27.
glad [*cp*. 16 22], when they saw the Lord [*cp*. 4 1; 6 23; 11 2; 20 2, 25; 21 7, 12].

cp. 28 17.
cp. 28 8.

cp. 16 11, 13, 14.
cp. 16 19, 20.

41 And while they still disbelieved [*cp*. 24 11, 38: *also* 24 25] for joy [*cp*. 24 52],
cp. 7 13, 19; 10 1, 39; *etc.*

cp. 21 5.

and wondered, he said unto them, Have ye here anything to eat? **42** And they gave him a piece of a broiled fish.³ **43** And he took it, and did eat before them. **44** And he

Matt. 28 18-20

21 Jesus

18 And Jesus

15 And he

John	Matthew	Mark	Luke
therefore said to them again, Peace *be* unto you [*cp.* 20 19, 26: *also* 14 27]:	came to them and spake unto them, saying,	said unto them,	said unto them,
cp. 14 25; 16 4.			These are my words which I spake unto you, while I was yet with you, how that all things must needs be fulfilled, which are written in the law of Moses, and the prophets, and the psalms, concerning me. **45** Then opened he their mind, that they might understand the scriptures [*cp.* 24 27, 32]; **46** and he said unto them, Thus it is written, that the Christ should suffer, and rise again from the dead the third day;
cp. 5 39.			
cp. 5 27; 17 2: *also* 3 35; 13 3: *and* 10 18.	All authority [*cp.* 7 29; 9 6, 8; 21 23-27: *also* 11 27] hath been given unto me in heaven and on earth.	*cp.* 1 22, 27; 2 10; 11 27-33.	*cp.* 4 32, 36; 5 24; 20 1-8: *also* 10 22.
cp. verse 23.	*cp.* 26 28.	*cp.* 1 4.	**47** and that repentance [4]and remission of sins [*cp.* 1 77; 3 3] should be preached in his name [*cp.* 9 48, 49; 10 17; 21 8]
cp. 14 13, 14, 26; 15 16; 16 23, 24, 26.	[*cp.* verse 19: *also* 7 22; 18 5, 20; 24 5] **19** Go ye therefore, and make disciples of all the	[*cp.* 16 17: *also* 9 37, 38, 39; 13 6] Go ye into all the world, and	unto all the [5]nations [*cp.* 2 30-32; 3 6: *also* 13 29; 14 21-24; 20 16],
cp. 10 16; 11 52.	nations [*cp.* 24 14; 26 13: *also* 8 11; 10 18; 21 31, 41-43; 22 7-10],	preach the gospel to the whole creation	beginning from Jerusalem.
	baptizing them into the name of the Father and of the Son and of the Holy Ghost:	**16** He that believeth and is baptized	*cp.* verse 47.
cp. 14 15, 23.	**20** teaching them to observe all things whatsoever I commanded you:	shall be saved; but he that disbelieveth shall be condemned.	
cp. 15 27.			**48** Ye are witnesses of these things. **49** And behold, I send forth the promise of my Father upon you:
cp. 14 16, 26; 15 26; 16 7.			
as the Father hath sent me [*cp.* 3 17, 34; 5 36-38; *etc.*], even so send I you [*cp.* 17 18].		*cp.* 5 30.	but tarry ye in the city, until ye be clothed with power [*cp.* 1 17, 35; 4 14, 36; 5 17; 6 19; 8 46; 9 1] from on high [*cp.* 1 78].
cp. 14 23.	and lo, I am with you [*cp.* 1 23] [1]alway [*cp.* 18 20], even unto [2]the end of the world.		
	[1] Gr. *all the days.* [2] Or, *the consummation of the age*		[1] Some ancient authorities omit *and saith unto them, Peace be unto you.* [2] Some ancient authorities omit ver. 40. [3] Many ancient authorities add *and a honeycomb.* [4] Some ancient authorities read *unto.* [5] Or, *nations. Beginning from Jerusalem, ye are witnesses*
22 And when he had said this, he breathed on them, and saith unto them, Receive ye the [1]Holy Ghost [*cp.* 7 39: *also* 14 17, 26; 15 26; 16 13: *and* 14 16; 16 7: *and* 1 33; 3 34]:	Matt. 16 **19** I will give	Matt. 18 **18** Verily I say	

23 whose soever sins ye forgive, they are forgiven unto them; whose soever *sins* ye retain, they are retained.	unto thee the keys of the kingdom of heaven: and whatsoever thou shalt bind on earth shall be bound in heaven: and whatsoever thou shalt loose on earth shall be loosed in heaven.	unto you, What things soever ye shall bind on earth shall be bound in heaven: and what things soever ye shall loose on earth shall be loosed in heaven.	*cp.* 24 47.

¹ Or, *Holy Spirit*

§ 88. Thomas doubts

John 20 24-25

24 But Thomas [*cp.* 11 16; 14 5; 20 26-29; 21 2], one of the twelve, called ¹Didymus [*cp.* 11 16; 21 2], was not with them when Jesus came. **25** The other disciples therefore said unto him, We have seen the Lord [*cp.* 20 18: *also* 4 1; 6 23; 11 2; 20 2, 20; 21 7, 12]. But he said unto them, Except I shall see in his hands the print of the nails, and put my finger [*cp.* 20 27] into the print of the nails, and put my hand into his side [*cp.* 20 20, 27: *and* 19 34], I will not believe [*cp.* 20 27].	*cp.* 10 3. *cp.* 28 17.	*cp.* 3 18. *cp.* 16 19, 20. *cp.* 16 11, 13, 14.	*cp.* 6 15. *cp.* 7 13, 19; 10 1; *etc.* *cp.* 24 11, 25, 38, 41.

¹ That is, *Twin.*

§ 89. The Second Appearance to the Disciples: Thomas believes

John 20 26-29

26 And after eight days again his disciples were within, and Thomas [*cp.* 11 16; 14 5; 20 24-25; 21 2] with them. Jesus cometh, the doors being shut [*cp.* 20 19], and stood in the midst [*cp.*20 19], and said, Peace *be* unto you [*cp.* 20 19, 21: *also* 14 27]. **27** Then saith he to Thomas, Reach hither thy finger [*cp.* 20 25], and see my hands; and reach *hither* thy hand, and put it into my side [*cp.* 20 20, 25: *and* 19 34]: and be not faithless [*cp.* 20 25: *also* 3 12; 6 64; 14 10], but believing. **28** Thomas answered and said unto him, My Lord and my God. **29** Jesus saith unto him, Because thou hast seen me, ¹thou hast believed: blessed *are* they that have not seen, and *yet* have believed.	*cp.* 10 3. *cp.* 28 17: *also* 6 30; 8 26; 14 31; 16 8: *and* 17 20; 21 21.	*cp.* 3 18. *cp.* 16 11, 13, 14: *also* 4 40; 11 22.	*cp.* 6 15. *cp.* 24 36. *cp.* 24 39. *cp.* 24 11, 25, 38, 41: *also* 8 25; 12 28; 17 5-6; 22 32.

¹ Or, *hast thou believed?*

§ 90. The Gospel has been written that others may believe

John 20 30-31

30 Many other signs therefore did Jesus [*cp.* 21 25: *also* 2 11; 4 54; *etc.*] in the presence of the disciples, which are not written in this book: **31** but these are written, that ye may believe [*cp.* 19 35: *also* 11 15; 13 19; 14 29: *and* 11 42: *and* 6 69; 9 38; 11 27; 16 27, 30; 17 8] that Jesus is the Christ [*cp.* 1 41; 4 25, 26, 29; 7 26, 41; 9 22; 10 24; 11 27], the Son of God [*cp.* 1 34, 49; 11 27: *also* 3 18; 5 25; 9 35; 10 36; 11 4; 19 7: *and* 1 18; 3 16-17, 35-36; *etc.*], and that believing ye may have life in his name [*cp.* 3 15, 16, 36; 5 24; 6 40, 47; 11 25-26].	*cp.* 16 16; 26 63, 68; 27 17, 22: *and* 4 3, 6; 8 29; 14 33; *etc.*	*cp.* 8 29; 14 61; 15 32: *and* 1 1; 3 11; 5 7; *etc.*	*cp.* 9 20; 22 67; 23 2, 35, 39: *and* 1 35; 4 3, 9, 41; *etc.*

(ii) The Final Appearance in Galilee (§§ 91-92)

§ 91. **Jesus is manifested through a miraculous Draught of Fishes**

John 21 1-14

1 After these things Jesus manifested himself [*cp. verse* 14: *also* 1 31; 2 11; 7 4; 14 21, 22: *and* 3 21; 9 3; 17 6] again to the disciples at the sea of Tiberias [*cp.* 6 1: *also* 6 16; *etc.*];

cp. 16 12, 14.

cp. 4 18; 15 29: *also* 8 24; *etc.*

cp. 1 16; 7 31: *also* 2 13; *etc.*

and he manifested *himself* on this wise. **2** There were together Simon Peter, and Thomas [*cp.* 11 16; 14 5; 20 24, 26-29] called [1]Didymus [*cp.* 11 16; 20 24], and Nathanael [*cp.* 1 45-51] of Cana in Galilee [*cp.* 2 1, 11; 4 46], and the *sons* of Zebedee, and two other of his disciples [*cp.* 1 35]. **3** Simon Peter saith unto them, I go a fishing. They say unto him, We also come with thee. They went forth, and entered into the boat; and that night they took nothing. **4** But when day was now breaking, Jesus stood on the beach:
    howbeit the disciples knew not that it was Jesus [*cp.* 20 14].

cp. 10 3.

cp. 3 18.

5 Jesus therefore saith unto them, Children, have ye aught to eat? They answered him, No. **6** And he said unto them,
    Cast the net
on the right side of the boat, and ye shall find

verse 3

They cast therefore, and now they were not able to draw it for the   multitude of fishes.

verse 11

7 That disciple therefore whom Jesus loved [*cp.* 13 23; 19 26; 20 2; 21 20: *also* 11 36] saith unto Peter, It is the Lord [*cp. verse* 12: *also* 4 1, 6 23; 11 2; 20 2, 18, 20, 25]. So when Simon Peter   heard that it was the Lord, he girt [*cp.* 21 18] his coat about him (for he was naked), and cast himself into the sea.

cp. 16 19, 20.

cp. 14 28-29.

8 But the other disciples came in the little boat [*cp.* 6 22] (for they were not far from the land, but about

cp. 3 9.

Luke 5 1-11

1 Now it came to pass, while the multitude pressed upon him and heard the word of God,

cp. 6 15.

verse 5
        that he   was standing by the lake of Gennesaret [*cp.* 5 2; 8 22, 23, 33];

cp. 24 16.
2 and he saw two boats standing by the lake: but the fishermen had gone out of them, and were washing their nets. **3** And he entered into one of the boats, which was Simon's, and asked him to put out a little from the land. And he sat down and taught the multitudes out of the boat. **4** And when he had left speaking, he

cp. 24 41.

said unto Simon, Put out into the deep, and let down your nets for a draught.

5 And Simon answered and said, Master, we toiled all night, and took nothing: but at thy word I will let down the nets. **6** And when they had this done,

they inclosed a great multitude of fishes; and their nets were breaking; **7** and they beckoned unto their partners in the other boat, that they should come and help them. And they came, and filled both the boats, so that they began to sink.

cp. 7 13, 19; 10 1; *etc.*
                8 But
Simon Peter, when he saw it,

fell down at Jesus' knees, saying, Depart from me; for I am a sinful man, O Lord. **9** For he was amazed, and all that were with him,

two hundred cubits off), dragging the net *full* of   fishes.

                    at the draught of the fishes which they had taken; **10** and so were also James and John, sons of Zebedee, which were partners with Simon. And Jesus said unto Simon, Fear not; from henceforth thou shalt [1]catch men. **11** And when they had brought their boats to land, they left all, and followed him [*cp.* 5 28; 18 28: *also* 5 27; 9 23, 59; 18 22].

9 So when they got out upon   the land,
cp. 1 37: *also* 1 43; 12 26; 21 19, 22.
    they see [2]a fire of coals [*cp.* 18 18] there, and [3]fish [*cp. verses* 10, 13; *and* 6 9, 11] laid thereon, and [4]bread. **10** Jesus saith unto them, Bring of the fish [*cp. verses* 9, 13; *and* 6 9, 11] which ye have now taken. **11** Simon Peter therefore went [5]up, and drew the net to land, full of great fishes, a hundred and fifty and three: and for all there were so many, the net was not rent. **12** Jesus saith unto them, Come *and* break your fast. And none of the disciples durst inquire of him [*cp.* 4 27], Who art thou [*cp.* 1 19; 8 25]? knowing that it was the Lord [*cp. verse* 7 *above*]. **13** Jesus cometh, and taketh the [6]bread, and giveth them [*cp.* 6 11], and the fish [*cp. verses* 9, 10; *and* 6 9, 11] likewise [*cp.* 6 11]. **14** This is now the third time [*cp.* 20 19, 26] that Jesus was manifested [*cp. verse* 1] to the disciples, after that he was risen from the dead.

		verse 6
	cp. 16 19, 20.	*cp.* 7 13, 19; *etc.*
cp. 14 19; 15 36; 26 26.	*cp.* 6 41; 8 6; 14 22.	*cp.* 24 30: *also* 9 16; 22 19.
	cp. 16 12, 14.	

Cross-reference columns for verses 9-10:

cp. 4 20, 22; 9 9; 19 27: *also* 4 19; 8 22; 9 9; 16 24; 19 21.	*cp.* 1 18, 20; 2 14; 10 28: *also* 1 17; 2 14; 8 34; 10 21.

[1] Gr. *take alive*.

[1] That is, *Twin*.   [2] Gr. *a fire of charcoal*.   [3] Or, *a fish*   [4] Or, *a loaf*
[5] Or, *aboard*   [6] Or, *loaf*

§ 92. The Commission to Peter and to the Disciple whom Jesus loved

John 21 15-23

15 So when they had broken their fast, Jesus saith to Simon Peter, Simon, *son of* [1]John [*cp. verses* 16, 17, *and* 1 42], [2]lovest thou me [*cp.* 14 21, 23; 16 27] more than these? He saith unto him, Yea, Lord; thou knowest that I [3]love thee. He saith unto him, Feed my lambs [*cp. verses* 16, 17: *also* 10 11-16, 26-27]. **16** He saith to him again a second time, Simon, *son of* [1]John, [2]lovest thou me? He saith unto him, Yea, Lord; thou knowest that I [3]love thee. He saith unto him, Tend my sheep. **17** He saith unto him the third time, Simon, *son of* [1]John, [3]lovest thou me? Peter was grieved because he said unto him the third time, [3]Lovest thou me? And he said unto him, Lord, thou knowest all things [*cp.* 16 30: *also* 2 24, 25: *and* 1 48; 4 19, 29; 5 6, 42; 6 61, 64; 11 14; 13 11, 18; 16 19; 18 4]; thou [4]knowest that I [3]love thee. Jesus saith unto him, Feed my sheep. **18** Verily, verily, I say unto thee, When thou wast young, thou girdedst thyself [*cp.* 21 7], and walkesdt whither thou wouldest: but when thou shalt be old, thou shalt stretch forth thy hands, and another shall gird thee, and carry thee whither thou wouldest not. **19** Now this he spake, signifying by what manner of death [*cp.* 12 33; 18 32] he should glorify God. And when he had spoken this, he saith unto him, Follow me [*cp. verse* 22 *below and* 13 36: *also* 1 43; 12 26]. **20** Peter, turning about, seeth the disciple whom Jesus loved [*cp.* 13 23; 19 26; 20 2; 21 7: *also* 11 36] following; which also leaned back on his breast [*cp.* 13 25] at the supper, and said, Lord, who is he that betrayeth thee [*cp.* 13 25]? **21** Peter [*cp.* 13 36: *also* 6 68] therefore seeing him saith to Jesus, Lord, [5]and what shall this man do? **22** Jesus saith unto him, If I will that he tarry till I come [*cp.* 14 3, 18, 28], what *is that* to thee [*cp. verse* 23 *below*]? follow thou me [*cp. verse* 19 *above*]. **23** This saying therefore went forth among the brethren, that that disciple should not die: yet Jesus said not unto him, that he should not die; but, If I will that he tarry till I come, what *is that* to thee [*cp. verse* 22 *above*]?

cp. 16 17: *also* 17 25.	*cp.* 14 37.	*cp* 22 31.
cp. 16 18, 19: *also* 9 36; 10 6; 15 24: *and* 26 31.	*cp.* 6 34: *and* 14 27.	*cp.* 22 32.
cp. 9 4; 12 25; 16 8.	*cp.* 2 8; 8 17.	*cp.* 5 22; 6 8; 9 47; 11 17.
cp. 4 19; 8 22; 9 9; 16 24; 19 21.	*cp.* 1 17; 2 14; 8 34; 10 21.	*cp.* 5 27; 9 23, 59; 18 22.
cp. 14 28; 15 15; *etc.* *cp.* 10 23; 16 28.	*cp.* 8 32; 9 5; *etc.*	*cp.* 8 45; 9 33; *etc.* *cp.* 19 13.
cp. 27 4.		

[1] Gr. *Joanes*. See ch. 1. 42, margin. [2], [3] *Love* in these places represents two different Greek words. [4] Or, *perceivest* [5] Gr. *and this man, what?*

E. Concluding Notes (§§ 93-94)

§ 93. The Disciple whom Jesus loved is the Author of the Gospel

John 21 24

24 This is the disciple which beareth witness [*cp.* 19 35: *also* 15 27] of these things, and wrote these things: and we know [*cp.* 3 2; 4 42; 9 24, 29, 31; 16 30] that his witness is true [*cp.* 19 35: *also* 5 31, 32; 8 13, 14].	*cp.* 22 16.	*cp.* 12 14.	*cp.* 24 48. *cp.* 20 21.	

§ 94. The Author of the Gospel has provided only a Selection from the available Material

John 21 25

25 And there are also many other things which Jesus did [*cp.* 20 30], the which if they should be written every one, I suppose that even the world itself would not contain the books that should be written.			

INDEX OF SYNOPTIC PARALLELS
printed in the text in full

MATTHEW

INDEX TO SECTION HEADINGS